BREAKING
FREE

BREAKING
FREE

MAKING LIBERTY IN CHRIST A REALITY IN LIFE

BETH
MOORE

WITH
DALE MCCLESKEY

in association with

Broadman & Holman Publishers
Original hardcover edition: 1-85345-334-X

This edition published by CWR, Farnham, England in
association with Broadman & Holman Publishers, Nashville,
Tennessee, USA © 2004 UK Edition.
For sale and distribution in the UK only.

Printed in Singapore by C.O.S. Printers Pte Ltd

Unless otherwise stated all Scripture citation is from the
NIV, the Holy Bible, New International Version,
copyright © 1973, 1978, 1984 by
International Bible Society. Also cited is KJV,
the King James Version.

1 2 3 4 5   04 03 02 01 00

DEDICATION

To the wonderful people of Franklin Avenue Baptist Church,
my home away from home. I will never be able to think about
the message of *Breaking Free* without thinking of you.
Words are inadequate to express my gratitude for your loving
share in this vision. You have stolen my heart.

ACKNOWLEDGMENT

I am deeply indebted to my dear friend and editor, Dale McCleskey, for his willingness to reformat the in-depth Bible study God has given me into this reader-friendly version. Dale, you have been trustworthy with the most personal and gloriously painful journey God has even entrusted to me. May every captive who turns these pages discover the only true Deliverer.

CONTENTS

PREFACE

Welcome to *Breaking Free*.

Somehow I think a writer should never appear desperate for the reader to care about her work. It just isn't seemly. She should just do her best and place the result out there. I believe that, but in this case I just can't do it. The contents of these pages are so important to me that I desperately want them to be important to you. The message in this volume is so precious to me that I desperately desire for it to be precious to you.

I want the process described here to grab your heart. I want it to pull at your life so powerfully that the bondage of mediocre discipleship will never again be acceptable. Christ calls us to a place of breaking free. He woos us to the place of absolute freedom—the only kind of freedom that is real. Let me start by pulling back the curtain just a bit to give you a preview of the road ahead. I have divided the journey into six segments.

We start in part I with the prophet Isaiah. I believe God's Word brings freedom. His incarnate Word through His written Word. So we begin with Bible study. We'll see how captivity came to the kings of ancient Israel, and we'll see how freedom comes through the King of kings.

Part II of our journey together is called "Benefits and Obstacles." We'll encounter the benefits of the Christian life that make freedom possible. We'll see how the Father intends these benefits for every one of His children, and we'll see the major obstacles in the way of that freedom.

In part III we'll explore some personal matters. We'll take a look back for the right reasons. We'll see how strongholds take such deep root in believers' lives. Only by facing some ancient ruins and broken hearts will we find the freedom God promises.

After we've dealt with some matters of the past, we get to turn to the future. We all have dreams. Some of those dreams may seem impossible. In part IV we'll see that God wants to surpass our best dreams, and He wants to bring us to the place of obedience that lasts.

Part V touches upon the deepest need of every human heart. We all long for a love that will not fade or fail. Genuine freedom can grow only in the light of that unfailing love.

Finally we will seek the place where we can gaze over into the promised land. Like Moses we will scale the heights to see the land of freedom and splendor, but unlike Moses, we have the opportunity to cross into the land. God shows us His splendor that He may beckon us. Come with all haste. Come to the place of breaking free. The place where we know Him and believe Him. The place where we seek His glory and forget our own. The place where satisfaction comes from the only true satisfier of our souls. The place where we experience His peace no matter what the world may throw our way. And the place where His presence is our constant desire and our daily joy.

Yes, I am desperate for you and for your freedom. I long for you to join the unshackled multitude that is breaking free.

WELCOME TO A JOURNEY

TO FREEDOM

I have never written anything that meant more to me than the message of this book. When I was eighteen, I surrendered to God's call to vocational ministry. Some years later, God spoke to my heart and said something like this: "I sent my Son to set the captives free. You will go forth and ring the liberty bell." Sweet thought. Even a little poetic for a romantic like me, but it sounded awfully evangelistic. I was fairly certain my calling was in the area of discipleship.

I shake my head and marvel now that I thought the only people captive were the spiritually lost. God pried open my comfortably closed mind in the most effective way possible: from the inside out.

I had no idea I was in captivity until God began to set me free. If anyone had told me Christians could be in bondage, I would have argued with all the volume a person can muster when a yoke of slavery is strangling her neck. I was the worst kind of captive: a prisoner unaware. The kind of prisoner most vulnerable to her captors. The easiest prey there is.

The following statement will constitute our definition of captivity throughout our study: *A Christian is held captive by anything that hinders the abundant and effective Spirit-filled life God planned for him or her.*

In the first steps of our journey, we will begin with an introduction both to the prophet Isaiah and to our subject of breaking free. We will make this beginning using two methods. You might think of them as the microscopic and the macroscopic. The microscopic view comes from an examination of a phrase from Isaiah 9:4 in this introduction. The broad overview in chapter 1 will be a look at the kings who ruled during the prophet's lifetime. Both views will give us the biblical tools to consider how to gain freedom in Christ.

Come and join me as we begin with a phrase from the pen of the "Prince of the Prophets." Isaiah 9:4 contains a most intriguing reference: "As in the day of Midian's defeat, / you have shattered / the yoke that burdens them, . . . / the rod of their oppressor." If you know your Bible, you may recognize the reference to Gideon, in the Book of Judges. Something happened in the days of Midian's defeat that was extremely important, not only to the Book of Isaiah, but to the Savior coming to set captives free.

In the Book of Judges, God told the people, "I will always go before you and bring you victory, but do not do one thing. Don't ever start worshiping other gods." Naturally, that is exactly what they did. Judges 6 begins with the unsettling words, "Again the Israelites did evil in the eyes of the LORD." Let's consider a series of lessons that lay the groundwork for our discussion of breaking free. I will list them as nine lessons about captivity and freedom.

LESSON 1

The people of God can be oppressed by the enemy. The Israelites had done evil in the eyes of the Lord. Judges 6:1 uses the incriminating word *again.*

So God handed them over for a season to the enemy to learn better. You may be like I once was. I thought, *If I just ignore Satan and desire to walk with God, I'm going to be fine.* We find out that doesn't work for very long, especially if you're beginning to be a threat to Satan's dark kingdom.

LESSON 2

When oppressed, the children of God tend to prepare shelters for themselves rather than do what liberty demands. Shelters can easily turn into strongholds. Often when we're oppressed, instead of cooperating with God and going to a place of freedom, we hide in shelters. Sometimes we just go into isolation. We hide behind our jobs. We hide behind busy things at church; we hide behind activities—the captivity of activity. Anything that treats the symptoms instead of going to the source is a shelter.

LESSON 3

The people of God have little defense against the destructive nature of the enemy without the power of God working in their favor. The Israelites prepared shelters for themselves, but verses 5 and 6 tell us that when the Midianites came they were like swarms of locusts—impossible to count. They invaded the land and ravaged it. We can be saved, the Holy Spirit can dwell in us, and yet we can continually live in defeat because the enemy can outwit us if we do not depend on the Holy Spirit and the Word of God. We've got to know that we're being swarmed, wise up in the Word of God, learn what our rights are, and learn to use the equipment God has given us.

LESSON 4

God did not allow His people to be oppressed so that they would be defeated but so that they would ultimately be victorious. God will sometimes allow things to get bad enough that we will be forced to look up.

Victory always begins with a cry for help. When we come to the end of ourselves and cry out for help, amazing things happen.

LESSON 5

God willingly tells His children why they are being oppressed if they are willing to listen. God wants us to know the reasons we continue being oppressed. In verses 7 through 10, He sent a prophet to the Israelites to tell them they were oppressed because they had worshiped other gods. We would rather God just fix our messes. We don't want to get into the reasons why. "Lord, just set me free! I don't need to know why I got in this mess; let's not dig up all those old bones. Just set me free." God says, "I want you to know what went wrong, so the next time you're in the same situation, you'll make different choices."

LESSON 6

God sees the potential of His children. In Judges 6:11–16 Gideon was hiding from the Midianites in a winepress. The angel of the Lord came and said to Gideon, "The LORD is with you, mighty warrior." Of all things, while Gideon trembled in fear, God called him a mighty warrior—long before he was one.

God is calling you a mighty warrior. This study is about God's teaching us to live like the mighty warriors we can be in Him. Are you sick of deceit and ready to learn how to live like a mighty warrior?

LESSON 7

Any sacrifice we make in our quest for freedom will be wholly consumed and blessed by God. Notice something extremely important: Gideon prepared a sacrifice. Then we read in verse 21: "With the tip of the staff that was in his hand, the angel of the LORD touched the meat and the unleavened bread. Fire flared from the rock, consuming the meat and the bread."

To be liberated in Christ, we've got some sacrifices to make. Make sure He's the one asking for it, but if He is, any sacrifice you make will be wholly consumed by Him as such a sweet sacrifice. He will bless.

We fear making sacrifices. But the irony is that we make a lot of sacrifices when we are not living the will of God. How many things have we placed on the altar to Satan's kingdom? We live sacrificially when we're outside the will of God, giving up all sorts of things that were meant to be ours in Christ. We want to claim those things back, but in the process we're going to be putting a few other things on the altar.

LESSON 8

To live in the freedom God has purposed, we must recognize and forsake all other gods. God told Gideon, "Tear down your father's altar to Baal" (v. 25). I love verse 27. Gideon took ten of his servants and did as the Lord said, but because he was afraid, he did it at night rather than in the daytime. Do you just love it? This is God's mighty warrior! Are you getting encouraged? He did it at night. But at least he did it. Now we're going to be asked to do exactly the same thing.

We're going to discover idols we did not even know we had. We're also going to be looking back a few generations to see what idols in our lineage need to be forsaken and torn down so we can know the freedom God has for us.

LESSON 9

God wants to remove all doubts concerning who brings the victory. God did this dramatically with Gideon. You probably know the rest of Gideon's story. He assembled an army. The enemy numbers were like locusts, and God said Gideon's army was too big. So God took Gideon through the world's first reduction-in-force. He reduced Gideon's army from 32,000 to 300 men.

No amount of determination will bring freedom. We're going to learn to be victorious by surrendering our lives completely to the Spirit of God, not by gritting our teeth and trying harder.

God showed who brought the victory in Judges 7:9–18. The Lord said, "If you are afraid to attack, go down to the camp . . . and listen to what they are saying" (vv. 10–11). The dust didn't settle until Gideon was up and running. He rushed to see what the Lord was speaking about, because he was scared to death. And you know what? That's OK with God. He recognizes our fears and our insecurities. I feel the Spirit of God sometimes says to me: "You know Beth, I understand that you're not very happy about this. I understand that you're scared to death of this. I understand that you may be crying over this. Cry, shake, whatever, but do My will, Child. Do My will; I have victory for you." So that's what Gideon did, and he found out the Midianites were scared to death of him!

Gideon returned to the camp of Israel and led the army to victory. What happened to the wimp we saw earlier? If you stick with God, you will be so unique in the body of Christ that whether or not you ever wanted to lead, you will. That's what happens when people become victors.

Now will you pray a prayer of dedication with me? We're going to give God this study, allow Him to do a work in us, release freedom in our lives, look into the deepest parts of our hearts, and teach us how to live in victory.

Oh God, as we begin this journey, our hearts are so full of anticipation. God, we want to be different. We invite You to do a work in us that we cannot even explain. We dedicate this study entirely to You. We pray, Father, that we will not raise up a hand to hinder or stop

You, because sometimes the truth is going to hurt. We know, God, that You desire to have the fullness of our lives so You can cause us to live in the victory Your Son died for us to have. Now, God, we humble ourselves before You, and we ask You to do a mighty work in us and through us, so we can proclaim Your name for the rest of our lives. You alone are God. There is no other Savior. Thank You in advance, Lord, for everything You're going to do. We give You every bit of the glory. In Jesus' name, Amen.

AUTHOR'S NOTE

I have used several resources for study of Greek and Hebrew words. Definitions taken from the *Complete Word Study Dictionary: New Testament and the Lexical Aids*[1] are enclosed in quotation marks with no reference. I have also used *Strong's Exhaustive Concordance of the Bible.*[2] Words taken from *Strong's* are enclosed in quotation marks with the word *Strong's* in parentheses.

PART I

FROM CAPTIVITY TO FREEDOM

As we begin our study, I need to challenge you. We will consider biblical keys to liberty, but don't expect to find a magic potion. Real freedom requires real work. A key part of the work involves God's Word. We hide God's Word in our hearts so that we might not sin against Him (Ps. 119:11). The memory verses for our study, in the order you will encounter them, are the following passages from Isaiah 61:1–4; 43:10; 43:6–7; 55:2; 26:3; and 43:2–3. I encourage you to copy these verses onto cards. Work on one verse at a time. Carry them with you. Practice reciting them often. Seek to have all the Scriptures memorized by the time you turn the last page. Begin your memorization with Isaiah 61:1. Then proceed with verses 2, 3, and 4.

> The Spirit of the Sovereign LORD is on me,
>   because the LORD has anointed me
>   to preach good news to the poor.
> He has sent me to bind up the brokenhearted,
>   to proclaim freedom for the captives
>   and release from darkness for the prisoners,

to proclaim the year of the LORD's favor
 and the day of vengeance of our God,
to comfort all who mourn,
 and provide for those who grieve in Zion—
to bestow on them a crown of beauty
 instead of ashes,
the oil of gladness
 instead of mourning,
and a garment of praise
 instead of a spirit of despair.
They will be called oaks of righteousness,
 a planting of the LORD
 for the display of his splendor.
They will rebuild the ancient ruins
 and restore the places long devastated;
they will renew the ruined cities
 that have been devastated for generations.
(Isa. 61:1–4)

CHAPTER 1

FROM KINGS TO CAPTIVITY

After Uzziah became powerful, his pride led to his downfall.

(2 CHRON. 26:16a)

I want to ask you to begin our very personal journey to breaking free in what may seem like a peculiar place. We will consider a brief overview of the kings who reigned during the ministry of Isaiah the prophet. We will do so for three reasons:

• First, each of the kings embodies the problems we too must encounter on the trail to freedom. By learning how they wandered into captivity, we can begin to see ourselves. I hope we will also begin to spot the first clues to how we can escape captivity.

• Second, studying these kings will give us a starting place for understanding the prophet Isaiah and his message.

• Third, I just believe Bible study carries its own rewards. God has used the study of His Word to set me free. Time studying the Bible is always well spent.

Before we turn to the first king, consider a few facts about Isaiah. He ministered as a prophet during the period when Israel was a divided kingdom. After King Solomon's death in 931 B.C., the kingdom of Israel divided into the north and the south. The southern kingdom took on the name Judah. The northern kingdom continued to be called Israel.

The prophets Hosea and Micah were Isaiah's contemporaries. Isaiah's name means "the Lord saves" and the word *salvation* is used in his book twenty-seven times—twice as many as the other prophets combined. Isaiah was married, and I think you might be blessed by the title he gave his wife. In Isaiah 8:3, he called her the "prophetess."

Can you imagine them being introduced as the prophet Isaiah and his beloved wife, the prophetess? I like Isaiah already, don't you? He and the Mrs. had two sons: Shear-Jashub and Maher-Shalal-Hash-Baz. Had they been mine, I would have nicknamed them Jash and Hash to save time. I doubt that he did. Under normal circumstances he may have had a playful side, but these were not funny times. Nothing is humorous about the impending judgment of God.

Isaiah was well educated, most likely came from an upper-class family, and was probably related to the royal house of Judah. God inspired him to write one of the longest books in the Bible. His ministry extended for over forty years, bridging 740 B.C. to at least 701 B.C.

Isaiah's calling came, not coincidentally, right after the death of the first king we'll consider: King Uzziah. The name *Uzziah* means "the Lord is my strength." Much of his reign was a reflection of his name. Uzziah became king when he was sixteen years old. He reigned in Jerusalem for fifty-two years. He brought Judah to its greatest heights economically and militarily. He might be remembered as the greatest king between David and Christ except for one thing. In 2 Chronicles 26:16–23 we discover that the sin of pride became his downfall. He usurped the role saved exclusively for the priests. He took upon himself the forbidden task of burning incense in the holy place within the temple of God. As a result God struck Uzziah with leprosy. Uzziah had been a good man. Yet when his life was over, all people could say was, "He had leprosy."

Pride can lead to captivity (Jer. 13:15–17). We certainly see that it led to a real and tangible captivity in Uzziah's life. Thus Uzziah's tragic end signals our first warning. Pride will be an obstacle every believer must face on the freedom trail.

Uzziah died in seclusion after a prosperous reign. His son Jotham resembled his father in that he grew powerful and ruled effectively. He differed in a crucial way: "Jotham grew powerful because he walked steadfastly before the LORD" (2 Chron. 27:6). Jotham seems to have learned from the downfall of his once-great father.

Jotham "did what was right in the eyes of the LORD " (2 Kings 15:35), but he overlooked one critical matter. The people worshiped the other gods like Baal and Asherah. These places of worship were called "high places." Jotham allowed the high places to continue in Judah. Jotham sought God faithfully and walked steadfastly before Him, but he refused to demand respect for the one and only God. So Jotham serves as the poster boy for another path to captivity. To be free in Christ, our high places will have to fall. We must be willing to take a stand against idolatry.

In the lives of Uzziah and his son, Jotham, we see huge obstacles of *pride* and an unwillingness to take a stand against *idolatry*. We also see a continuous suggestion of *unbelief* because they were warned over and over about the consequences of their defiance. The same obstacles they faced confront us as we seek to enjoy the benefits of salvation.

Ahaz became king after the death of his father Jotham, but Ahaz "did not do what was right in the eyes of the LORD" (2 Chron. 28:1). He made idols, worshiped the Baals, and offered sacrifices at the high places. In an abyss of personal evil I cannot even imagine, verse 3 says he even sacrificed his sons in the fire. Can you even comprehend such behavior on the part of one of the kings of God's people?

Please do not miss the fact that Ahaz offered sacrifices at the high places. The high places were accessible to a young and impressionable Ahaz because his father Jotham did not have them removed. Not coincidentally, the atrocity Jotham chose to ignore was exactly the one that snared his own son. Later in our study we will concentrate on the sins parents and grandparents pass along to children.

Next we consider the fourth king and a remarkable phenomenon that is highly improbable without God—the righteous son of an unrighteous father. Hezekiah turned out to be an exact opposite of his father Ahaz. He did something critically important that Jotham failed to do. Hezekiah destroyed the high places. Hezekiah wholeheartedly sought both reformation and restoration. I wonder when Hezekiah's attitudes and philosophies began to depart from his father's. Is it possible he resented losing brothers on a pagan altar and distrusted any father who could do such a thing?

In 2 Chronicles 32 we read one of the remarkable stories of deliverance in Scripture. King Sennacherib of Assyria invaded Judah and laid siege to the cities. The Assyrian army surrounded Jerusalem, and the officials sought to discourage the inhabitants of the city. In the process they made a crucial mistake: they taunted Israel's God.

The Assyrian messenger tried to convince the people of Jerusalem that God could not save them. He said the gods of the other nations could not save those nations and Israel's God would be the same. He asked the wrong question: "How then can your god deliver you from my hand? . . . for no god of any nation or kingdom has been able to deliver his people from my hand or the hand of my fathers. How much less will your god deliver you from my hand!" (2 Chron. 32:14b–15).

From the tone of 2 Chronicles 32:20, Hezekiah and Isaiah were obviously frightened, but they did something brilliant with their fears: they cried out to the Lord. "And the LORD sent an angel, who annihilated all the fighting men and the leaders and officers in the camp of the Assyrian king. So he withdrew to his own land in disgrace" (2 Chron. 32:21).

Hezekiah may have considered Sennacherib's attack to be the most frightening experience of his life . . . until he was hit with a different kind of fear, a far more personal kind.

In Isaiah 38 God told Hezekiah he was going to die, but Hezekiah turned his face to the wall and cried out to God. In response, God added fifteen years to the king's life. Isaiah said, "Prepare a poultice of figs and apply it to the boil, and he will recover" (v. 21). I find it fascinating that God healed Hezekiah through medical treatment. Obviously God did not build a wall between faith and using medicine.

No sooner had Hezekiah recovered than he started sounding as if his close encounter with death came with an automatic doctorate. He said things like, "In your love you kept me / from the pit of destruction" (v. 17), as if the decision to spare one of God's own has anything to do with loving one person more than another. God cannot love us any more or any less than He does at this moment. He chooses to heal or not to heal for His own reasons. All His decisions come from His love, but whether He chooses to heal or take us home, His love remains constant.

Hezekiah also assumed God gave him fifteen more years because only those living on this earth can praise Him (v. 19). Only a few people in the Old Testament seem even to have glimpsed the Resurrection. Hezekiah obviously thought this world was all there is. All these years I've figured my best abilities to praise God would come with my death and, until then, I was severely limited.

Neither of these statements by Hezekiah was the biggy, though. Someone should have stuffed that fig poultice in his mouth before he was able to utter, "I will walk humbly all my years / because of this anguish of my soul" (v. 15).

We have a crippling tendency to forget what God has done for us. For a while, we're humbled. Then, if we do not guard our hearts and minds, we begin to think we must have done something right for God to have been so good to us. Therein lies another road to captivity. It is the road of legalism. Hezekiah believed he was right with God because of what he had done.

We don't have to look far to see that Hezekiah's self-generated righteousness didn't work well or long. Emissaries from the seemingly insignificant city of Babylon came to Jerusalem to congratulate Hezekiah on his restored health. In arrogance and foolish pride, he showed the envoys all the treasures of the city. Babylon would be the very nation to take Judah into captivity. Hezekiah let down his guard and enjoyed the approval of the godless.

Hezekiah's life is a blatant reminder that no one is immune to foolish actions fueled by pride. We may be afraid to ask God on a daily basis to keep us humble because humility involves discomfort. We may have to suffer some embarrassment, even some failure. Why are we not far more frightened of what pride can do? Pride can cost us—and probably those after us.

Several years ago I began developing the habit of confessing and repenting of pride daily, even if I may not have been aware of its presence. I asked God to show me where it was raising up its head or sneaking up on me. So often God will show me little bits of pride that, if left to grow, could be devastating. Let me share a recent example.

Not long ago, I decided to purchase a new Bible. My old one looked like someone had put it in the dishwasher on "pot scrubber." I told my coworkers that I was going to keep the new Bible at work until I could get accustomed to it and still take my old one on speaking engagements for awhile. As the words came out of my mouth, the Holy Spirit seemed to whisper in my ear, "Sounds like pride to Me." He was right. I didn't want to have to struggle to find Scriptures in front of a group. I felt sick to my stomach. That very moment I put up my old Bible. I've flip-flopped my way through the new one ever since.

Have you noticed that the godly kings seemed to struggle with issues of pride more than the ungodly kings? May we learn to guard ourselves against all the lures to captivity. Pride, idolatry, unbelief, legalism, these will prove obstacles we too must confront.

CHAPTER 2

THE REIGN OF CHRIST

The Spirit of the Sovereign LORD is on me,
because the LORD has anointed me
to preach good news to the poor.

(ISA. 61:1a)

We began our study by getting to know the kings in Isaiah's lifetime. In chapters 1–35, Isaiah preached about the rebellion of God's people and the threat of the Assyrians against Judah and Jerusalem. Assyria took the northern kingdom captive in 722 B.C. In chapters 36–39, Isaiah recorded Assyria's defeat by the southern kingdom as King Hezekiah rightly responded to Sennacherib's attack. Isaiah also recorded the illness of Hezekiah, his bout with pride, and the future rise of Babylon.

We've learned something important from Judah's kings. Not even the best were perfect. Not even the most honorable were holy. Not even the most humble were immune to pride. No earthly leader is incapable of misleading. If our liberty in Christ is going to be a reality in life, we are going to have to learn to walk in the freedom of Christ, independent of everyone else we know.

We need more than a leader on our road to freedom. We need a Savior—One who keeps on saving. Although we need to be saved from eternal separation from God only once, Christ continues His saving work in us for the rest of our lives. If you're like me, you can think of more than a few potential disasters from which Christ has saved you since your initial experience of salvation.

Chapters 40–66 begin a new theme in Isaiah. Isaiah spoke to the time when the captivity would end; Israel would be comforted by God and restored to her appointed purpose. I love the way God worded the turning point in the Book of Isaiah after He declared her grievous sins and chastisements. Isaiah 40:1 expresses the theme of this later section: "Comfort, comfort my people, says your God."

The next verse begins, "Speak tenderly to Jerusalem." Oh, how I thank Him for tender words He has spoken to me after I have been chastened for sin. Many of them have come from the Book of Isaiah. Sometimes I wonder why He continues to be so faithful. Yes, He is faithful to chastise, or how would we learn from our rebellion? But He is also so compassionate in His comfort.

God chose the Book of Isaiah, a treatise on captivity, to record some of the most remarkable prophecies about Christ in the entire Old Testament. In a book through which God prophesied the horrors of a foreign yoke, He introduced the Deliverer. In some instances God fulfilled prophecies temporarily through a human agent while ultimately fulfilling them in Christ.

I want to ask you to give utmost attention to Isaiah 61:1–4. Read these verses aloud if possible. Then I want you to see several important points from these wonderful Scriptures.

1. *God hears the cry of the oppressed.* He even hears the cries of those whose oppression is a result of sin and rebellion. We must never cease believing that God cares about those in physical, emotional, mental, or spiritual prisons. God issued Isaiah 61:1–4 as a response to the captivity He foresaw as He looked down on rebellious Judah. God always

cares more for our freedom than even we do. He initiated the saving relationship between the people and the Liberator. "I have surely seen the affliction of my people which are in Egypt, and have heard their cry by reason of their taskmasters; for I know their sorrows"(Exod. 3:7, KJV). God is intimately acquainted with the sorrows and suffering that result from slavery. He also has a remedy. He is the meeter of our needs.

Whether the Israelites fell victim to their taskmasters as in Exodus or walked into slavery because of disobedience and idolatry as in Isaiah, God had deliverance in mind for them. As long as the sun comes up in the morning, God will keep offering to deliver His children.

God's liberating words in Isaiah 61:1–4 apply just as surely to us as they did to the Israelites. They will continue to apply as long as God looks down from the height of His sanctuary, views the earth, and hears the groaning of the prisoner.

2. *God fulfills Isaiah 61:1–4 in Christ alone.* In Luke 4:14–21 Jesus quoted Isaiah 61 as His personal charter. Think about the fulfillment of Isaiah 61:1–4 in Christ. Both Isaiah 61:1 and Luke 4:14 tell us that Christ Jesus would be empowered by the Spirit. We are going to see how important the Holy Spirit is to freedom in Christ. Second Corinthians 3:17 will become a vital truth to us. It tells us that "where the Spirit of the Lord is, there is freedom."

Christ sets us free by the power of His Spirit; then He maintains our freedom as we learn to live from day-to-day in the power of His free Spirit. Isaiah and Luke agree that only Christ was appointed to offer this kind of freedom.

3. *Christ's ministry is a ministry of the heart.* Did you notice all the parts of Jesus' job description in Isaiah 61:1–4? Christ came forth to "bind up the brokenhearted, / to proclaim freedom for the captives / and release from darkness for the prisoners / . . . to comfort all who

mourn / . . . to bestow on them a crown of beauty / instead of ashes / . . . a garment of praise / instead of a spirit of despair" (Isa. 61:1–3).

Based on 2 Peter 3:9, Christ's first priority is setting captives free from the bondage of eternal destruction, but saved people can still be in bondage (Gal. 5:1). When I think of bondage, I most often imagine yokes that come from some area of childhood trauma or victimization because the yoke formed in my childhood has been the primary area of captivity I have had to combat. I make this point because most of us unknowingly limit our perceptions of captivity to those bonds we've personally witnessed or experienced. For this study to be most effective, let's expand our thinking about captivity.

When I realized God was calling me to write this study, I asked the group of women I teach to broaden my horizon in terms of areas of captivity believers face. I asked any of them who had been set free from an area of bondage to share with me two pieces of information through a letter: (1) the specific area of captivity they faced; and (2) the specific ways and lengths of time God employed to set them free.

I'm not sure anything could have prepared me for their responses. Although they will remain unnamed, you know women just like them. These respondents are bright, educated Christian women. They serve faithfully in their churches. They come from all economic backgrounds. For fear of judgment many of them have never told anyone but a godly counselor what they battled.

I heard painful testimonies of bondage to lust and a pattern of falling into sexual sin. I tearfully read about struggles with homosexuality and a fear of men because of childhood abuse. Some spoke about a previous inability to love people fully, including their own husbands and children. One wrote me about the victory God had given her over a compulsion to steal. Another had been freed from habitual dishonesty. A friend I never would have suspected wrote me about her freedom from the bitterness flowing from physical abuse she endured as a child. My heart broke for one woman who described how deep insecurity had stolen friendships, church work, and a contented marriage from her. I've heard from many who were held captive by a critical and judgmental heart toward people. Others wrestled terribly with anger toward God. Doubt. Discouragement. Loneliness. A chronic lack of satisfaction.

Please keep in mind that these letters were only from those who had found freedom in Christ. Imagine how many are still struggling! I firmly believe:

- Christ came to set the captive free—no matter what kind of yoke binds them.
- He came to bind up the brokenhearted—no matter what broke the heart.
- He came to open the eyes of the blind—no matter what veiled their vision.

PART II

BENEFITS AND OBSTACLES

You have examined the rule of the four kings of Isaiah's day and compared the reign of the King of kings. You may already be recognizing the symptoms of captivity in your life. Now we are ready to begin the core of our journey. In the following chapters you will get to know your birthright. God intends five benefits to be the daily experience of every child of God. They are not prizes for an elite few believers. He wants you to live and breathe each of these blessings.

Since many Christians today obviously are not living in the five benefits, we will also consider five primary obstacles. These are hindrances that keep us from the birthright God intends.

I hope you have been working on hiding God's Word in your heart. And because the five benefits are so important to our journey, I want to ask you to begin to memorize them also:

1. To know God and believe Him
2. To glorify God
3. To find satisfaction in God

4. To experience God's peace

5. To enjoy God's presence

Five obstacles block our access to the benefits God wants for us:

1. *Unbelief,* which hinders knowing God

2. *Pride,* which prevents us from glorifying God

3. *Idolatry,* which keeps us from being satisfied with God

4. *Prayerlessness,* which blocks our experience of God's peace

5. *Legalism,* which stops our enjoyment of God's presence

The remainder of our Scripture memory in this book will be the scriptural source of these benefits. The verse for the first benefit is Isaiah 43:10. Copy and memorize the verse for Benefit 1:

"You are my witnesses," declares the LORD,
 "and my servant whom I have chosen,
so that you may know and believe me
 and understand that I am he." (Isa. 43:10)

Continue to work on memorizing our theme passage: Isaiah 61:1–4. Don't get discouraged. The Scripture memory work will get lighter. You've begun well.

CHAPTER 3

TO KNOW GOD AND BELIEVE HIM

Since ancient times no one has heard,
no ear has perceived,
no eye has seen any God besides you,
who acts on behalf of those who wait for him.

(ISA. 64:4)

I love the apostle Paul's rendition of Isaiah 64:4 in 1 Corinthians 2:9. He wrote: "No eye has seen, / no ear has heard, / no mind has conceived / what God has prepared for those who love him." Did you notice the comment Paul added to Isaiah's description of what God has prepared for us?

God wants to do in your life what your mind has never conceived. But just as the children of Israel were held captive by the Babylonians, areas of captivity can keep us from living out the reality of Isaiah 64:4 and 1 Corinthians 2:9.

Take a moment to reread the definition of captivity I gave you previously: *A Christian is held captive by anything that hinders the abundant and effective Spirit-filled life God planned for him or her.* One of the most effective ways we can detect an area of captivity is to measure whether or not we are enjoying the benefits God intends for each of His children. In the following pages, I want to introduce you to five important benefits of your relationship with God. We will seek to get to know each one intimately. Then we will seek to use those benefits as diagnostic tools to determine what God wants to do in our lives to enable us to experience true liberty in Christ.

Let me ask you a question. Are you experiencing the benefits of your covenant relationship with God through Christ, or do the benefits you read in Scripture seem more like warm, fuzzy thoughts?

Just as the Israelites were in bondage, a foreign yoke may be keeping you from personally realizing five primary benefits that God intends for His children to enjoy. The absence of any benefit is a helpful indicator of captivity. According to the Book of Isaiah, God has graciously extended these five benefits to His children.

1. To know God and believe Him
2. To glorify God
3. To find satisfaction in God
4. To experience God's peace
5. To enjoy God's presence

These five benefits and their scriptural references will serve as a road map to lead you home any time you've been carried away captive. Let's begin with a general consideration of the first benefit; then we will examine each of the other four.

Read the wonderful words of Isaiah 43:10: "'You are my witnesses,' declares the LORD, / and my servant whom I have chosen, / so that you may know and believe me / and understand that I am he.'"

Did you note why we have been "chosen"? He chose us specifically so that we may know and believe Him and understand who He is.

In Isaiah 43:10, the Hebrew word for "know" is *yadha*. The ancient term encompassed a personal level of familiarity and was often used to depict the close relationship between a husband and a wife. One of your chief purposes on this planet is to know God intimately and with reverent familiarity. That intimate relationship begins, but was never intended to end, with what we call the "salvation experience." So the first question to ask yourself is, Have you received Christ as your personal Savior?

If you have not, I cannot think of a better time than right now to do so, because Christ is the only entrance to the freedom trail. John 8:36 expresses the truth so simply: "If the Son sets you free, you will be free indeed."

One of the most beautiful elements of salvation is its simplicity. Christ has already done all the work on the cross. Your response includes four elements:

1. Acknowledge that you are a sinner and that you cannot save yourself.
2. Acknowledge that Jesus Christ is the Son of God and only He can save you.
3. Believe that His Crucifixion was for your personal sins and that His death was in your behalf.
4. Give Him your life and ask Him to be your Savior and Lord.

If you already know Christ, is your relationship distant, or close and personal, or somewhere in the middle? If you enjoy a close relationship with God, this study will be an opportunity to deepen that relationship. I deeply desire for you to say when you turn the last page, "And I thought I knew Him and loved Him when I first began." If you don't have a close and familiar relationship with God, don't despair! We will have many priceless opportunities to get in tune with His heart.

Isaiah 43:10 tells us that God not only desires for us to know Him, He wants us to believe Him! The Hebrew word for "believe" in this verse is *aman,* which means "to be firm, to be enduring, to trust."

The level of trust we have for God is a monumental issue in the life of every believer. Many variables in our lives affect our willingness to trust God. A loss or betrayal can deeply mark our level of trust. A broken heart never mended handicaps us terribly when we're challenged to trust. Trusting an invisible God doesn't come naturally to any believer. A trust relationship grows only by stepping out in faith and making the choice to trust. The ability to believe God develops most often through pure experience. "I found Him faithful yesterday. He will not be unfaithful today."

As we study together, I want to ask you to consider how you would characterize your level of trust at the present. We will examine what kinds of experiences have had an impact on your present level of trust.

I would encourage you to copy our working definition of captivity on a card and memorize it: *A Christian is held captive by anything that hinders the abundant and effective Spirit-filled life God planned for him or her.*

I am immeasurably thankful for your willingness to join me on this freedom trail. I am praying for you as you read and study.

CHAPTER 4

To Glorify God

Everyone who is called by my name,
whom I created for my glory,
whom I formed and made.

(ISA. 43:7)

One of our goals in *Breaking Free* is to identify our personal hindrances to abundant life. We noted that the absence of the benefits God intends for us may indicate an area of captivity. I strongly encourage you not just to read *Breaking Free*. Ideally, I encourage you to do the workbook study with a group of fellow believers. Make memory work a part of your study. Copy and memorize the ten memory verses, the definition of *captivity*, and the five benefits. My prayer is that you will be gloriously liberated to pursue and trust Him by the time we turn the last page. Now we examine Benefit 2: To glorify God.

In Isaiah 43:7, what do you suppose God means when He refers to His glory? The more I study God's glory, the more convinced I become that it is almost indefinable. Let's look at several Scriptures and learn the meanings in Hebrew and Greek. However, keep in mind that God's glory far exceeds anything we can comprehend. His glory is everything we're about to learn and infinitely more.

First we see that the glory of God always has an impact. In Isaiah 6:3 the seraphim in the throne room of God called to one another: "Holy, holy, holy is the LORD Almighty; / the whole earth is full of his glory." When Moses and Aaron encountered the glory of God, they fell facedown (Num. 20:6). In 2 Chronicles 5:14, "the priests could not perform their service because of the cloud, for the glory of the LORD filled the temple of God." When God's glory appears, it just can't help but interrupt any routine.

Did you also note that God makes Himself known through His glory? Psalm 19:1 says, "The heavens declare the glory of God; / the skies proclaim the work of his hands." Psalm 29:9 demonstrates the power of God's self-revelation: "The voice of the LORD twists the oaks / and strips the forests bare. / And in his temple all cry, 'Glory!'"

God's glory doesn't just reflect Him. It is also part of who He is! In each of those Old Testament references, the Hebrew word for "glory" is *kavodh,* meaning "weight, honor, esteem." The word *kavodh* comes from another Hebrew term that greatly increases our comprehension. The word *kavedh* means to "be renowned . . . to show oneself great or mighty." In other words, God's glory is the way He makes Himself known or shows Himself mighty. God wants to reveal Himself to humans. Each way He accomplishes this divine task is His glory. God's glory is how He shows who He is.

Consider the following New Testament uses of *glory* and note what they add to our understanding. The apostle John told us that Christ displayed God's glory: "The Word became flesh and made his dwelling among us. We have seen his glory, the glory of the One and Only, who came from the Father, full of grace and truth" (John 1:14). "This, the first of his miraculous signs, Jesus performed at Cana in Galilee. He thus revealed his glory, and his disciples put their faith in him" (John 2:11).

Hebrews states the same concept in the form of propositional truth: "The Son is the radiance of God's glory and the exact representation of his being, sustaining all things by his powerful word. After he had provided purification for sins, he sat down at the right hand of the Majesty in heaven" (Heb. 1:3). Christ is the very glory of God.

Peter conveys the idea with a bit more application to our lives: "His divine power has given us everything we need for life and godliness through our knowledge of him who called us by his own glory and goodness" (2 Pet. 1:3). Not only is Christ the representation of God's glory, His glory also supplies our needs.

The Greek word for "glory" in these New Testament references is *doxa*. It is "the true apprehension of God or things. The glory of God must mean His unchanging essence. Giving glory to God is ascribing to Him His full recognition. . . . The glory of God is what He is essentially." God's glory is the way He makes Himself recognizable.

Look at Isaiah 43:7 once more: "Everyone who is called by my name, / whom I created for my glory, / whom I formed and made." Based on what we've learned from our Scriptures and definitions, I believe being created for God's glory means two marvelous truths to those who are called by His name:

1. God wants to make Himself recognizable to us.
2. God wants to make Himself recognizable through us.

First Corinthians 10:31 declares, "Whatever you do, do it all for the glory of God." God desires that He be recognizable in us in all that we do! Living a life that glorifies God is synonymous with living a life that reveals God.

If you're like me, you're probably overwhelmed by the enormous responsibility of such a calling. We're imperfect creatures! How are we to help others recognize something about God just from watching our lives and knowing us? Consider another portion of the definition of *doxa* that relates the term to human beings: "The glory of created things including man is what they are meant by God to be, though not yet perfectly attained."

Not yet perfectly attained . . . God intended that we show forth His glory, but we "all have sinned and fall short of the glory of God" (Rom. 3:23). We've fallen short, missed the mark, sinned; but anyone who knows our God knows He is far too tenacious to be thwarted by our sin. Paul declared that "God has chosen to make known among the Gentiles the glorious riches of this mystery, which is Christ in you, the hope of glory" (Col. 1:27). The apostle Paul announced the mystery that Christ Himself dwells in the life of every believer. Christ in us! Romans 8:9 tells us that "if anyone does not have the Spirit of Christ, he does not belong to Christ." In other words, the moment each of us received Christ as our Savior, the Holy Spirit of Christ took up residence in our inner being.

Do you see the key? We have no hope whatsoever of God's being recognizable in us if the Spirit of Christ does not dwell in us. If we are not occupied by the Holy Spirit, we have nothing of God in us for Him to show. Christ is a human being's only "hope of glory"!

We glorify God to the degree that we externalize the internal existence of the living Christ. A life that glorifies God is not something we suddenly attain. As we spend time in the presence of God, His glory both transforms us and radiates from us.

Paul used the example of Moses' meeting with God to illustrate this practical truth. When Moses had been in the Lord's presence, his face glowed with God's glory so much that Moses put a veil over his face (Exod. 34:33). Paul wrote of Christians: "We, who with unveiled faces all reflect the Lord's glory, are being transformed into his likeness with ever-increasing glory, which comes from the Lord, who is the Spirit" (2 Cor. 3:18).

I hope you didn't miss the fact that we are being changed into Christ's "likeness with ever-increasing glory." I love the King James Version's words: "from glory to glory"! You see, people who are living out the reality of their liberation in Christ (Gal. 5:1; 2 Cor. 3:17) progress in their spiritual lives in an "ever-increasing glory." As they grow in spiritual maturity, the Spirit of Christ becomes increasingly recognizable in them. Likewise, when Christ is not recognizable in a redeemed life, we need to identify and allow God to treat the area of captivity.

We were created for the purpose of giving Christ's invisible character a glimpse of visibility. If we grasp all the eternal implications of such a destiny, we would want to do anything possible to make sure all hindrances were removed. Remember the definition of *doxa* as it relates to human beings?—"what they are meant by God to be." Now reflect once again on the words of Isaiah 43:7: "Everyone who is called by my name, / . . . I created for my glory." Allow me to attempt to summarize:

- We were created for God's glory.
- We have no hope of God's glory without the indwelling Spirit of Christ that comes at our salvation.
- We fulfill what we were meant to be when God is recognizable in us.
- A life that glorifies God or makes Him recognizable is a process that ideally progresses with time and maturity.

You may be wondering how a person could recognize whether or not his or her life was glorifying God. I want to ask you to think about the following Scriptures and statements. They help me to determine whether Benefit 2 is a present reality in my life. Please don't be dismayed if you feel you are not already living a life that glorifies God! He never sheds light on our weaknesses or shortcomings for the sake of condemnation (Rom. 8:1). God makes us aware of hindrances so He can set us free!

Here is my personal checklist of Scriptures and evaluations. I seek to apply these to my life on a regular basis:

- Is my most important consideration in every undertaking whether or not God could be glorified? (1 Cor. 10:31).
- Do I desire God's glory or my own? (John 8:50, 54).
- In my service to others, is my sincere hope that they will somehow see God in me? (1 Pet. 4:10–11).
- When I am going through hardships, do I turn to God and try to cooperate with Him so He can use them for my good and for His glory? (1 Pet. 4:12–13).
- Am I sometimes able to accomplish things or withstand things only through the power of God? (2 Cor. 4:7).

Don't worry! None of us consistently glorify God in everything we say and do, but we can experience genuine liberation in Christ. God wants to do more than we've ever heard, seen, or imagined in each life (1 Cor. 2:9). God protects us from pride by keeping us somewhat unaware of the degree to which we are effectively glorifying Him at times. However, when we are able to respond to the questions with an affirmative answer of "Yes" or "I'm making progress," God is being glorified! Just be sure to turn around and give Him the glory!

This chapter may have been difficult for you. You may feel like you have a long way to go before you are fulfilling His purpose. Instead, I hope you can see the magnificent potential He planned for you to fulfill. On the other hand, you may be able to celebrate some progress in your pursuit of a God-glorifying life. No matter what God has exposed to you, relish the wonderful words of Christ that pertain to you. From the shadow of the cross, He said of you:

> I pray for them. I am not praying for the world, but
> for those you have given me, for they are yours. All I
> have is yours, and all you have is mine. And glory has
> come to me through them. (John 17:9–10)

In this context, Christ used the word *glory* to indicate wealth and riches He had received. No matter where you are on the journey to the glorifying, liberated life in Christ, you are His treasure. He does not want to take from you. He wants to give to you and free you from any hindrance.

Please conclude this chapter with a time of prayer about the God-glorifying life. Share with Him your sincere response to what you have been reading.

CHAPTER 5

TO FIND SATISFACTION
IN GOD

Then you will know the truth, and the truth will set you free.

(JOHN 8:32)

Christ continually uses the truth of John 8:32 as the means to our destination. Not only is God's truth an absolute necessity in our progress toward complete freedom, but our truthfulness is also a necessity. Psalm 51:6 says God desires "truth in the inner parts." A combination of two vehicles—God's truth and our truthfulness—will drive us to our desired destination.

I mention the importance of honesty because I may be about to get more honest than some of us can stand. I ask you to hear me out and consider what I have to say: Many Christians are not satisfied with Jesus. Before you call me a heretic, let me set the record straight: Jesus is absolutely satisfying. In fact, He is the only means by which any mortal creature can find true satisfaction. However, I believe a person can receive Christ as Savior, serve Him for decades, and meet Him face-to-face in glory without ever experiencing satisfaction in Him. If you have indeed discovered genuine satisfaction in Christ, I am going to assume that—like me—you are so zealous for others to find Him satisfying that you will gladly participate in this segment of our study anyway.

The Bible uses the word *soul* in a number of ways. One of those ways is to refer to the nonmaterial part of us. When I speak of soul hunger, I am referring to our need for spiritual satisfaction. Is your soul, your spirit, your own inmost place—the real you—entirely satisfied with Christ? As we meditate on our answers, let's consider the biblical meaning of *satisfaction* through several Old Testament Scriptures.

Isaiah recorded God's issuing a poetic and classic invitation:

> Come, all you who are thirsty,
>   come to the waters;
> and you who have no money,
>   come, buy and eat!
> Come, buy wine and milk
>   without money and without cost.
> Why spend money on what is not bread,
>   and your labor on what does not satisfy?
> Listen, listen to me, and eat what is good,
>   and your soul will delight in the richest of fare.
>   (Isa. 55:1–2)

The prophet contrasts the world's attempt to find satisfaction with what God provides. The Hebrew word used for "satisfy" is *sob'ah,* meaning "to have enough, be full . . . sufficiently" (*Strong's*). In effect, God is asking, "Why do you work so hard for things that are never enough, can never fill you up, and are endlessly insufficient?"

Can you think of anything you've worked hard to attain that ultimately failed to bring the satisfaction you were expecting? We've each been disappointed by something we expected to bring satisfaction.

Jeremiah 31 contains another intriguing reference to satisfaction. God said He will refresh the weary and satisfy the faint—when He brings them home from captivity (Jer. 31:23–25). In Jeremiah 31:25, the Hebrew word for "satisfy" is *male*, meaning "to fill, accomplish, the filling of something that was empty . . . the act of replenishment as well as the experience of satiation." The word for "faint" is *da'ab*, meaning "to pine" (*Strong's*). Do you see the connection to captivity and to lack of satisfaction in Christ? We can easily be led into captivity by seeking other answers to needs and desires that only God can meet. Perhaps we each have experienced an empty place deep inside that we tried our best to ignore or to fill with something other than God.

A crucial part of fleshing out our liberation in Christ means allowing Him to fill the empty places in our lives. Satisfaction in Christ can be a reality. I know from experience, and I want everyone to know how complete He can make us feel. I'm not talking about a life full of activities. I'm talking about a soul full of Jesus.

The filling only He can give does not automatically accompany our salvation. I was in my early thirties before I understood the huge difference between salvation from sin and satisfaction of soul. Salvation secures our lives for all eternity. Soul satisfaction ensures abundant life on earth.

We can learn several truths about satisfied souls by drawing a parallel between the soul and the physical body. I know this seems simplistic, but humor me for a moment. How do you know you are hungry? When you are thirsty? What do you usually do when you're hungry or thirsty? *You seek what will meet your need.* If you ignore your physical needs long enough, not only will you be miserable; you will be ill. You can easily recognize the signals the body gives, but great wisdom lies in learning to discern the signals your spiritual nature gives.

Psalm 63 offers insight into the satisfied soul. Look at David's descriptions of satisfaction: "My soul thirsts for you, / my body longs for you, / in a dry and weary land" (v. 1). "Because your love is better than life, / my lips will glorify you" (v. 3). "My soul will be satisfied as with the richest of foods" (v. 5). The most obvious symptom of a soul in need of God's satisfaction is a sense of inner emptiness. The awareness of a "hollow place" somewhere deep inside—the inability to be satisfied.

The soul can also manifest physical symptoms of need. I like to think of it this way: Just like my stomach growls when I'm hungry for physical food, my spirit tends to growl when I'm in need of spiritual food. When a checker at the grocery store seems overtly irritable or grouchy, I sometimes grin and think to myself, "I bet her kids woke up before she had a chance to have her quiet time!" I can certainly assure you that my personality is distinctively different when I haven't had the time I need with the Lord. My soul can do some pretty fierce growling!

How about you? Does your hungry soul ever manifest physical symptoms such as irritability, selfish ambitions, anger, impure thoughts, envy, resentments, and eruptions of lust?

Here's a similar analogy. When a soul is thirsty for the Living Water (John 4), just as my mouth gets dry when I am thirsty, my spiritual mouth gets dry when I need the satisfying refreshment only God can bring. The following Scriptures suggest a few symptoms of a mouth wet with God's Living Water.

My mouth is filled with your praise,
    declaring your splendor all day long. (Ps. 71:8)

May my tongue sing of your word,
    for all your commands are righteous. (Ps. 119:172)

The Sovereign LORD has given me an instructed tongue,
    to know the word that sustains the weary. (Isa. 50:4)

Our final point is very important. We can positively assume that our soul is hungry and thirsty for God if we have not partaken of any spiritual food or drink in a long while. Souls accustomed to soul food are more likely to have a highly developed appetite. In Psalm 63, David was accustomed to beholding the power and glory of God. He was so acquainted with God's love, he considered it "better than life" (v. 3). Therefore, he missed God's refreshment when he didn't have it.

I think we have the same tendency. The more we've been satisfied by God's love, His Word, and His presence, the more we will yearn for it. On the other hand, we can spend so much time away from the Lord that we no longer feel hungry or thirsty. I know from personal experience that if you fail to partake of the spiritual food and drink of God for a while, you are hungry and thirsty for His satisfaction whether or not you know it!

God can satisfy your yearning soul. Satisfying your innermost places with Jesus is a benefit of the glorious covenant relationship you have with God in Christ. Open the door; He waits to satisfy your hungry soul.

CHAPTER 6

To Experience God's Peace

*Now may the Lord of peace himself give you peace at all times
and in every way. The Lord be with all of you.*

(2 Thess. 3:16)

I can't overemphasize the importance of peace as a real and practical benefit of our covenant relationship with God. His peace should not be an infrequent surprise but the ongoing rule of our lives.

The apostle Paul underscored the essential nature of peace in 2 Thessalonians 3:16. Did you notice how crucial he considered peace to be? "At all times." "In every way." Peace can be possible in any situation, but we cannot produce it on demand. In fact, *we* cannot produce it at all. It is a fruit of the Spirit (Gal. 5:22).

We have Christ's peace. It has already been given to us if we have received Christ. We just don't always know how to activate it. We're about to discover the key to experiencing the practical reality of God's peace. Then throughout the course of our journey, we're going to work on becoming more free to turn that key.

Isaiah used the word *peace* twenty-six times. God continually promised peace when His captives returned wholeheartedly to the Lord. The familiar messianic passage, Isaiah 9:6, identifies peace with Christ as "Prince of Peace." The next verse connects the Prince of Peace to His reign: "Of the increase of his government and peace / there will be no end. / He will reign on David's throne." Many of us have memorized the words of Isaiah 26:3: "You will keep in perfect peace / him whose mind is steadfast, / because he trusts in you." Isaiah 32:17 identifies yet another aspect of God's peace: "The fruit of righteousness will be peace; / the effect of righteousness will be quietness and confidence forever." And who can think long about peace in the Book of Isaiah without bringing to mind the awesome prediction of Christ's suffering for us? "He was pierced for our transgressions, / he was crushed for our iniquities; / the punishment that brought us peace was upon him" (Isa. 53:5).

Did you see any hints of a common denominator tying several of these Scriptures together? Isaiah 9:6–7 perfectly portrays the key to peace: authority. When we allow the Prince of Peace to govern our lives, peace either immediately or ultimately results. Peace accompanies authority.

Have you experienced a time when you were surrendered to Christ in difficult times and you found His peace beyond understanding? Can you also say, as I can, that you have had an absence of peace in much less difficult circumstances? Have you ever wondered what the difference was?

Peace comes in situations that are completely surrendered to the sovereign authority of Christ. Sometimes when we finally give up trying to discover all the answers to the whys in our lives and decide to trust a sovereign God, unexpected peace washes over us like a summer rain. We sometimes lack peace in far less strenuous circumstances because we are not as desperate or as likely to turn them over to God.

I finally had to turn some of the hurts of my childhood over to God's sovereign authority because I realized they would consume me like a cancer. When at last I allowed Him to govern everything concerning my past, not only did the Prince give me His peace, He actually brought good from something horrible and unfair. If you have not yet bowed the knee to God's authority over areas of your past, something is holding you captive.

Christ desperately wants His people to experience His peace. The Greek word *klaio* is the strongest word used in the New Testament for grief. It means "to weep, wail, lament, implying not only the shedding of tears, but also every external expression of grief." Christ wept on several occasions, but on only one occasion is His grief described with the word *klaio*. That occasion is found in Luke 19:41–42. As Jesus approached the city of Jerusalem, He wept over it and said, "If you, even you, had only known on this day what would bring you peace—but now it is hidden from your eyes."

I believe Christ still grieves when He sees hearts in unnecessary turmoil. You can have the peace of Christ, believer, no matter what your circumstances; but you must believe, bend the knee, and learn to receive.

We hopefully will be able to discover a few reasons why we are so reluctant to submit to God's authority, but we must remember that bending the knee is ultimately a matter of pure obedience. You may never feel like giving your circumstance, hurt, or loss to Him; but you can choose to submit to His authority out of belief and obedience rather than emotion. Obedience is always the mark of authentic surrender to God's authority.

When I finally bent the knee to the Prince of Peace over hurts in my childhood, I realized He was directing me to forgive the person who hurt me. God did not insist on my forgiving for the sake of that person but for peace in my life. Once I began to surrender to Him in this painful area, He began to give me a supernatural ability to forgive. A segment of Scripture in Isaiah beautifully reveals the relationship between obedience, authority, and peace. God has a right to all authority because of who He is: "This is what the LORD says— / your Redeemer, the Holy One of Israel: / 'I am the LORD your God, / who teaches you what is best for you, / who directs you in the way you should go'" (Isa. 48:17).

Did you notice the titles by which the Lord refers to Himself in the passage? Allow me to reverse the order and share my outlook on His right to complete authority. He is God, the Creator of the heavens and the earth, the supreme Author of all existence. He reigns over all, and in Him all things exist. He is Lord, the Master and Owner of all living creatures. He is the covenant Maker and Keeper. He is holy. As Lord, He will never ask anything of us that is not right, good, and open to the light. He is perfect and undefiled. Lastly, He is Redeemer, the One who bought us from sin's slave master so we could experience abundant life. He bought us to set us free. "What, then, shall we say in response to this? If God is for us, who can be against us?" (Rom. 8:31).

What do you suppose would happen if we paid attention to God's commands? We don't have to wonder, because He told us clearly: "If only you had paid attention to my commands, / your peace would have been like a river, / your righteousness like the waves of the sea" (Isa. 48:18).

Consider the following applications as you imagine peace like a river.

1. *A river is a moving stream of water.* God's Word does not say we'll have peace like a pond. If we were honest, we might admit to thinking of peaceful people as boring. We might think, *I'd rather forego peace and have an exciting life!* When was the last time you saw white-water rapids?

Few bodies of water are more exciting than rivers! We can have active, exciting lives without suffering through a life of turmoil. To have peace like a river is to have security and tranquility while meeting many bumps and unexpected turns on life's journey. Peace is submission to a trustworthy Authority, not resignation from activity.

2. *A river is a body of fresh water fed by springs or tributary streams.* To experience peace, we must be feeding our relationship with God. I've found that I can't retain peace in the present by relying on a relationship from the past. As a river is continually renewed with the moving waters of springs and streams, so our peace comes from an active, ongoing, and obedient relationship with the Prince of Peace. This and other Bible studies are examples of ways God desires to feed a peaceful river in your soul.

3. *A river begins and ends with a body of water.* Every river has an upland source and an ultimate outlet or mouth. Rivers depend on and are always connected to other bodies of water. Likewise, peace like a river flows from a continuous connection with the upland Source, Jesus Christ, which is a timely reminder that this life will ultimately spill out into a glorious eternal life. The present life is not our destination, hallelujah! We who know Christ move over rocks and sometimes cliffs, through narrow places and wide valleys to a heavenly destination. Until then, abiding in Christ (John 15:4, KJV) is the key to staying deliberately connected with our upland Source.

Take pleasure in knowing that God inspired His Word with great care and immaculate precision. He chose every word purposely. When He said we could have peace like a river in Isaiah 48:18, He wasn't drawing a loose analogy. He meant it. What does it take to have this peace? Attention to God's commands (by obedience) through the power of the Holy Spirit. Obedience to God's authority not only brings peace like a river but righteousness like the waves of the sea. Not righteous perfection. Righteous *consistency.*

You see, God's way is the safe way. The right way. And the only peaceful way in a chaotic world. I hope you've discovered that peace is not beyond your reach. It's not a goal to meet one day. You can begin a life of authentic peace today. Right now. The path to peace is paved with kneeprints. Bend the knee to His trustworthy authority. "Let the peace of Christ rule in your hearts" (Col. 3:15).

CHAPTER 7

TO ENJOY GOD'S PRESENCE

When you pass through the waters,
I will be with you;
and when you pass through the rivers,
they will not sweep over you.
When you walk through the fire,
you will not be burned;
the flames will not set you ablaze.
For I am the LORD, your God,
the Holy One of Israel, your Savior.

(ISA. 43:2–3)

I doubt any believer feels God's wonderful presence every second of every day. Sometimes we're challenged to believe He's with us simply because He promised (Heb. 13:5). That's faith.

God's Word often tells us not to fear, yet not all of our fears are unfounded. Think about it. Our present society poses many real threats. Did you notice Isaiah 43:2 said, "*When* you pass through the waters"? God is not suggesting that difficult things don't happen to His children.

If nothing frightening will happen to us, how could the assurance of God's constant presence still be the quieter of our fears?

Psalm 139:7–12 assures us that God's presence is with us always. "Even the darkness will not be dark" to our God (v. 12). Hebrews 13:5 assures us: "Never will I leave you; / never will I forsake you." We cannot escape God's presence, but we do not always sense His presence.

God's presence in our lives is absolutely unchanging, but the evidence of His presence is not. On some occasions God may purposely alter the evidences of His presence to bring the most benefit from our experience. Sometimes we receive the most benefit from seeing many visible "prints" of His invisible hands during a difficult season. Other times we profit most from seeing fewer evidences. God does not love us less when He gives us fewer evidences. He simply desires to grow us up and teach us to walk by faith.

In Matthew 14:25–32 in the midst of a storm, Jesus came walking on the water. To his terrified disciples, He said: "Take courage! It is I. Don't be afraid" (v. 27), but the storm continued to rage until He got into the boat. The point is not that we have nothing to fear but that His presence is the basis for our courage. Christ did not say, "Take courage! I am calming the storm. Don't be afraid." Instead, with the winds still raging, He said, "Take courage! It is I. Don't be afraid."

Christ does not always immediately calm the storm, but He is always willing to calm His child on the basis of His presence. "Don't worry! I know the winds are raging and the waves are high, but I am God over both. If I let them continue to swell, it's because I want you to see Me walk on the water." We'll probably never learn to enjoy our storms, but we can learn to enjoy God's presence in the storm!

In Psalm 16:11, David confidently proclaimed: "You will fill me with joy in your presence." The Hebrew word for "joy" is *simchah,* which means "glee, gladness, joy, pleasure, rejoice(-ing)." We can learn to enjoy God's presence even when life is not enjoyable. I can't explain it, but I've experienced it over and over.

Before we can begin to enjoy God's presence in our lives, we must accept His presence as an absolute fact. The most wonderful assurance of God's presence is probably within your reach this very moment—His Word. When it all comes down, we either choose to believe or disbelieve God. Once we choose to accept His presence as a fact, we can be free to go on to enjoyment.

Are you ready to accept His ever-abiding presence in your life as an absolute fact? Are you ready to begin enjoying God in your life more than ever? If so, take time to pray, asking Him to strengthen your faith and teach you how to enjoy Him to the fullest.

Enjoying your relationship with Christ both leads to and reinforces the five benefits of that covenant relationship. These benefits obviously relate to each other. Here's a comparison that may help you relate to them.

My husband Keith and I have been married for twenty-plus years. I know my husband very well, and I believe him when he tells me something (Benefit 1). In an earthly sense, I glorify (revere) him because I've lived with him so long that some of his traits now show up in me (Benefit 2). He satisfies virtually every need a husband should (Benefit 3). I often get to experience peace while he assumes the responsibility in matters of finances and future security (Benefit 4). I could not experience the last primary benefit of our marriage without the other four, yet it is completely distinct: I purely enjoy my husband's presence (Benefit 5).

As much as I enjoy my husband, daughters, family, and friends, no relationship in my life brings me more joy than my relationship with God. I certainly haven't "arrived" in some mystical place, nor have I made even these few steps quickly or casually. I've grown to enjoy God with time. Not every minute I spend with Him is gleeful or great fun.

Intimacy with God grows through sharing every realm of experience. I've wept bitterly with Him. I've screamed in frustration. Sometimes I thought He was going to break my heart in two. But I've also laughed out loud with Him. Wept with unspeakable joy. Left the chair and gone to my knees in awe. Squealed with excitement.

I have been to every extreme and back with God. But if I had to define my relationship with Him by one general statement, I would tell you that He is the absolute joy of my life. I don't just love Him. I love loving Him. Surrendering my heart to Him has not been a sacrifice. I don't know any other way to say it: He works for me.

I am hesitant to say all of this because I would be sickened to think I might sound proud of my relationship with God. Please hear my heart: the greatest joy in my life is the very thing I have deserved the least. I consider the ability to love Him and enjoy Him an absolute gift of grace . . . one He will gladly extend to anyone who offers his or her whole heart.

I know a little of what the apostle Paul meant when he said "I am jealous for you with a godly jealousy" (2 Cor. 11:2). My friend, I am "jealous" for you to enjoy God. I want God to be the greatest reality in your life. I want you to be more assured of His presence than any other you can see or touch. This can be your reality. This is your right as a child of God. We were destined for this kind of relationship with God, but the enemy tries to convince us that the Christian life is sacrificial at best and artificial at worst.

We've established a five-part checklist of priority benefits based on the Book of Isaiah. The enemy has no right to hold you back from realizing any of these benefits. They are yours. In this study we are going to reclaim some surrendered ground. As you reflect over the list, do any of these benefits suggest that you may have something holding you back? Is God pointing to the possibility of an area of captivity in your life?

Conclude with an assignment to take very seriously. Commit yourself entirely to God that He may set you free to be everything He planned. Ask Him in Jesus' name not to let the enemy steal one bit of the victory God has for you. We must not allow intimidation or fear to imprison us in any area. Remember, Satan can presume no authority in your life. He will do his best to bluff you. Don't let him. "The one who is in you is greater than the one who is in the world" (1 John 4:4).

Listen closely. The liberty bell is ringing.

CHAPTER 8

THE OBSTACLE OF UNBELIEF

"Build up, build up, prepare the road!
Remove the obstacles out of the way of my people."

(ISA. 57:14)

We identified five primary benefits of our covenant relationship with God. The absence of any of these benefits is a possible indicator of some form of captivity. Isaiah records a promise and a statement that speaks powerfully to me about liberty. God said through Isaiah, "'The man who makes me his refuge / will inherit the land / and possess my holy mountain.' / And it will be said: / 'Build up, build up, prepare the road! / Remove the obstacles out of the way of my people'" (Isa. 57:13–14).

In Isaiah's day villages prepared weeks in advance for a visit by their king. Workmen cleared a path and built a road to provide the easiest access for the king's entourage. If the king did not find the path adequately prepared, he would bypass the village and withhold his blessing.

God inspired Isaiah 57:14 with a different entourage in mind, however. Look closely at the Scripture. Notice that God emphasized the commoner as the traveler. Instead of calling for all obstacles to be removed for his own journey, the King commanded the removal of all obstacles for His people's journey. He wanted no obstructions hindering the journey of His people into His presence.

We want to accomplish the task described in Isaiah 57:14. Yes, we face a few obstacles that need to be removed, but we have the approval and blessing of the matchless King in our favor. We don't have to wonder if He's willing and able to deliver us from the bonds that are withholding abundant life. Remember, it is for freedom Christ has set us free. He's more than willing. He's ready. The question is whether or not we are ready to cooperate and prepare the way for our Liberator.

Throughout this study, we will seek to remove many obstacles between us and the practice of freedom. As we begin, however, we specify five primary obstacles to freedom that correspond with our five primary benefits. These five obstacles are so prohibitive that if they are not addressed and removed in advance the personal visitation of our King will be greatly hindered. These are the five obstacles that stand in the way of our benefits: unbelief, pride, idolatry, prayerlessness, and legalism.

Let's begin with Benefit 1: To know God and believe Him. The fact that you are reading this volume is evidence of your desire to know God. Let's focus, then, on the second portion of Benefit 1—To believe Him.

What do you think would be the most obvious obstacle to believing God? As simple as this seems, the largest obstacle is unbelief, choosing not to believe God. We're not talking about believing *in* God. We're talking about believing God, believing what He says. We can believe in Christ for salvation in a matter of seconds and yet spend the rest of our days believing Him for little more. Eternity can be well secured while life on earth remains shaky at best. Let's pinpoint what "believing God" means, and we'll have a better understanding of its greatly hindering antonym.

I have come to pay special attention when the New Testament quotes a verse from the Old. Genesis 15:6 says, "Abram believed the LORD, and he credited it to him as righteousness." Paul quoted the verse in Romans 4:3. The verses show a congruency between both testaments regarding the concept of believing God.

In Genesis 15:6, the Hebrew word for "believed" is *'aman,* meaning "to make firm, . . . to stand firm, to be enduring; to trust, to believe." In Romans 4:3, the Greek word for "believed" is *pisteuo,* meaning "to be firmly persuaded as to something, to believe . . . with the idea of hope and certain expectation." It comes from the Greek word *pistis,* translated into the English word *faith* throughout the New Testament. As you can see, in both testaments, belief and faith represent the same concept.

We can easily assume the definition of unbelief, but let's take a look at an interesting Scripture to further our understanding and offer us encouragement. In Mark 9:21–24 the father of a demon-possessed boy asked Jesus to help—if He could. Jesus told him, "Everything is possible for him who believes." Immediately the boy's father exclaimed, "I do believe; help me overcome my unbelief!"

What refreshing honesty this admission must have been to Christ! The father gave the right answer, "I do believe!" But right answers don't help much with a wavering heart. As the father stood in the presence of Christ, he could no longer hold back his honest heart: "Help me overcome my unbelief!" The Greek word for "unbelief" is *apistos,* meaning "not worthy of confidence, untrustworthy . . . a thing not to be believed, incredible."

We can believe in Christ, accepting the truth that He is the Son of God, and we can believe on Christ, receiving eternal salvation, yet fail to stand firm in belief and choose to find Him trustworthy day to day.

The phrase "not worthy of confidence" makes me shudder. God is so deserving of our trust. Moses expressed the truth so well: "God is not

THE OBSTACLE OF UNBELIEF

a man, that he should lie, / nor a son of man, that he should change his mind. / Does he speak and then not act? / Does he promise and not fulfill?" (Num. 23:19).

Can you think of a time when God proved unworthy of your confidence? If we think we've discovered unfaithfulness in God, I believe one of three things has happened: (1) we misinterpreted the promise, (2) we missed the answer, or (3) we gave up before God timed His response.

I see good and bad news involving the issue of a believer's practice of unbelief. The bad news? Unbelief is crippling. The steps we take forward with God we take through faith. Therefore, unbelief literally cripples our spiritual "walk," casting huge obstacles in the way of a victorious life.

Do you believe God? Or somewhere along the way have you ceased believing God is able? Do you secretly approach Him with the attitude, "*if* you can do anything, take pity on me."

Now for the good news! If we're willing to admit our lack of confidence in Him, Christ is more than willing to help us overcome our unbelief. Belief—or faith in the abilities and promises of God—is a vital prerequisite for fleshing out the liberty we've won through Jesus Christ.

Let's take a simple self-test to measure our state of belief. Think carefully about each of the following six statements. If you were rating your belief from 1 to 10 (10 being "strongly believe") to indicate how strongly you believe or disbelieve each statement, what number would you give them? Think seriously about each statement before you read on to see what the Scripture says about the issues.

1. Christians can have areas of captivity.
2. Christ can set anyone free from captivity.
3. God is fully acquainted with you personally and wants what is best for you.
4. Christians have an invisible but very real enemy called Satan who is a personality of evil rather than a "principle" of evil.

5. Your heart can sometimes want what is desperately wrong for you.

6. The Bible is the inspired Word of God and true.

Compare the six statements with what the Scripture says to each one:

1. Speaking specifically to those who had been set free, Paul warned the Galatians, "Do not let yourselves be burdened again by a yoke of slavery" (Gal. 5:1).

2. Jesus said the Father "has sent me to proclaim freedom for the prisoners" (Luke 4:18).

3. In one of the greatest statements of God's personal involvement in our lives, David wrote:

O LORD, you have searched me
    and you know me.
You know when I sit and when I rise;
    you perceive my thoughts from afar.
You discern my going out and my lying down;
    you are familiar with all my ways. (Ps. 139:1–3)

4. Paul the apostle wrote that "our struggle is not against flesh and blood, but against the rulers, against the authorities, against the powers of this dark world and against the spiritual forces of evil in the heavenly realms" (Eph. 6:12). Peter declared, "Your enemy the devil prowls around like a roaring lion looking for someone to devour" (1 Pet. 5:8).

5. Remember that Jeremiah described the heart as "deceitful above all things / and beyond cure" (Jer. 17:9).

6. Paul assures us that "all Scripture is God-breathed and is useful for teaching, rebuking, correcting and training in righteousness"

(2 Tim. 3:16). And David proclaimed that "the word of the LORD is flawless" (Ps. 18:30).

At one time I could not have answered any of the questions with a confident 10; but in recent years, I can assure you that God has made a full believer out of me. If we believe the Bible, we can believe the concepts represented by each question.

Your struggle may be that you are not utterly convinced that the Bible is God's inspired Word. If so, scriptural "proofs" may mean little to you. Believe it or not, I was not always convinced either—although I never would have admitted it. Not coincidentally, my uncertainty accompanied a sizable lack of knowledge. I knew what I had been taught and wholeheartedly believed the basics; but I did not become convinced about the glorious inspiration of God's complete Word until I really began to study. Instead of discovering loopholes and worrisome inconsistencies, I have been awed to my knees over the beauty of God's Word and the perfect blending of the Old and New Testaments. The study of Scripture has increased my faith at least a hundredfold. I grow increasingly amazed at His Word.

In Scripture we clearly see how important belief can be in the matter of freedom. For example, Matthew 9:27–29 records Jesus' encounter with two blind men. He asked them, "Do you believe that I am able to do this?" When they said yes, He touched their eyes and told them, "According to your faith will it be done to you."

Please understand. Christ is fully God. He can heal anyone or perform any wonder, whether the belief of the person is great or small. Christ isn't asking us to believe in our ability to exercise unwavering faith. He is asking us to believe that He is able.

When it comes to bringing us to a life of freedom, I believe He is also willing. If we were focusing on physical healing, I would not have such certainty. Sometimes God heals physical sicknesses, and sometimes

He chooses greater glory through illness. He always can heal physical diseases, but He does not always choose to bring healing on this earth.

Scripture is absolutely clear, however, that God always wills the spiritual captive to be free. God's will is for us to know Him and believe Him, glorify Him, be satisfied by Him, experience peace in Him, and enjoy Him. For God to have utmost cooperation from us on this freedom trail, we must believe that He is willing and completely able.

If you are not struggling with belief, be careful not to judge another's weaker faith (Rom. 14:1). Some believers have been in chains for so long and have tried so hard to break free in the past, they have almost given up hope for the future.

If you are having difficulty believing you really could live out the liberty of Christ, would you make the same plea the father made in Mark 9:24? Spend some time in prayer asking the Father to overcome your unbelief.

Glance back at Isaiah 43:10 one more time. God wants us to know and believe Him. The most effective key to believing God is right before our eyes: the more we know Him, the more we will believe Him. The apostle Paul said it best: "I know whom I have believed, and am convinced that he is able to guard what I have entrusted to him for that day" (2 Tim. 1:12). We tend to run to God for temporary relief. God is looking for people who will walk with Him in steadfast belief. Choose to believe. Those who trust in Him will not be put to shame.

CHAPTER 9

THE OBSTACLE OF PRIDE

*"I live in a high and holy place, but also with him
who is contrite and lowly in spirit, to revive the spirit
of the lowly and to revive the heart of the contrite."*

(ISA. 57:15)

Next we consider the primary obstacle hindering Benefit 2: To glorify God. Remember what it means to glorify God. In simple terms, God is glorified in anyone through whom He is allowed to show Himself great or mighty. How can we be assured of living a God-glorifying life? By adopting a God-glorifying attitude. God tucked a wonderful Scripture in the Book of Isaiah that beautifully illustrates an attitude through which God will undoubtedly be glorified. Isaiah 26:8 says: "Your name and renown / are the desire of our hearts."

God will show Himself "great and mighty" in those whose heart's desire is His name and renown. The original word for "renown" is *shem,* which means "definite and conspicuous position . . . honor, authority, character . . . fame" (*Strong's*).

According to Isaiah 43:7, we are called to allow the King of all creation to reveal Himself through us. He will not share His glory with another, not even with His own children. Not because He's egotistical but because He's interested in our eternal treasures. By demanding that we seek His glory alone, He calls us to overcome the overwhelming and natural temptation to seek our own. So what do you think would be the biggest obstacle to glorifying God? Pride.

Alexander Pope called it "the never-failing vice of fools."[1] Pride—a destroyer of ministries, marriages, friendships, jobs, and character. God will be most readily seen through those who desire His fame above all else. Sounds simple, but it's not. Few things are more contrary to our human natures than desiring anyone's fame above our own. Even when we desire the fame of our spouses or children, deep inside we are often yearning for the fame they might lend to us.

To fulfill our God-given destinies—to allow the King of all creation to show Himself through us—we must overcome the temptation to seek our own glory by desiring His instead. If we are to recognize and allow God to free us from any areas of captivity, we must recognize pride as more than self-promotion. Pride is a dangerous lure to captivity.

God's command to give Him glory does not come without a warning. Feel the weight of Jeremiah's words about pride:

> Give glory to the LORD your God
> before he brings the darkness,
> before your feet stumble
> on the darkening hills.
> You hope for light,
> but he will turn it to thick darkness
> and change it to deep gloom. (Jer. 13:16)

In verse 17 God went on to warn that captivity would come to His people, due to pride, if they did not listen to Him. "Because of your pride / . . . the LORD'S flock will be taken captive."

Beware of the fact that pride often disguises itself. For example, I have known people who thought they were too far gone to save, too wicked, too sinful. Such people would be shocked to hear that their attitude is a form of pride as well. They think their sin or problem is bigger than God.

Pride is a boulder in the road on our journey to freedom. The size of this boulder differs with each of us according to the degree to which we struggle with pride. I can hardly imagine that any of us see only a small pebble in our way. To go forward from here, God must empower each of us to roll the boulder of pride off our road to liberty. I believe this stone will roll if we give it three mighty shoves.

1. *View pride as a vicious enemy.* Proverbs 8:13 quotes God as saying: "I hate pride and arrogance." Proverbs 11:2 proclaims, "When pride comes, then comes disgrace, / but with humility comes wisdom." Proverbs 13:10 adds, "Pride only breeds quarrels, / but wisdom is found in those who take advice." And most of us are familiar with the words of Proverbs 16:18: "Pride goes before destruction, / a haughty spirit before a fall."

Let me see . . . God hates it, it brings disgrace, it breeds quarrels, and it points us to destruction like a compass needle seeking north. Obadiah 1:3 caps it all off: "The pride of your heart has deceived you," the prophet wrote. And though you may dwell in the "clefts of the rocks" and "say to yourself, 'Who can bring me down' . . . 'from there I will bring you down' declares the LORD" (Obad. 1:3–4). The first shove to move the obstacle of pride is to view it as the vicious enemy it is.

2. *View humility as a friend.* Often our society looks on biblical humility as a sign of weakness. Nothing could be further from the truth. Being filled with pride is easy. It comes naturally. Humility takes a supply of supernatural strength that comes only to those who are strong enough to admit weakness.

Scripture only occasionally repeats itself, but you glimpse the value of humility in that both James and Peter quoted Proverbs 3:34, that "God opposes the proud / but gives grace to the humble" (James 4:6; 1 Pet. 5:5).

Our prophet Isaiah quoted God, saying, "I live in a high and holy place, / but also with him who is contrite and lowly in spirit" (Isa. 57:15). And God said, "This is the one I esteem: / he who is humble and contrite in spirit, / and trembles at my word" (Isa. 66:2). *Esteem* basically means to "have respect" (*Strong's*). Can you imagine being one whom God "respects"? What a wonderful thought! To remove the obstacle of pride we must view it as a bitter enemy and view humility as a dear friend.

3. *Humbling yourself before God.* James 4:10 and 1 Peter 5:6 plainly tell us to humble ourselves. You see, humility is not something we have until humbling ourselves is something we do. This step necessitates action before possession. Humbling ourselves certainly does not mean hating ourselves. Humility can be rather easily attained by simply opening our eyes to reality. Just read a few chapters of Scripture boasting in the greatness of God; Job 38 is one of my favorites.

We certainly don't have to hate ourselves to see how small we are and to respond appropriately by bowing down before Him. In a nutshell, that's what humbling ourselves before God means: bowing down before His majesty. We don't have to hang our heads in self-abasement to humble ourselves. We simply must choose to lower our heads from lofty, inappropriate places. We choose to humble ourselves by submitting to His greatness every day.

The last sentence of Daniel 4:37 provides one of the most effective motivations for humility in my personal life: "Those who walk in pride he is able to humble."

I look at it this way: I'd rather humble myself than force God to humble me. Let's allow the circumstances and weaknesses, and any thorns in the flesh God has chosen to leave, to do the job they were sent to do—provoke humility. Not so we can be flattened under God's door-mat, but so He can joyfully lift us up. Take a moment today to find a private place, get down on your knees, and humble yourself before your glorious God. The hosts of heaven are sure to hear a thunderous rumble as boulders of pride roll off our road to freedom.

CHAPTER 10

THE OBSTACLE OF IDOLATRY

"Who shapes a god and casts an idol,
which can profit him nothing?"

(ISA. 44:10)

The third obstacle blocks our access to Benefit 3: To find satisfaction in God. God wants us to find our satisfaction in Him rather than waste our time and effort on things that cannot satisfy. But when we look to other sources for satisfaction, we are guilty of idolatry.

Isaiah contains one of the most poetic and comely expressions of grace in either Testament:

Come, all you who are thirsty,
come to the waters;
and you who have no money,
come, buy and eat!
Come, buy wine and milk
without money and without cost. (Isa. 55:1)

On the heels of the invitation, God posed the question that haunts every generation of Adam's descendants. "Why spend money on what is not bread, / and your labor on what does not satisfy?" Then, like a frustrated parent determined to get through to his child, He said, "Listen, listen to me, and eat what is good, / and your soul will delight in the richest of fare." I believe God's prescription for those who possess an inner thirst (Isa. 55:1) and hunger they cannot fill is implied in Isaiah 55:6. Those who are spiritually thirsty and hungry need only to do this: "Seek the LORD while he may be found; / call on him while he is near."

I believe God creates and activates a nagging dissatisfaction in every person for an excellent reason. According to 2 Peter 3:9, God doesn't want anyone to perish. Rather, He wants everyone to come to repentance. He gave us a will so we could choose whether or not to accept His invitation, but God purposely created us with a need that only He can meet.

Have you ever noticed that one of the most common human experiences is the inability to be completely satisfied? Unfortunately, salvation alone does not completely fill the need. Many come to Christ out of their search for something missing; yet after receiving His salvation, they go elsewhere for further satisfaction. Christians can be miserably dissatisfied if they accept Christ's salvation yet reject the fullness of daily relationship that satisfies. God offers us so much more than we usually choose to enjoy.

Dissatisfaction is not a terrible thing. It's a God-thing. It's only a terrible thing when we don't let it lead us to Christ. He wants us to find the only thing that will truly satiate our thirsty and hungry hearts.

Realizing that God desires for us to find genuine satisfaction in Him helps us discover the third primary obstacle in our road to freedom: settling for satisfaction with anything else. God gave this practice a name I was unprepared to hear: idolatry. After serious meditation, I realized the label made perfect sense no matter how harsh it seemed. Anything we try to put in a place where God belongs is an idol.

To travel forward on the road to freedom, we must remove the obstacle of idolatry. We begin by recognizing the obstacle as idol worship, but we may find removing it difficult. The first two obstacles to freedom—unbelief and pride—can be removed effectively by a matter of choice: we can choose to believe God, and we can choose to humble ourselves before God. I am not minimizing the difficulty, but I am suggesting that the obstacles are removed by volition. Some of the idols in our lives—things or people we have put in God's place—can take much longer to remove. Some of them have been in those places for years, and only the power of God can make them budge. We must begin to remove idols by choosing to recognize their existence and admitting their inability to keep us satisfied.

The nation of Israel struggled horribly with the sin of idolatry. We saw some of the results in the lives of Uzziah, Jotham, Ahaz, and Hezekiah. In the second chapter, Isaiah recorded what he saw when he looked at Judah and Jerusalem. The passage sounds hauntingly like prosperous America. He said of the people of Israel:

They are full of superstitions from the East;
    they practice divination like the Philistines
    and clasp hands with pagans.

Their land is full of silver and gold;
    there is no end to their treasures.
Their land is full of horses;
    there is no end to their chariots. (Isa. 2:6–7)

In the first words of verse 6, Isaiah said, "You have abandoned your people." Isaiah concluded that he saw no sign of God's presence there. God had promised not to abandon them, and He didn't. But where sin is rampant He is certainly capable of shrinking the presence of the Holy Spirit and leaving virtually no signs of His presence. I've experienced the withdrawing of God's obvious presence in my own life in seasons of sin.

The nation of Israel had been given everything, yet they refused to receive and be satisfied. They traded in what their hearts could know for what their eyes could see. Isaiah 44:10 reminds us that a person's idols can profit him nothing. In fact, the next verse says that idols ultimately reap shame. The chapter gives us several glimpses at the destructiveness of idols. For example, look at verse 12:

> The blacksmith takes a tool
>   and works with it in the coals;
> he shapes an idol with hammers,
>   he forges it with the might of his arm.
> He gets hungry and loses his strength;
>   he drinks no water and grows faint. (Isa. 44:12)

People can become so engrossed in their idols that they no longer pay attention to their physical needs. Verse 13 tells us that idols can also take the form of humans.

> [The carpenter] shapes it in the form of man,
>   of man in all his glory,
>   that it may dwell in a shrine. (Isa. 44:13)

We can apply this point literally. At some time each of us has exalted someone to a place where only God belonged.

Even after such a catalog of idolatry, in verse 21 God promised: "I will not forget you." The mercy of God is indescribable, isn't it? Even when His people turned to idols, He swept away their offenses like a cloud, their sins like the morning mist. As we face some of the idols we have worshiped in our quest for satisfaction, we need never doubt the mercy of God. He asks one thing: "Return to me, / for I have redeemed you" (v. 22).

Can you see the strong tie between our quest for satisfaction and the worship of idols? The void God created in our lives for Himself will demand attention. We look desperately for something to satisfy us and fill the empty places. Our craving to be filled is so strong that the moment something or someone seems to meet our need, we feel an overwhelming temptation to worship it.

In my opinion, one of the most thought-provoking verses in Isaiah 44 is verse 20. Read it carefully.

He feeds on ashes, a deluded heart misleads him;
> he cannot save himself, or say,
"Is not this thing in my right hand a lie?"

Fresh conviction washes over me like a squall. How many times have I fed on ashes instead of feasting on the life-giving Word of God? How many times has my deluded heart misled me? How many times have I tried to save myself?

I could fall on my face this moment and praise God through all eternity for finally awakening me to say, "This thing in my right hand is a lie." I can remember one thing in particular I held on to with a virtual death grip. I also remember the harrowing moment God opened my eyes to see what a lie I had believed. I cried for days.

I originally thought this lie was a good thing. My heart, handicapped in childhood, had deluded me. Although I didn't realize it at the time, I eventually bowed down and worshiped it. My only consolation in my idolatry is that I finally allowed Him to peel away my fingers and to my knowledge, I have grasped only His hand since.

Sadly, I often learn things the hard way. Yes, I plunged to the depths before I discovered satisfaction. I pray to settle for nothing less the rest of my days. I am very aware that Satan will constantly cast idols before me. I hope never to forget that I could fall again.

Beloved, whatever we are gripping to bring us satisfaction is a lie—unless it is Christ. He is the Truth that sets us free. If you are holding anything in your craving for satisfaction right now, would you be willing to acknowledge it as a lie? Even if you feel you can't let go of it right this moment, would you lift it before Him—perhaps literally lifting your fisted hand as a symbol—and confess it as an idol? God does not condemn you. He calls you. Will you open your hand to Him? He is opening His to you.

CHAPTER 11

THE OBSTACLE OF
PRAYERLESSNESS

*". . . all who keep the Sabbath without desecrating it and who
hold fast to my covenant—these I will bring to my holy mountain
and give them joy in my house of prayer."*

(ISA. 56:6–7a)

The fourth benefit of our relationship with God is to experience His peace. The key to peace is authority—peace is the fruit of an obedient, righteous life.

The issue of disobedience and rebellion against the authority of God complicates the life of a captive. I can tell you from personal experience that at times of greatest captivity, I wanted more than anything to be obedient to God. I was miserable in my rebellion, and I could not understand why I kept making wrong choices. Yes, they were my choices, and I've taken full responsibility for them as my sins. However, Satan had me in such a viselike grip that I felt powerless to obey, although I wanted to desperately. Of course, I wasn't powerless; but as long as I believed the lie, I behaved accordingly.

You are probably familiar with Philippians 4:6–7: "Do not be anxious about anything, but in everything, by prayer and petition, with thanksgiving, present your requests to God. And the peace of God, which transcends all understanding, will guard your hearts and your minds in Christ Jesus."

I decided that to bring home the impact of the verses I would have a little fun and paraphrase the passage from a negative standpoint. In other words, I turned this prescription for peace into a no-fail prescription for anxiety. My result looked like this: "Do not be calm about anything, but in everything, by dwelling on it constantly and feeling picked on by God, with thoughts like 'and this is the thanks I get,' present your aggravations to everyone you know but Him. And the acid in your stomach, which transcends all milk products, will cause you an ulcer, and the doctor bills will cause you a heart attack and you will lose your mind."

Without a doubt, avoiding prayer is a sure prescription for anxiety, a certain way to avoid peace. To experience the kind of peace that covers all circumstances, the Bible challenges us to develop active, authentic (what I like to call "meaty") prayer lives. Prayer with real substance to it—original thoughts flowing from a highly individual heart, personal and intimate. Often, we do everything but pray. We tend to want something more "substantial." Even studying the Bible, going to church, talking to the pastor, or receiving counsel seems more tangible than prayer.

What victory the enemy has in winning us over to prayerlessness! He would rather we do anything than pray. He'd rather see us serve ourselves into the ground, because he knows we'll eventually grow resentful without prayer. He'd rather see us study the Bible into the wee hours of the morning, because he knows we'll never have deep understanding and power to live what we've learned without prayer. He knows prayerless lives are powerless lives, while prayerful lives are powerful lives!

In Ephesians 1, Paul named specific blessings that can come through prayer. He prayed that his spiritual offspring would receive "the Spirit of wisdom and revelation, so that you may know him better" (v. 17). He asked God to open the eyes of their hearts so they could "know the hope to which he has called you, the riches of his glorious inheritance in the saints, and his incomparably great power for us who believe" (vv. 18–19). The better we know God (v. 17), the more we trust Him. The more we trust Him, the more we sense His peace when the wintry winds blow against us.

At the grocery store recently I was amused by the label on a lotion that claimed it was an effective stress reliever. I could hear a baby screaming on the next aisle. I had a brief impulse to offer the lotion to the poor mom pushing the cranky cargo. I was too afraid I might get a little stress reliever thrown on my face. You see, this world can't seem to come up with a real, lasting solution to the stresses and strains of life.

A few days ago I again saw the best advice the world seems to have: "Just remember two things: (1) Don't sweat the small stuff. (2) It's all small stuff." That advice is so shallow. It's not all small stuff. I have a friend whose son was paralyzed in an accident his senior year in high school. I pray almost daily for a list of people, from age four to seventy-four, who are battling cancer. Two recently came off my list and into heaven. My precious friend's husband, an honest, hardworking believer with a son in college, just lost his job—again. Not long ago, three tornadoes whipped through my hometown—stealing, killing, and destroying. No, it's not all small stuff.

Worldly philosophy is forced to minimize difficulty because it has no real answers. You and I know better than the small-stuff philosophy. We face a lot of big stuff out there. Only through prayer are we washed in peace.

It's time to roll away the stone of prayerlessness. It is the most prohibitive obstacle in the road to a believer's victory, no matter what our specific pursuit may be.

Let me share with you one of the reasons I believe prayerlessness is such an obstacle. When Satan takes perfect aim at our "Achilles heel," picks the perfect time, and wears the perfect disguise, none of the following will work effectively to keep us out of a snare:

- *Discipline.* Somehow, at times of great temptation and weakness, discipline can fly like a bird out the nearest window.

- *Lessons from the past.* Somehow we don't think that straight when we get a surprise, full-fledged attack.

- *What is best for us.* Our human nature is much too self-destructive to automatically choose what is best at our weakest moments.

Our strongest motivation will be the Person with whom we walk. Staying close to Him through constant communication, we receive a continual supply of strength to walk victoriously—in peace even as we walk through a war zone.

Let me give you another reason we need prayer as we seek to break free. Satan will try to stir up what our faithful Refiner wants to skim off. Remember, Christ came to set the captive free. Satan comes to make the free captive. Christ wants to cut some binding ropes from our lives. Satan will want to use them to tie us in knots.

We must walk with Christ step-by-step through this journey for the sake of protection, power, and a resulting unparalleled passion in our lives. None of these three will be realities any other way. The enemy will be defeated. Believe it. Act on it.

Prayer matters. The Spirit of God released through our prayers and the prayers of others turns cowards into conquerors, chaos into calm, cries into comfort. The enemy knows the power of prayer. He's been watching it furiously for thousands of years. In preparation for this lesson, I searched for all the uses of the word *pray* in its various forms from Genesis to Revelation. I nearly wept as I saw hundreds of references.

> Abraham prayed . . . Isaac prayed . . . Jacob prayed . . . Moses left Pharaoh and prayed . . . So Moses prayed for the people . . . Manoah prayed to the Lord . . . Samson prayed . . . Hannah wept much and prayed . . . David prayed . . . Elijah stepped forward and prayed . . . And Elisha prayed, "O, Lord" . . . After Job had prayed for his friends . . . And Hezekiah prayed to the Lord . . . Daniel got down on his knees and prayed . . . From inside the fish Jonah prayed . . . Very early in the morning, while it was still dark, Jesus got up, left the house and went off to a solitary place, where He prayed . . . Going a little farther, He fell with his face to the ground and prayed.

If Christ sought to have the divine life strengthened in Him through solitary times of intimacy with the Father, how much more should I? I am hopeless to live the victorious life without prayer.

The Bible is a book of prayer. And as Isaiah 56:7 reminds us, God's presence is a house of prayer. When our lives are over and the record of our days stands complete, may the words have been written of us, "Then he or she prayed . . ."

CHAPTER 12

THE OBSTACLE OF LEGALISM

The Lord says: "These people come near to me with their mouth and honor me with their lips, but their hearts are far from me. Their worship of me is made up only of rules taught by men."

(ISA. 29:13)

We have one last boulder to roll off the road before we are free to move ahead on our journey to liberation. As you recall, each obstacle we are studying in this section is a direct hindrance to one of the five primary benefits of our salvation.

The fifth and final benefit is to enjoy God's presence. Many situations or conditions can keep us from truly enjoying God's presence. For instance, not spending adequate time with Him will greatly affect our pure enjoyment of His presence. Having an underdeveloped prayer life will also rob our joy, as could harboring bitterness or anger at another person. But the person who studies God's Word in depth and experiences a consistent lack of enjoyment of God often suffers from a condition with an ugly name—legalism.

The term *legalism* does not appear in Scripture, but perfect illustrations of it are scattered throughout the Word. Each of the following Scriptures teach us something about legalism.

Matthew 12:9–14 tells how Jesus healed a man who had suffered since birth with a withered hand. Now with a word Jesus restored it. But because He healed the man on the Sabbath, "the Pharisees went out and plotted how they might kill Jesus" (v. 14).

Acts 15 tells of a crucial decision in the early church, a decision that vitally affects you and me. The church was growing, and Gentiles were coming to know Christ. "Then some of the believers who belonged to the party of the Pharisees stood up and said, 'The Gentiles must be circumcised and required to obey the law of Moses'" (v. 5). The leaders had to determine whether we become Christians by faith in Christ alone or by keeping the law. In the discussion that followed, Peter delivered the ultimate verdict. He said, why should we put "on the necks of the disciples a yoke that neither we nor our fathers have been able to bear? No! We believe it is through the grace of our Lord Jesus that we are saved, just as they are" (vv. 10–11).

Legalism appeared again in the Galatian churches. Teachers came telling the new Christians they must keep the Jewish law to be saved. Paul "laid down the law" on the issue.

> We who are Jews by birth and not "Gentile sinners" know that a man is not justified by observing the law, but by faith in Jesus Christ. So we, too, have put our faith in Christ Jesus that we may be justified by faith in Christ and not by observing the law, because by observing the law no one will be justified. (Gal. 2:15–16)

In the passages above and many others, we get a clear picture of legalism. Ecclesiastes 7:20 clearly sounds the futility of legalism: "There is not a righteous man on earth / who does what is right and never sins." We cannot please God or find freedom in rule-keeping. Never have. Never will. Tragically, self-generated righteousness will always appeal to the human heart. In my opinion, legalism results when three conditions occur:

1. *Regulations replace relationship.* The Pharisees had a superficial understanding of God and no enjoyment of His presence. The Sabbath belonged entirely to God. He established it for our benefit, not our imprisonment. The greatest benefit Christ could bring to the man with the shriveled hand was a relationship with the Savior. He initiated that relationship through healing. We don't have to wonder who enjoyed Christ more that day, the Pharisees or the man with the shriveled hand!

We must beware. A student of God's Word can squeeze the enjoyment out of his or her Christian walk by replacing relationship with regulations. Legalism also occurs when:

2. *Microscopes replace mirrors.* Note the words from Matthew 12:10: the Pharisees were "looking for a reason to accuse." Modern-day Pharisees sometimes practice religious voyeurism, looking for a reason to accuse others. They tend to love a church "soap opera" because their own relationship with God is so unexciting. They look to the faults of others to keep things interesting.

I am so thankful to testify that I have seen far more genuine examples of true Christianity in the church than unfeeling legalists. Unfortunately, I also have seen many caring Christians intimidated by the occasional legalist. Concentrating on the shortcomings of others can cheat a Christian of truly enjoying the presence of God. Legalism also results from a third cause:

3. *Performance replaces passion.* If our motivation for obedience is anything other than love for and devotion to God, we're probably up to

our eyeballs in legalism and in for disaster. Obedience without love is nothing but the law. God gave a perfect description of legalism in Isaiah 29:13:

> These people come near to me with their mouth
> and honor me with their lips,
> but their hearts are far from me.
> Their worship of me
> is made up only of rules taught by men.

Let's search our hearts for a moment. God does not take our spiritual temperature under the tongue by the words we say, nor in our ear by the impressive teachings we hear, nor under our arms by the service we perform. God takes our spiritual temperature straight from the heart.

Three strong reasons exist for rolling the large obstacle of legalism out of our way before we go any further in our study.

1. *This journey is about a relationship—not regulations.* I want you to thoroughly enjoy God's presence. God is going to get very personal with us if we take breaking free seriously. Sometimes you're going to have your eyes opened to things you'd rather not see. How do I know? Because I've been on this journey! When this study is complete and someone asks you if you enjoyed it, I want you to be able to say with all sincerity, "I enjoyed God!"

2. *This journey is about you.* In the past I've written studies on biblical figures like Moses, David, and Paul. This time each of us is the human protagonist.

3. *This journey is about the heart.* I pray you will grow in knowledge, but that is not our purpose. This Bible study is for the heart—to loosen any chains withholding the heart from enjoying the abundant liberty in

Christ's salvation. I plead with you to withhold nothing from God as you journey toward freedom in Christ.

Precious student of God's Word, you've worked hard shoving those obstacles off the road in these chapters. Are you still having trouble budging one or two? Then remember, God's specialty is rolling away a stone. Show Him which one is causing you trouble, put your hands on top of His, and on the count of three . . .

PART III

ANCIENT RUINS AND BROKEN HEARTS

We now begin the more personal portion of our journey to freedom. The trail leads through some places where pain dwells, but we will find these places bear rich fruits as well.

Continue to memorize Isaiah 61:1–4; 43:10, and the benefits of our great salvation. Next memorize Isaiah 43:6–7, the scriptural reference for Benefit 2:

> Bring my sons from afar
>> and my daughters from the ends of the earth—
> everyone who is called by my name,
>> whom I created for my glory,
>> whom I formed and made.

CHAPTER 13

TOURING THE ANCIENT RUINS

They will rebuild the ancient ruins
and restore the places long devastated;
they will renew the ruined cities
that have been devastated for generations.

(ISA. 61:4)

Learning from the mistakes of others is the essence of wisdom. The captivity Isaiah foretold literally happened to the Jews when the Babylonians captured the people of Judah. We want to apply to our internal captivities the principles related to their physical captivity.

In Isaiah 61:4 did you notice what was to be rebuilt and restored? Did you note how long the ancient ruins had been devastated? Isaiah spoke of rebuilding, restoring, and renewing ruins that were ancient and cities that had been devastated for generations. Allow the Holy Spirit to meddle for a moment. Can you think of any ruins in your life that have been in your family line for generations?

I can think of a few ancient ruins in mine. You may be able to identify ruins like alcoholism, gambling, pornography, racism, or family feuding, paralyzing phobias, or the suicide of a relative. We'll be discussing some of these as we continue our study. Until then, let's explore this concept to clarify how we can personally apply the idea of rebuilding ancient ruins in our lives and families.

I am so thankful for God's uncanny sense of timing; as I write this portion of the study, I have just returned from Greece and Rome. God allowed us to trace many of the apostle Paul's travels, and we gazed on the ruins of ancient cities like Ephesus, Corinth, and Rome.

Why do people flock to see ancient ruins? Because unlocking any society's heritage is important to understanding the development of its present inhabitants. Looking back for the right reasons with the right attitude helps us become better equipped to look forward. That's exactly what this portion of our study is all about—looking back. Don't get antsy on me, now. We need to muster the courage to stop by the ancient ruins and see what we can learn about ourselves.

We need to examine areas of devastation or defeat that have been in our family lines for generations. Then we can explore resulting generational bonds that need breaking. Yokes can often be caused by severed relationships, lives left in ruins because of a loss or a tragedy, ancient family arguments and inheritances of hate, or generational debris scattered by a bomb that dropped and a life that refused repair.

A crucial reason exists for facing generational strongholds head-on: unless we purposely seek them, they can remain almost unrecognizable, but they don't remain benign. Family ruins continue to be the seedbed for all sorts of destruction. We tend to think of generational hand-me-down baggage as part of who we are rather than how we're bound. In many cases we grew up with these chains, so they feel completely natural. We're apt to consider them part of our personalities rather than a yoke squeezing abundant life out of us. Consider the following example:

> In the early 1900s, Claire's parents died in an epidemic. She was forced to live with her older brother.

Money was scarce, so in Claire's behalf and without her consent, the brother accepted an offer of marriage from a prosperous older man. This husband turned out to be cruel and abusive; and after fathering two daughters, he left the family penniless because she did not give him a son. Claire found refuge in Christ as her Savior, but she never let Him rebuild her life. Claire died before her granddaughter and great-granddaughters ever knew her. They were never orphaned nor beaten by a spouse, yet all but one of them battled a distrust and fear of men that they hardly recognized, let alone understood.

You may respond, "But, Beth, that scenario seems more like a learned behavior than a stronghold." I reply that anything passed down to us that inhibits the full expression of freedom we should have in Christ qualifies as bondage. Our aim is not to argue genetics versus environment; our aim is to be loosed from anything limiting our lives in Christ.

Can you think of any examples of generational bondage you have observed in families? You may think of prejudice, addiction, or bitterness—what a host of malignant legacies families sometimes share!

You and I would both quickly agree that these are sad scenarios. Do you know what makes them even sadder? They were unnecessary to those in Christ. The cross of Calvary is enough to set us free from every yoke; and His Word is enough to make liberty a practical reality, no matter what those before us left as an "inheritance." But His Word must be applied to specific life needs.

Let's allow the Word of God to help us formulate the right approach to our ancient ruins through two considerations. We can see the first in Matthew 1:1–16—the genealogy of our Lord. Jesus' family tree includes such imperfection as Rahab the prostitute (Josh. 2:1–7) and Manasseh, an indescribably vile king (2 Chron. 33:1–17).

1. *Even Christ had a blend of the negative and positive in His lineage.* We each have a concoction of good, bad, and ugly in our family lines. Our purpose is not to drag old skeletons out of the closet or engage in family bashing of any kind. We just need to make sure we didn't inherit any hand-me-down chains that interfere with the priceless benefits of our covenant relationship with Christ. He broke the chains of all kinds of bondage when He gave His life for us on the cross; however, many of us still carry them in our hands or have them dangling from our necks out of pure habit, lack of awareness, or lack of biblical knowledge. We need to recognize any generational bonds and ask God to remove them.

When I refer to something we may have inherited, I mean anything we may have learned environmentally, anything to which we may be genetically predisposed, or any binding influence passed down through other means. Again, I don't come to you on the basis of science or psychology but on behalf of a statement declared emphatically in Galatians 5:1: "It is for freedom that Christ has set us free."

You may have inherited so much bondage that you can hardly stand looking back. My special prayer for you is that God will help you see some positives, also. I can remember when I first dealt with the memories of my childhood victimization. My first inclination was to believe Satan's lie and think my entire childhood was ruins. Eventually, I realized that I was wrong. Yes, I experienced some very ugly things, but I also can see the merciful hand of God in many positives.

If you will compare Matthew 1 and Galatians 3 carefully, you will see something wonderful about our lineage in Christ. Matthew 1:1 says, "A record of the genealogy of Jesus Christ the son of David, the son of Abraham." Paul wrote about our lineage in Christ: "If you belong to Christ, then you are Abraham's seed, and heirs according to the promise"

(Gal. 3:29). When we recognize our lineage in Christ's own family line, we can rejoice in the words of Psalm 16:6: "The boundary lines have fallen for me in pleasant places; / surely I have a delightful inheritance."

2. *We don't have to disinherit or dishonor our physical lineage to fully accept and abide in our spiritual lineage.* God fully recognizes and desires to use both "lines" to His glory. Our spiritual lineage can overpower and disable any continuing negative effects of our physical lineage. We all have a "goodly heritage" in Christ (Ps. 16:6, KJV). For those who feel they inherited many negatives, joyfully accepting this truth takes the edge off the pain of looking back.

I want you to take a first look back at both the positive and the negative in your heritage. Do not let the enemy get to you with a spirit of heaviness. We are going to stand on a positive approach even to our negatives, because bringing them before God is the first step to healing exposure and gaining freedom. If you encounter anything painful, thank God immediately that He is ready and willing to diffuse all things in your heritage that are binding you.

First recall the five benefits of our covenant relationship with Christ. God intends that both you and I know and believe Him, glorify Him, find satisfaction in Him, experience His peace, and enjoy His presence.

Please remember, our purpose is to recognize what we've inherited or how we've been rightly or wrongly influenced—not to cast blame. When I ask you to review positives and negatives, think in terms of the influence on enhancing or inhibiting the five benefits in your life. Please pause and ask God to reveal to you or remind you of any information pertinent to our study.

I want to ask you to do more than just read the following exercise. At the least, spend some time thinking about each of these parts of your family legacy. You will benefit more if you write these questions and responses in a journal. Review both the positive and negative influences from your grandparents and parents. If you never knew your parents or grandparents, substitute the caregivers you have experienced.

Think about your maternal grandparents. How did your grandfather positively influence your life? How did he negatively influence you? What about your maternal grandmother? With what positives did she bless you? What negative attitudes or behaviors did you learn from her?

How did they affect your feelings about God? How did they impact your feelings about love and the opposite sex? Did they help you to feel secure in the world, or did they tear down your sense of security? If you had a trash bag and a trophy case, what would you display as a blessing they brought to your life? What do you need to consign to the trash?

Can you think of any reasons why the negatives may have been present in their lives? If so, do those factors help you understand or possibly forgive offenses or neglect?

After you have considered your maternal grandparents, stop to pray about them and their influence. If they are still alive, pray for them. Thank God for the items in the trophy case. Ask Him to help you dispose of the trash. Please don't rush through this exercise.

Now repeat the exercise above with your paternal grandparents. After you have prayed for and about their influence, repeat it for your parents. Again, you may need to substitute others who cared for you when you were a child.

You may find this to be a difficult exercise. You might need to spend time on each part of your family separately. Consider marking this spot and coming back to it as necessary. Do not get bogged down here, but don't rush through it too quickly either.

You may have recognized some ancient ruins in generations of your family. Thank God that, although you cannot change the past, He can help you change what you're doing with it! And the changes He makes in you in the present can certainly change the future!

CHAPTER 14

THE ANCIENT BOUNDARY STONE

Do not move an ancient boundary stone
set up by your forefathers.

(PROV. 22:28)

As we journey toward the land of the free, we may have to become the brave! Our tour will take us by the ancient ruins in this segment of our journey for a few history lessons. Again, our purpose is not to condemn or dishonor people of our heritage but to recognize barriers in our present caused by bondage from our families' past. In our previous lesson, we highlighted two considerations that we want to remember:

1. Even Christ had a blend of the negative and positive in His lineage.
2. We don't have to disinherit or dishonor our physical lineage to fully accept and abide in our spiritual lineage.

When we think of Exodus 20, we automatically think of the Ten Commandments. Let's look at the chapter in its proper context. Before God delivered the Ten Commandments to the children of Israel, He identified Himself. He said, "I am the LORD your God, who brought you out of Egypt, out of the land of slavery" (v. 2). One vital way we can look at the Ten Commandments is as a plan for staying out of slavery. They serve the function as boundaries for our safety and protection.

Proverbs says: "Do not move an ancient boundary stone / set up by your forefathers" (Prov. 22:28). An ancient boundary stone was similar to a fence. It served as a visual reminder of what belonged to the landowner and what was beyond the legal limits. It reminded people when they were crossing the line. God's Ten Commandments are the ultimate boundary stone. We are not free to move them around to fit our lifestyles.

You may be wondering what ancient boundary stones have to do with a study on ancient ruins—practically everything. Those who live beyond the boundaries will return to bondage. Not only will they return to bondage; they will leave a well-trodden path for the next generations to follow. To understand generational bondage, let's risk the discomfort of taking a look at generational sin. They are very closely intertwined for at least two reasons:

1. *All bondage begins with sin.* In the Book of Exodus, the nation of Israel was in bondage because of its cruel taskmasters' sins. In the Book of Isaiah, the nation of Judah was heading into bondage because of their own sin.

2. *All bondage promotes sin.* Not necessitates but promotes. Let me use an illustration to explain. All television commercials promote products. I don't have to buy, but realistically I'd have to be pretty strong to watch without buying into at least some of the products. Likewise, all bondage highly intensifies the pull toward sin. I believe that a person raised in generational bondage generally struggles in some way with the sin it promotes.

The tie between generational bondage and generational sin is what creates such a difficult cycle. Someone moves the ancient boundary stone and decides to abide by his or her own set of rules. Life beyond the boundary stone leads to bondage. Bondage leads to sin. Sin leads to more bondage. The cycle does not stop until someone has enough courage to move back to the ancient boundary stone God ordained.

Exodus 20:5 reflects the cycle I have just identified: "You shall not bow down to them or worship them; for I, the LORD your God, am a jealous God, punishing the children for the sin of the fathers to the third and fourth generation of those who hate me."

I want to be part of breaking negative cycles in my family line. I believe you want the same for your family. One reason our study is called *Breaking Free* is because many of us are dealing with ancient cycles that need breaking. Perhaps on our own determination and strength we've bent them a little, but they'll never break without God. And He ordinarily will not rebuild what is not broken.

God's commands—His ancient boundary stones—were given not to enslave us but to keep us free. He is a good and wise God who knows what is best for us. Even His jealousy is for us and not against us. He is jealous for us with a godly jealousy (2 Cor. 11:2). Having a godly jealously means being jealous for someone, not of someone.

The idea of God's jealousy proves a stumbling block for some people. Obviously, when God referred to Himself as the jealous God in Exodus 20:4–5, He certainly wasn't jealous of idols. He is jealous for His children. He knows all other "gods" of this world are as nothing (Isa. 41:21–24). They possess no glory and can offer no salvation. All idols can do is detract attention from the one, true God, the only One worthy of our praise, the only real Deliverer.

God is also a Giver by His eternal nature. He desires to bless. When we turn away to other "gods," we often force Him to hold back His blessing and stay His giving hand.

The second stumbling block in Exodus 20:5 is the word *punishing*. *Visiting* (KJV) is a little more reflective of the Hebrew. The original word is *paqadh*, and some of its meanings are "inspect, review, number, to be deposited . . . to visit in the sense of making a call." It was a word also used for taking a census.

God does not punish children for their parents' sins. We will see this truth clearly in our study of Ezekiel 18 in chapter 19 of this book. In Exodus 20:5, I believe God says He will be able to review or take a census of all the times the effects of parents' sins can be seen in the next several generations. He will be able to number those who have been adversely affected by the sins of their parents or grandparents. For instance, if a pollster took a census of the number of alcoholics in three generations of an alcoholic patriarch's family, the head count would very likely be high. Why? Because alcoholism was deposited in the family line. It came calling, and an unfortunate number of children and grandchildren answered the door.

Before we parents die of fright, let's remember that God is the only perfect parent. He's not cursing three or four generations over a little parental irritability. In fact, I don't believe He's calling a curse down on anyone. I believe God is referring to a natural phenomenon placed in poignant words in Hosea 8:7, "They sow the wind / and reap the whirlwind." Parents and grandparents must be very careful what they sow because it may reap the wind in their own lives and the whirlwind in the lives that follow.

Notice the context of the warning in Exodus 20:5. God's edict concerning generational sin follows on the heels of the commandment against idols. Why do you think parents and grandparents must be seriously warned against seeking other "gods" and bowing down to idols?

Keep in mind that idolatry involves anything or anyone we worship, use as a replacement for God, or in any way treat as our god. Because only Christ can set us free, all other gods or idols can only enslave; therefore, enslaved parents teach their children how to live in bondage even with the best of intentions to do otherwise. For many years I have kept an excerpt from *It's Always Something* by the late Gilda Radner. The last few paragraphs share a lesson on life every parent should heed.

> When I was little, my nurse Dibby's cousin had a dog, just a mutt, and the dog was pregnant. I don't know how long dogs are pregnant, but she was due to have her puppies in about a week. She was out in the yard one day and got in the way of the lawn mower and her two hind legs got cut off. They rushed her to the vet and he said, "I can sew her up, or you can put her to sleep if you want, but the puppies are okay. She'll be able to deliver the puppies."
>
> Dibby's cousin said, "Keep her alive."
>
> So the vet sewed up her backside, and over the next week the dog learned to walk. She didn't spend any time worrying, she just learned to walk by taking two steps in the front and flipping up her backside, and then taking two steps and flipping up her backside again. She gave birth to six little puppies, all in perfect health. She nursed them and then weaned them. And when they learned to walk, they all walked like her.[1]

Go ahead and laugh a few seconds, then take it very seriously. The date I read this excerpt was exactly July 13, 1989. Do you know why I remember it so well? Because after crying myself into a heap, I resolved to do anything and everything God willed—no matter how difficult— to make sure my two precious pups would not grow up to walk like their mother, the victim. Or like her mother, the victim. I say this with deep love and all due respect. I was trying to do my best before that pivotal period in my life, but I still had areas of bondage I had convinced myself would not affect my children. I finally faced the fact that I had to break all chains. Even a thin chain can strangle the life out of you.

To the praise and glory of our redeeming God, as I write this study, Amanda is in college and Melissa is finishing high school. So far, I see no signs of their living like "victims," but don't worry, I intend to keep watching. With deep earnest, I pray that if they walk like me now, they will walk wholeheartedly in liberty with God. I have found freedom right next to His side. Breaking the cycle has been such hard work, but the glorious freedom God has given is worth it, because He is worth it. And He happens to think you are worth it.

I realize this lesson has been heavy, but our goal is not just to learn the Bible. God wants whole hearts, not big heads. We're taking a journey so we can pack up and move to a place where we can freely enjoy our covenant relationship with Christ, the place secured by the ancient boundary stones.

Take courage if these subjects are hard for you. The enemy is hoping we'd rather remain in denial than face the truth and let God's Word penetrate our lives and set us free. If the subject of generational bondage and sin doesn't seem to apply to you, ask God how He desires to use these lessons in your life. To grow compassion? Deeper understanding? In my opinion, few of our family "lines" couldn't use a little "realignment." Let's invite God into our private business. He's the perfect family Counselor.

CHAPTER 15

THAT ANCIENT SERPENT

In order that Satan might not outwit us.
For we are not unaware of his schemes.

(2 COR. 2:11)

I have several reasons for approaching Satan's role in bondage the way we will. I don't want him glorified in any way. This study is about who we are in Christ and learning to live in the freedom we've been given. We will focus on some of the enemy's schemes because he is deeply involved in matters of generational sin and bondage.

Notice how Revelation 12:9 portrays Satan: "The great dragon was hurled down—that ancient serpent called the devil, or Satan, who leads the whole world astray." Satan is both ancient and misleading. "That ancient serpent" has been around a long time. We can safely assume he and his cohorts know more about our family heritage than the most extensive genealogical research could uncover. If knowledge is power, our enemy is pretty powerful. If he can use our earthly heritage to lead us astray, I have little doubt he will.

Despite thousands of years of existence, though, I don't think the ancient serpent has a wealth of new ideas. Satan probably tries the same general lure on us that he used on those who came before us in our family lines. He starts with the obvious and sees if what worked with the parents will work with the children. Not very creative, maybe, but highly effective.

My husband was never close to one of his grandfathers. According to Keith, this grandfather allowed his unrestrained temper to totally destroy the family home. I can remember Keith saying, "The scariest times of my life were when I saw glimpses of that same kind of anger displayed in one of my parents."

When Keith became a father, every time he reacted to anything with the least degree of anger, the enemy would attack with accusing thoughts like, "See, you're just like them!" Keith would often feel depressed afterward. I admire my husband for the way he has taken this to the Lord and let Him treat it with Truth so the chain could be broken. You see, every time Keith got angry about something, Satan saw a dual opportunity. If he could tempt Keith to lose his temper and raise his voice or say more than he should, the enemy would win a double-header: he'd tempted Keith to sin in his anger and to feel hopeless about ever changing his behavior.

Personalize this experience for just a moment. What behavior might you see in your life that you disliked in your parents or grandparents?

Second Corinthians 11:3 gives us another picture of Satan. Paul wrote to those he had introduced to Christ: "I am afraid that just as Eve was deceived by the serpent's cunning, your minds may somehow be led astray from your sincere and pure devotion to Christ."

The verse shows that Satan is a deceiver, leading our minds astray. I want to zero in on the fact that he is cunning (NIV) or subtle (KJV). The more undetected Satan's work remains, the less we'll resist him. As we determined earlier, one of the dangers of a generational yoke is that it blends in so well with the rest of our lives and families. God gave me a frightening visual aid just a few days before writing this entry. Keith and I were walking our dog on a trail in the country. Keith suddenly grabbed me and said, "Don't move!" The biggest copperhead Keith had ever seen was curled up on the path just a few feet in front of us. Keith saw the snake because he is a hunter. He has an eye for camouflaged creatures!

We can think of Satan's subtleties as his camouflage. Generational yokes often go undetected because they blend in so well with our personalities. We excuse some of these yokes as simply being the way we are. We might even say, "My mother was like this and so was hers! We're just outspoken women who know our own minds!" Or, "My grandfather raised my father not to take a handout from anyone. We are proud people, and I'm not going to take a handout either."

You may be beginning to see a well-camouflaged chain you've inherited. You don't have to decide, "Well, I'm stuck with it, so I may as well be proud of it." In Christ we are not stuck with anything but Him; praise His Name!

You may be surprised to learn that the Scripture has a prescription for breaking one of the strongest forms of family bondage. That prescription is called forgiveness. Notice what Paul says about it in 2 Corinthians 2:10–11: "I have forgiven in the sight of Christ for your sake, in order that Satan might not outwit us. For we are not unaware of his schemes."

The enemy specializes in taking advantage of any refusal to forgive. I'll describe an all-too-common scenario. A family has a feud over the family business. The grown siblings cease speaking to one another and do not allow their children to associate. They harbor bad feelings so long that those who refused to forgive become unforgiving people. The cancer spreads to other relationships as well. The grandchildren and the great-grandchildren know very little about the original feud. In fact, they know very little about one another. They have little in common, except most of them are mad at someone all the time.

If we come from an extended family full of disassociations, we may feel unaffected by it, but we're probably not. A feeling of detachment is a negative effect all by itself. Perhaps alienation has been your family's way of life for so many generations—it doesn't even seem strange! Let's be courageous and ask God if we are perpetuating division and unforgiveness in the family line.

Of Satan, 1 Peter 5:8 says: "Your enemy the devil prowls around like a roaring lion looking for someone to devour." The implication is that Satan is looking to devour anything that is—if you'll allow me to make up a word—"devourable," or vulnerable.

The sins of the fathers increase the vulnerability of the children to the third and fourth generations (Exod. 20:5). As a child, my maternal grandmother lost both her parents. Years later she lost her husband and finished raising my mother all by herself during the Great Depression. My dear mother battled insecurities all her life. When I began to seek wholeness in Christ, I finally mustered the courage to ask Him where I was vulnerable. He revealed to me that I feared having no one to take care of me; and if I didn't let Him heal this part of me, I would be vulnerable to unhealthy relationships. This only makes sense in terms of a chain of insecurity passed down through several generations.

God and I worked very hard on this issue, and I am so glad we did. Although my parents have been wonderful and my husband is an excellent provider, the reality is this: God is my only guarantee. The Knower of all my needs is the sole Meeter of all my needs. Only He can fully and wholly provide, but we cannot drop chains we do not even know we're carrying! Remember John 8:32; just facing the truth of our past or present will not heal us. It's facing our truth in the light of God's Truth (His Word and His Son) that sets us free! Whenever the enemy tries to use your physical lineage against you, use your spiritual lineage against him! As a child of God and a joint heir with Christ, refuse the enemy a single inch of the ground we are taking back.

CHAPTER 16

SURVEYING THE ANCIENT RUINS

Yet you ask, "Why does the son not share the guilt of his father?" Since the son
has done what is just and right and has been careful
to keep all my decrees, he will surely live.

(EZEK. 18:19)

❧

We have identified some ancient ruins and gathered some intelligence
on the serpent, who specializes in ancient ruins. Now we are ready to
look at blueprints for rebuilding our ancient ruins. I promised biblical
proof that Exodus 20:5 does not mean children bear the guilt of their
forefathers' sins. Feeling the effects of their sins and shouldering the
guilt are very different repercussions. God brings healing to the former
and relieves the unnecessary burden of the latter.

Ezekiel 18 addresses the sins of the fathers and sons (not to the exclu-
sion of the mothers and daughters). The most obvious place to discover
ancient ruins is in the previous generation because it is more recent.

You may come from an unusually healthy family and relate very little from personal experience. Perhaps this lesson will help you understand a friend. On the other hand, you may have descended from the

opposite extreme and see nothing positive in your lineage. I pray that you will let God shed a little light on the shades of grace and goodness in your heritage. I assume, however, that most readers are somewhat like me. I am a blend of the best and worst of my earthly lineage. I am asking God to help me discern the difference and allow Him to break all negative bonds. I want to pass down the very best to my children, both physical and spiritual. In straining ahead for an ideal, we are sure to reach positive change.

The Israelites had a proverb that served to blame their present troubles on past generations. The saying was, "The fathers eat sour grapes, / and the children's teeth are set on edge" (Ezek. 18:2).

Do your children ever accuse you of being unfair about something? Every once in a while mine do—and it hurts! Then just in case I don't get the point, they'll go on and on with the subject until I'm weary of hearing it. At those times, I could be caught using words like these: "I've heard that out of your mouth more times than I ever wanted to! What you're accusing me of isn't even true! Now, let that be the end of it!" Ezekiel 18 quotes God responding in a similar way:

> As surely as I live, declares the Sovereign LORD, you will no longer quote this proverb in Israel. For every living soul belongs to me, the father as well as the son— both alike belong to me. The soul who sins is the one who will die. (Ezek. 18:3–4)

God went on to explain and illustrate the principle, but we can summarize it in two words: *personal responsibility.* God told of a righteous father and unrighteous son. His conclusion was simple. The father would live for his righteousness. The son would die for his unrighteousness.

We who have trusted Christ don't "die" for our sins. Thankfully, Christ has already done that for us. We can experience the death of self-respect over our sins or the death of an earthly relationship, but our physical deaths are only means of passing from this life to our citizenship in heaven.

Most of us probably have discovered a few ancient ruins. In this lesson and the next, we are going to study how to begin rebuilding our ancient ruins. We begin rebuilding when we do four things:

1. *We must agree to take an honest look back.* Many well-meaning Christians take out of context the exhortation in Philippians 3:13, "forgetting what is behind," and apply it as a command to never look at the past. Paul was talking about all the trophies of life he had to leave behind to follow Christ. God's Word clearly expresses what a good and effective teacher the past can be. The past will be a good teacher if we will approach it as a good student, from the perspective of what we can gain and how God can use it for His glory.

Ezekiel 18 illustrates very simply how the chain of destructive behavior must be broken.

> But suppose this son has a son who sees all the sins his father commits, and though he sees them, he does not do such things . . . He will not die for his father's sin; he will surely live. (Ezek. 18:14, 17)

> Rid yourselves of all the offenses you have committed, and get a new heart and a new spirit. Why will you die, O house of Israel? (Ezek. 18:31)

I see four important steps the son took toward breaking the cycle his father may have created or perpetuated:

1. He saw the sins his father committed.
2. He made the firm decision not to practice the same habits.
3. He got rid of his own offenses.
4. He pursued a new heart and new spirit.

You may be thinking, "Easier said than done!" You're right. I've never seen a construction worker who didn't sometimes get covered in sweat; but if he worked diligently, the result was something beautiful. Rebuilding happens no other way. We will work on each of these subjects over the course of our journey to breaking free, but let's look at the first one now. The Hebrew word for "sees" in Ezekiel 18:14 is *ra'ah,* which means to "view, inspect . . . to learn . . . gain understanding." Did you notice that gaining understanding has nothing to do with dishonoring a parent?

Proverbs 30:11 speaks of those "who curse their fathers / and do not bless their mothers." Such behavior is no option for believers. God told us to honor our parents in Exodus 20:12, just seven verses after He described generational sin, so we cannot pretend that our subject matter is the exception to the rule. As we consider any sins of our parents that we don't want to imitate or pass down, we should be careful not to curse them by demeaning and belittling them. We can be honest and still avoid belittling a parent. Would you be willing to ask God to help you view any sins of your parents for the opportunity to avoid repeating them in your life or your children's? Would you be willing to take a deeper inspection than we've taken so far to learn and gain understanding?

Without dishonoring anyone, what further enlightenment regarding chains you need to break has the Holy Spirit given you? What patterns have you seen in your parents' lives that you do not want repeated in your own? We need to take an honest look back, but we need to do more.

2. *We must believe the truth over the enemy's lies.* We can be freed from the effects and practices of the sins in our lineage. Allow me to say gently and with much compassion: you are not the exception, and neither is your situation. In all things we can be overcomers but, indeed, only through Him who loves us (Rom. 8:37).

In earlier chapters we talked about belief versus nonbelief. Down in the deepest part of our hearts, do we look at old habits and behaviors that have been snares to us and our parents and think, *It's no use?* Please turn from any unbelief or it will keep liberty from being a reality.

To break the bondage of generational sin, we need to take a look back, and we need to believe God's truth over the enemies' lies.

3. *We must discern the difference between rebuilding and preserving the ancient ruins.* You may be saying, "Beth, believe me, I've taken plenty of looks back, and I continue to get angrier or more depressed." I understand. I've done exactly the same. Then I learned the difference between rebuilding and preserving. I was reminded of the difference as I stood at the Acropolis in Athens. Our guide estimated how much money they spend every year "preserving the ruins." God never called us to preserve our ancient ruins. Rather than inspect the ancient ruins and then work with God to rebuild, sometimes we just keep revisiting and preserving, and we never get over it. Without God, our only sure Restorer, that's about the best we can do. If you have "ancient ruins," have you been preserving or working on rebuilding them?

4. *We must accept God's appointment as a reconstruction worker.* I hope you are memorizing Isaiah 61:1–4. Verse 4 says, "They will rebuild the ancient ruins / and restore the places long devastated." "They" refers to the captives who have been set free.

Once again, we can apply something figuratively that applied literally to Israel: Just as God appointed the Israelites to rebuild the wall around Jerusalem, He appoints you to rebuild your ancient ruins.

I believe one reason God requires our cooperation is that He deeply desires our involvement with Him. He created us for this purpose. Rebuilding ancient ruins is impossible for us without God. We are unqualified for the task; but as we draw near to Him, He rebuilds our lives and characters. Remember, God's primary purpose in healing us from our hurts is to introduce us to new depths of relationship with Himself.

Although we are focusing on rebuilding the ancient ruins, I am praying that every part of this study will place tools in your hands for this important and sometimes ongoing task. Perhaps you're still wondering how our ancient ruins can ever be rebuilt. After all, we can't change the past, right? As we begin cooperating with God in the process of rebuilding, we might not be able to change the past, but we can change a few things more impressive:

- We can change how we look at it.
- We can decide how we're going to build on it.

Let's make a covenant to stop preserving and start rebuilding. The hammer is passed down into our hands.

CHAPTER 17

THE ANCIENT OF DAYS

"I have revealed and saved and proclaimed—
I, and not some foreign god among you.
You are my witnesses," declares the LORD, "that I am God.
Yes, and from ancient days I am he."

(ISA. 43:12–13)

Just as God's primary agenda is redemption, Satan's primary agenda is to blind people to the Redeemer. But once we are redeemed, our completion becomes God's primary agenda. As God began stirring the tremendously heavy burden in my heart to write this study, He gave me two statements on which to build:

1. Christ came to set the captives free.
2. Satan came to take the free captive.

We are the free; our liberty is a fact. But according to Galatians 5:1, we can return to a yoke of bondage. One of the primary goals of this study is to help us learn to cease cooperating with the enemy and start living in the reality of our liberty.

Daniel 7:9 refers to God as the "Ancient of Days." The enemy, that ancient serpent, has been around a long time and knows our tendencies and vulnerabilities. Far more impressive, however, is the "Ancient of Days"!

When she was in the second grade, my daughter Amanda illustrated a truth about the centrality of God. She was telling me something she had prayed over at school that day. I said, "Oh, Amanda, do you know how much it means to Mommy for you to make God a part of your day?" I'll never forget her answer. "You're so silly, Mommy. You know God made the day. I'm just glad He made me part of His." I was stunned. She expressed the meaning of God's wonderful name, the "Ancient of Days."

Every day the sun rises by God's permission. He's never had a wink of sleep, and nothing has been hidden from His sight. God has been God through every single day of your heritage. If you're dealing with some ancient ruins, He was there when they crumbled. He knows every detail. He knows exactly how you've been affected, and His expertise is reconstruction. After all, Christ was a carpenter by trade. Nothing has ever been allowed to crumble in a Christian's life or heritage that God can't reconstruct and use. Let's consider several primary catalysts that take us from cursings to blessings in our family's lineage.

Psalm 78 speaks of multiple generations. It shows that every generation has a new opportunity to exert positive influence.

They would not be like their forefathers—
a stubborn and rebellious generation,
whose hearts were not loyal to God,
whose spirits were not faithful to him. (Ps. 78:8)

No matter what atrocity has taken place in your family line, God can raise up a new generation of godly seed. Your grandfather could serve a life sentence for murder, and your grandchild could serve a life sentence of faithful evangelism through which thousands come to know Christ!

Between every unfaithful generation and faithful generation is one person determined to change. You could be that link. So could I. Perhaps no one in your family was overtly sinful, but they were simply uninvolved in Christ's kingdom. Maybe you would like to be a link that takes your family line from an unfulfilling life of religion to a passionate life of relationship with Christ. Perhaps your prayer for your grandchildren and great-grandchildren might be a love for missions. Whatever it may be, you can be that link!

If your dream or desire for your grandchildren and great-grandchildren is in keeping with what you know of God's will, then you have the endorsement and approval of Christ to begin acting on it. Cooperate with God and pray toward the fulfillment of the dream.

You can be absolutely certain that God's will is for your generation to give way to godly seed. I aggressively pray for godly seed to come from my offspring. I love my parents and grandparents, and I want to pass down many wonderful things they've given me. We faithfully attended church, but my parents were never taught how to walk with God daily through prayer and His Word. They did not possess intimate relationships with God that released power to overcome some big obstacles. Keith and I hope to give our children some new gifts. I pray constantly for my children and theirs to love God passionately and serve Him fervently. I hope they will inherit a burden for world missions and a love for all races.

On the other hand, I'm not naive enough to think we won't hand down a few unwanted "gifts." I pray they also will be able to discern and reverse any negative cycles they see in Keith and me.

God certainly blesses our prayers and our hopes, but to break cycles and provoke lasting change we must also be willing to deliberately cooperate with Him. Among the most treasured gifts we could pass down is authenticity. We accomplish little good when we tell of the praiseworthy deeds of the Lord but live lives inconsistent with His Truth.

Here's a bold and challenging question for you: In what ways are you allowing the next generation to see authenticity in your life? We're about to see why the work is so very worth it! Look again at Exodus 20:5–6. Many readers are so disturbed by verse 5 that verse 6 never sinks in. God visits the sin to the third and forth generation, but he shows "love to a thousand generations of those who love me and keep my commandments" (Exod. 20:6).

Not much comparison between three or four and a thousand! God is clearly more gracious in His blessings than He is stern in His chastisements. Do you realize that your walk with God could affect many future generations? How many of your descendants could be blessed because you agreed to be a link to a new cycle of faithfulness to God?

We know from John 3:16 that God loves the entire world, but He shows love to those who love and obey Him. God lavishly loves every person, but He reserves the right to demonstrate His loving mercy to the obedient. John 14:21 expresses the same truth. Jesus said, "Whoever has my commands and obeys them, he is the one who loves me. He who loves me will be loved by my Father, and I too will love him and show myself to him."

In future chapters we will address in far more depth the subjects of loving God and obeying Him. For now, let's dig out a beautiful jewel embedded in Exodus 20:6. The Hebrew word for "showing" in this verse is *asah*. Guess what it means? It means "to construct, build." Right there in the context of generational influence, God promises to build blessing on the lives of those who love Him and obey Him.

The "Ancient of Days" is anxiously waiting to build a solid foundation that your descendants can live on for years to come if they choose. He's not asking us to rebuild ancient ruins by ourselves. He's simply asking us to be one of the tools He uses. God knows exactly what went wrong, exactly where the cracks are in the foundation. He was there, remember? He was completely God then, and He is completely God now.

Many people yearn to be part of something significant. We want to make useful contributions to society. We look at people who do and we're envious, yet do we realize what kind of contribution we can make to our own family lines? I can't think of anyone to whom I'd want my life to be a blessing more than my children's children and their children's children. Ten generations later our names might be forgotten, but one day in heaven they'll get to meet the link that changed the direction of the chain.

Sometimes we're willing to criticize what happened before us, but are we willing to take the challenge of positively affecting those after us? The little slice of time God offers each generation is a trust. Those before us who were unfaithful with their trust will be held accountable, but we're still here. We still have a chance to positively affect the generations that follow us. Remember Hezekiah? His actions caused his own children to be carried away captive. Many parents have done the same because they viewed their few years as the only years that mattered. The virus of self-centeredness is contagious, but each generation has the option not to catch it. I am praying that you and I will not be like Hezekiah.

If you do your part for one generation, He'll do His for a thousand. Sounds like a pretty good deal to me. I don't know how much longer Christ will tarry, but I don't expect Him to linger a thousand more generations. That means your life could affect every generation until He comes. Pretty impressive. The blood's already been shed. Isn't it worth a little sweat and tears?

CHAPTER 18

STRAIGHT TO THE HEART

He has sent me to bind up the brokenhearted.

(ISA. 61:1)

Can you remember when you lost your first tooth? Rode your first two-wheeler? Lived through your first day of junior high? These were monumental experiences, yet you may or may not recall them. But if I asked about the first experience that shattered your heart, you'd likely remember everything—down to the last detail. Somehow having your heart broken is an injury in a class all by itself.

As I think back on a few of my own heartbreaks, I can almost feel the ache all over again. Not only is a broken heart inevitable from time to time; it is one of the primary emotional rites of passage into maturity. Sadly, many individuals are introduced to mature emotions long before they should be.

One of the primary reasons God sent His Son to this earth was to bring tender salve and relief to those whose hearts have been broken. I believe that only God can truly and completely heal shattered hearts. He uses different methods; but according to Isaiah 61:1, one of His greatest priorities is binding up the brokenhearted.

Let's take an in-depth look at this wonderful part of the ministry He assigned to His Son in Isaiah 61:1. I pray that you will be as blessed as I am over the original meanings God led me to discover in Isaiah 61:1. Don't proceed quickly. Take in the following truths slowly. Meditate on them and feel vastly loved.

Take notice of the second active verb in the verse: "He has sent me." The Hebrew word for "sent" is *shalack,* meaning "to shoot (forth)" (*Strong's*).

Psalm 127:3–4 says that "sons are a heritage from the LORD, / . . . Like arrows in the hands of a warrior." We know from John 3:16 that Jesus is God's only begotten Son. John 3:17 tells us God gave His Son for the salvation of people by sending Him into the world.

You see, God only had one arrow in His quiver. The most perfect arrow ever to exist, a masterpiece, priceless to Him. Cherished far above all the hosts of heaven. Nothing could compare. His only heritage. His only Son. But as God looked on a lost world—desperate and needy and in the clutches of the enemy—His heart was overwhelmed. Though they had sinned miserably against Him and few sought Him, God had created them in love and could not love them less.

Love reached sacrificially into the quiver and pulled forth the solitary arrow. The quiver would now be empty, His cherished arrow in the hands of hateful men. Yes, God so loved the world; but God also loved His only begotten Son with inexpressible, divine affection. The divine dilemma: two loves. And one would demand the sacrifice of the other. He positioned the weapon, pulled back the bow, steadied His grip, aimed straight for the heart: "And she brought forth her firstborn son, and wrapped him in swaddling clothes, and laid him in a manger" (Luke 2:7, KJV).

Oh, what unfathomable love! What sacrifice! All who will lower their shields of unbelief and let the healing arrow penetrate shall be saved. I don't know if you're feeling what I am right now, but I've had to stop, picture, meditate, and respond to God.

The next Hebrew word I'd like you to see is the adjective we're using in this lesson continually for the heart. "He sent me to bind up the *broken*hearted." The Hebrew word for "broken" in Isaiah 61:1 is *shavar*, meaning "to burst, break into pieces, wreck, crush, smash; to rend, tear in pieces (like a wild beast)."

Have those words ever described your heart? Has your heart felt as if wild beasts were fighting over it? They certainly describe mine, and it hurts even to think about it! The definition also says, "This verb occurs with a broad range of violent meanings." Please don't misunderstand. This latter part of the definition does not mean that a broken heart occurs only when something violent happens to you. As you and I both know, broken hearts result more frequently from words than actions. The idea is that a heart is almost always broken in a specific moment over a single action. Let me explain by example.

David and Teresa struggled in their marriage almost from the start. David feared that Teresa married him for security rather than affection, but he loved her too much to face the problem. He hoped she would learn to love him but, sadly, she didn't. She grew colder and colder. For six years he fought for the marriage and carried most of the weight of the relationship. One day he walked in from work to find her clothes gone and a note on the table. "I'm sorry, David. I can't help the way I feel. I don't love you, and I never have. I tried for as long as I could. We'll both be better off."

Based on the definition of the word *broken* in Isaiah 61:1, at what point do you imagine David's heart was "smashed" or "torn into pieces"?

If your answer is "when he realized Teresa left him," you're probably right. This doesn't mean that he didn't hurt before, nor does it mean he hadn't suffered long-term misery. *Shavar* simply means that we can usually trace a time of heartbreak to a single moment.

Can you relate to this definition? Think of a time when you suffered through a season with a broken heart. Can you remember one particular moment when, figuratively speaking, you felt your heart break? Did you have any idea at the time that God cared so much that He aimed His Son straight toward your heart?

I'd like you to see the last Hebrew definition in Isaiah 61:1: "He has sent me to bind up the brokenhearted." The word for "bind up" is *chavash,* meaning "to bind on, wrap around; bind up as a wound, bandage, cover, envelope, enclose." *Strong's Dictionary* adds a visual definition to the same word: "to compress, . . . to stop." How can we biblically characterize the difference between an aching heart and a broken heart? God defines a broken heart in our context as one that is hemorrhaging.

Compressing the hemorrhaging heart is the idea of applying pressure to a badly bleeding wound. What a wonderful picture of Christ! A crushing hurt comes, and the sympathizing, scarred hand of Christ presses the wound; and for just a moment, the pain seems to intensify . . . but finally the bleeding stops. Are you beginning to see the intimate activity of Christ when we're devastated? And to think, this is the same One we accuse of not caring when the crushing moment occurs.

Let's conclude our chapter with a last thought on Christ's binding up the brokenhearted. Notice that the first definition includes the concepts of covering, enveloping, and enclosing. Life's way of reacting to a crushed heart is to wrap tough sinews of flesh around it and tempt us to promise we'll never let ourselves get hurt again. That's not God's way. Remember, self-made fortresses not only keep love from going out; they keep love from coming in. We risk becoming captives in our own protective fortresses. Only God can put the pieces of our hearts back together again, close up all the wounds, and bind them with a porous bandage that protects from infection . . . but keeps the heart free to inhale and exhale love.

Are you in bondage to a broken heart that you have never let Christ bind and heal? Right now, you could conclude this lesson with a bandage instead of bondage. Go ahead. Expose your heart one more time . . . just to Him. After all, this is what His Father sent Him to do. The bow's stretched back and the Arrow's ready. But it's up to you to drop your shield.

CHAPTER 19

HEARTS BROKEN IN
CHILDHOOD

At that time the disciples came to Jesus and asked, "Who is the greatest in the kingdom of heaven?" He called a little child and had him stand among them.

(MATT. 18:1–2)

We will spend two chapters on hearts broken by childhood victimization or abuse. God does not minimize the things that break our hearts. He is not looking down on us thinking how petty we are because things hurt us. If we're so "heavenly minded" that we grow out of touch with earthly hardships, somewhere we've missed an important priority of Christ. God left our bare feet on the hot pavement of earth so we could grow through our hurts, not ignore and refuse to feel our way through them.

In Matthew 18, Jesus' disciples were concerned with who would be greatest in the kingdom. Jesus called a little child, saying that to be great the disciples must become like such a child. Then Christ made a statement significant to our subject. He said, "If anyone causes one of these little ones who believe in me to sin, it would be better for him to have a large millstone hung around his neck and to be drowned in the depths of the sea" (v. 6).

Based on Christ's statement, how do you think one person could cause another person to sin? I believe Christ's words specifically apply to child victimization or abuse. Anything that directly causes a child to have an increased tendency toward sin can be characterized as victimization or abuse.

I never share the details of my childhood victimization for two reasons: first, I want the Healer glorified, not the hurt; and second, a greater number of people can relate to more general terms.

Unfortunately, many of you have suffered abuses much like mine. If you asked those of us who have been victimized whether or not the experience qualifies as heartbreaking, we'd answer with a resounding yes!

God used Matthew 18 mightily to answer some questions for me. Let me tell you how I deal with "whys" to which I can't find answers: I find as many answers as I can in God's Word, fill in those blanks, and trust Him with the rest. Sounds simple but it's not. It's something I practice by faith every single day of my life and find great solace and rest in this method. Go with me through Matthew 18:1–9, and let's see if we can fill in enough blanks concerning childhood victimization to trust God with the rest.

1. *Children are the apple of Christ's eye.* Based on Luke's account of the same scene in 9:46, the disciples were arguing over who would be greatest in the kingdom. Instead of pointing out one of them when asked this question, Jesus "called a little child and had him stand among them" (Matt. 18:2). Christ essentially said, "You want to see my idea of greatness? Take a look at this child."

Savor Christ's tenderness toward children. He could have simply spoken a blessing over the children, but He chose to demonstrate His love for them instead by taking them in his arms, putting his hands on them, and blessing them (Mark 10:16). I believe Christ not only loved children, but they also loved Him. How many children would be willing to leave their playtime and step up in front of thirteen men to be used as an example? Not many, unless they completely loved and trusted the One who summoned them.

I think Christ was one of those people who attracted all the kids in the neighborhood. I think He probably went few places without swinging around several kids in a quick game of "Flying Dutchman." In fact, the attraction children had to Christ may have been the very reason the disciples rebuked them in Mark 10:13. The disciples may have been sick of constantly maneuvering around a bunch of kids.

Maybe I'm wrong, but based on the blanks we can fill in, I have a feeling the missing blanks are in favor of children. I find humor in the fact that Christ pulled a real child forward to express His idea of greatness, while His chosen twelve were acting like a bunch of children. I also notice another fact about Christ and the children.

2. *Children are uniquely accompanied by Christ.* What do you suppose Christ meant in Matthew 18:5 when He said, "Whoever welcomes a little child like this in My name welcomes Me"? Christ basically said, "What you do for them, you do for Me."

3. *Abuses to children may as well have been personally applied to Christ.* Based on the context, I believe He was saying not only, "What you do for a child, you do for Me," but also "What you do to a child, you do to Me." He obviously takes harm to children very personally.

If you were victimized as a child, did you ever think about how Christ felt about what happened to you? How could the enemy benefit from tempting you to believe wrongly about Christ's attitude toward child victimization? From all we have seen, Christ obviously cares very deeply for children and all that happens to them. Zechariah portrays God's defensiveness toward His own: "Whoever touches you touches the apple of his eye" (Zech. 2:8).

4. *Christ is never the author of abuse.* The Bible teaches us that some hardships are specifically ordained by God for the purpose of our

growth and refining. Child abuse is not one of them. When you are try-ing to discern whether God or Satan is the author of a hardship, one of your best clues is whether sin is involved. God never entices us to sin, nor does He employ sin or perversion as a means of molding us into the image of Christ. Impossible!

Allow me to use my own experience as an example. Two of the fac-tors that most affected my childhood were abuse and a fall that mangled my teeth. My teeth became a source of insecurity and embarrassment for years. I know without a doubt that Satan was the author of my child-hood abuse because such heinous sin was involved and because shame resulted. Remember, shame is Satan's "stamp of approval."

On the other hand, my fall placed many difficult challenges in front of me, but sin played no part in the cause. As a result of the fall, God allowed me to experience what I call the "underdog syndrome" and placed in me a deep compassion for people who are teased harshly and treated unmercifully. God somehow made the truth register in my young heart that He thought I was beautiful. Without a doubt, I gained abundantly from that childhood disaster.

Think about your own childhood. Can you identify an experience that would be characteristic of God at work? Can you identify a handi-work of Satan?

I want to make a point that may be difficult but which is necessary for our liberation. I'll personalize it to my own experience: God per-mitted both of those childhood experiences whether or not He authored them. No, God could not have authored my childhood victimization because it was opposite of His character, but obviously He allowed it. Why? He may have other reasons I do not yet know; but until those blanks are filled in, I know the following:

1. He knew that I would have to seek Him diligently for healing; and in healing, I would come to know my Healer.

2. He knew glory would come to His name through the miracle of restoration and subsequent ministry.
3. He knew I would be compassionate to people who have been hurt in childhood.
4. He knew that the crime of childhood victimization would "come out of the closet" in this generation, and He desired to call forth Christian spokespeople to address it from His Word.
5. He wanted me to teach how to make freedom in Christ a reality in life from the passion of personal experience.

I know no better way to say it. Until the rest of the blanks are filled in, those are enough for me. God's good from life's bad is one of the most liberating concepts in the entire Word of God.

I so much encourage you to completely surrender your hurt to Him, withholding nothing, and invite Him to work miracles from your misery. Then be patient and get to know Him through the process of healing. You will see fruit. I promise! But more than that, *Christ* promises.

We've filled in four blanks about childhood victimization. In the next chapter we will consider two more. You may or may not have experienced childhood victimization, but virtually everyone has suffered some kind of hurt in childhood. Have you surrendered every single part of that hurt to Him? If not, would you surrender the hurt now? Take time right now to pray, offering something that hurt you as a child to the One who loves children so much. You are His child, no matter your age.

CHAPTER 20

HEARTS MENDED BY TRUTH

Woe to the world because of the things that cause people to sin! Such things must come, but woe to the man through whom they come!

(MATT. 18:7)

Christ healed in many different ways. Sometimes through touch. Sometimes through speech. Matthew 18 shows Christ offering healing through truth. I found significant healing in the study of this Scripture. I learned how important I was to Christ when I was a child and accepted how much He despised what had happened to me. Scripture is the strongest bandage God uses to bind hearts that were broken in childhood.

I believe that those who have fallen victim to abuse are less likely to find instantaneous healing. They are more likely to find progressive healing through the study and application of truth. Renewed minds and positive habits are a necessity to lives pressing onward in victory. We saw four truths in the last chapter. Matthew 18 teaches another healing truth about Jesus and children.

5. *Christ avenges the abuse or victimization of children.* I believe Christ is referring to childhood victimization in Matthew 18:6–10 for at least a couple of reasons:

- He specifically implies something one person can do to another. In this reference, the "other" is a child.
- He speaks of an action that "causes one of these little ones . . . to sin."

Each of us who has been victimized in childhood can testify that the tendencies toward certain sins dramatically increase as a result. As part of my healing, I had to take responsibility for my own sin, whether or not another person's actions escorted me to those sins.

Perhaps you are like I was at one time. You don't want to take responsibility for your sins because you don't think they were your fault. You may wonder, "How else would I have responded after my reference point was so distorted?" But, you see, I don't think confessing sin is primarily about fault. It's about freedom!

Yes, my sins were my own fault. But more important to God, I believe, was my willingness to confess how badly I hated those sins and how I wanted to be free from the power the abuse held over my decisions. Confession allowed me to bring sinful behaviors to the table for open discussion with God. He instantly forgave me and completely cleansed me; then He began to teach me how to change my responses.

You may be thinking, *But the complications and repercussions of victimization are so overwhelming. It's just so hard to deal with!* I agree. And that is one of the reasons it would be better for any victimizer "to have a large millstone hung around his neck and to be drowned in the depths of the sea." Undoubtedly, childhood victimization is a giant to battle, especially if the person was someone who was supposed to protect you. However, just as surely as God empowered young David to slay Goliath, He'll empower you if you let Him. Just remember David's words in

1 Samuel 17:47: "For the battle is the LORD's." Lamentations speaks powerfully to God's attitude toward abuse: "You have seen, O LORD, the wrong done to me" (Lam. 3:59).

Forgiving my perpetrator didn't mean suddenly shrugging my shoulders, muttering, "OK, I forgive," and going on as if those things hadn't happened. They did happen. And they took a terrible toll on my life. Forgiveness involved my handing over to God the responsibility for justice. The longer I held on to it, the more the bondage strangled the life out of me. Forgiveness meant my deferring the cause to Christ and deciding to be free of the ongoing burden of bitterness and blame.

You know one of the primary reasons I finally forgave my perpetrator? This may be hard for you to stomach, but it is the absolute truth: I finally came to a place where I felt more sorry for him than I did for myself. I can tell you that if I had to be in the scenario of Matthew 18:6, I'd rather be the loved and cherished victim than the victimizer. As my nephew used to say when he was little, "Dat dude's in bid trouble."

We also find a sixth truth about victimization.

6. *We can sadly assume victimization will continue in this present world system.* See the words of Matthew 18:7: "Woe to the world because of the things that cause people to sin! Such things must come, but woe to the man through whom they come!"

Some level of child victimization will probably continue in our world because the vile prince of this world system (John 12:31) and his evil underlings are at work. Until Christ's kingdom comes, we can and must reach out to victims and support laws that restrain evil and "expose deeds of darkness"; but we will never be able to completely stop it. Satan has far too much to gain from it. The next word may help you understand why the enemy benefits so viciously from these kinds of hurts.

In the King James Version, Matthew 18:7 says: "Woe unto the world because of offences!" Look at the meaning of the word *offences.*

Skandalon means "the trigger of a trap on which the bait is placed, and which, when touched by the animal, springs and causes it to close causing entrapment. . . . *Skandalon* always denotes an enticement to conduct which could ruin the person in question." You don't have to have your doctorate in biblical studies to recognize the work of the enemy in victimization. Have you ever considered how childhood victimization could eventually trap someone by enticing them into sin?

We know from research that large numbers of both men and women who turn to scandalous behaviors such as prostitution, promiscuity, and homosexuality were victims of sexual abuse in childhood. I'm not making excuses, but sometimes explanations for such a lack of self-respect help us understand and know how to respond to such destructive behaviors.

Satan wants to keep people from receiving Christ as Savior. Certainly, childhood victimization is an effective deterrent. Since the enemy cannot keep salvation from anyone who wants to believe, he tries to ensure that people will be either too emotionally handicapped to turn into an effective witness or too broken to avoid falling into scandalous sin. The enemy's hope for Christians is that we will either be so ineffective we have no testimony, or we'll ruin the one we have.

Isn't the enemy's gain one more reason we must refuse to let him have another inch of ground over something in our past? It's time to direct our indignation toward the author of abuse: Satan himself. I want to make a statement I believe with my whole heart concerning childhood victimization: Ultimately the accuser (Satan) is the chief abuser.

I was abused more times than I would like to count, but Satan accused me every day of my life from that time on until I finally said, "Enough!" and agreed to let God bring healing and forgiveness. My friend, read these words carefully and accept them with your whole heart: You are not defined by anything that happened to you or anything you have done. You are defined by who you are in Christ. You are God's beloved child. He has seen any wrong done to you, and He will uphold your cause. As for that perpetrator? "Dat dude's in bid trouble."

We've talked about a difficult subject, but until the truths of our pasts converge with the truth of God's Word, we will never be whole. When Christ said, "You will know the truth and the truth will set you free," He was referring to His truth, the Word of God. If I am a believer in Christ, I cannot know the truth about myself until I know the truth of God's Word. Please make me a promise. Do not allow Satan to get an inch of ground from this lesson. The last thing your enemy wants is for you to be free. Remember, Christ came to set the captives free, and Satan came to make the free captive. He could try to counterfeit what we've learned by trying to sow fear in you regarding your children or heaviness in you because of difficult reminders. Refuse to let him pluck away any of the seeds God has planted. Let these truths take root in your heart, then water and cultivate them with belief.

As we conclude this chapter, you may be thinking, "But I still don't have all the answers." Neither do I, but God has filled in enough of the blanks to invite us to trust Him with the rest. I invite you to read the following. In each of the blanks, insert your first name.

My child, _____, I loved you
before you were born. I knew what your first and last
words would be. I knew every difficulty you would face.
I suffered each one with you. Even the ones you didn't
suffer with Me. I had a plan for your life before you were
born. The plan has not changed, _____,
no matter what has happened or what you have done.
You see, I already knew all things concerning you before
I formed you. I would never allow any hurt to come

into your life that I could not use for eternity, _____. Will you let Me? Your truth is incomplete unless you view it against the backdrop of my Truth. Your story will forever remain half-finished . . . until you let Me do My half with your hurt. Let Me perfect that which concerns you.

I remain,

Your Faithful Father

CHAPTER 21

HEARTS BROKEN BY BETRAYAL

If an enemy were insulting me,
I could endure it;
if a foe were raising himself against me,
I could hide from him.

(PS. 55:12)

Next we focus on another painful catalyst for a broken heart. In the verse above, David was in great distress. He had felt surrounded by enemies. Earlier in the psalm he had cried out in despair:

Oh, that I had the wings of a dove!
    I would fly away and be at rest—
I would flee far away
    and stay in the desert. (Ps. 55:6–7)

According to verse 12, David found his situation almost unendurable. The reason for his anguish of heart may surprise you.

But it is you, a man like myself,
  my companion, my close friend,
with whom I once enjoyed sweet fellowship
  as we walked with the throng at the house of God.
  (Ps. 55:13–14)

Only a person with intimate access to your heart can betray you to the point David described. If you've ever been betrayed by a sibling, parent, spouse, child, or good friend, you've probably experienced the kind of anguish we're discussing.

Please do not retreat emotionally from this issue. I want to ask you to work with the Holy Spirit to ensure you've healed properly. If you haven't, perhaps this lesson will help.

Recall that the Hebrew word for heartbreak—*shavar*—means we can usually trace a time of heartbreak to a single moment. Can you recall a specific moment when your heart broke over betrayal? Whether or not you fell to the temptation, chances are good you were tempted to react destructively over the days, weeks, or even months that followed.

Hebrews 4:15–16 tells us that in Jesus we have a great high priest "who has been tempted in every way, just as we are—yet was without sin." I see at least four reasons why Christ is the perfect choice to turn to when I am betrayed and want to react destructively:

1. *He is sympathetic.* We can't always count on sympathy from others when we're suddenly shattered. Our heartbreaks really aren't anyone else's responsibility. They are Christ's. Remember, He came to bind up the brokenhearted. All anyone can really do is sit with us and watch our hearts bleed! Others can only take that kind of intimacy for a short time!

2. *He knows I am weak.* Unlike people, Christ is never intimidated by the depth of our need and the demonstration of our weakness. I am

so glad that I don't have to have a "stiff upper lip" and set a good example for others to follow when I'm all alone with God and hurting.

3. *He has been tempted in every way I have.* What things have you either done or wanted to do? If I'm reading Hebrews 4:15 correctly, Christ also has been tempted to react just like you were. I find great comfort in knowing Christ doesn't throw His hand over His mouth in shock when I wish I could act a certain way.

4. *He met my same temptation without sin.* No matter how I have reacted to betrayal or any other kind of heartbreak in the past, I am so glad to know that a way exists to be victorious. Christ has already done it. If I follow Him through my situation, I too can do it. If I blow it or react wrongly, I can choose to follow Him the rest of the way; and in His mercy He will still bless and honor my choice. It's never too late to start following His lead in your crisis.

We've established the fact that Jesus has walked in the sandals of those sinking in the sand of betrayal. Now let's take a look at the specifics. You probably know the story, but don't let familiarity cause you to miss a fresh application.

During the supper (Matt. 26) Jesus said of Judas, "I tell you the truth, one of you will betray me" (v. 21). Later Jesus said to the other disciples, "This very night you will all fall away on account of me" (v. 31). Christ said that one would betray and all would fall away. Why do you think Christ considered only Judas a betrayer even though all the disciples deserted Him and fled? (v. 56).

I don't know the correct answer, but clearly Judas's actions were planned and deliberate while the remaining disciples reacted in fear. Judas showed premeditation. I usually think of betrayal as something the betrayer knew would devastate but did not care enough to act differently.

If you've ever felt betrayed, wasn't part of your injury knowing that the other person would have been aware of how hurt you would be?

Judas was a betrayer in every sense of the word. A true betrayer is motivated by selfishness. Judas knew what his betrayal would cost Jesus, but he decided it was worth it.

A second reason Christ may have considered only Judas's actions betrayal appears in Matthew 9:4: "Knowing their thoughts, Jesus said, 'Why do you entertain evil thoughts in your hearts?'" Christ could see evil in Judas's heart. I don't believe He saw evil in the disciples. Rather, I think He saw fear. Big difference.

Betrayal is motivated by selfishness but not always by evil. I don't believe every spouse who has an extramarital affair means to devastate the betrayed husband or wife. Indeed, a betrayer may be sincerely regretful of the pain selfishness caused. Sometimes betrayal is a matter of perception.

In Christ's case, however, Judas's betrayal took the worst of forms. Even though Christ knew Judas would betray Him, I believe He was still devastated by it. He came to this earth in the form of human flesh not only to die in our behalf but also to live in our shoes. Heart-shattering betrayal is one of the hardest experiences we encounter. To know how best to bind up the heart broken by betrayal, Christ chose to experience it. That's what Hebrews 4:14–16 is all about. Christ ministers to the betrayed through His example.

Philippians 2:5 says: "Your attitude should be the same as that of Christ Jesus." Let's see if we can determine Christ's attitude as He faced betrayal "yet was without sin."

Jesus said, "Do you think I cannot call on my Father, and he will at once put at my disposal more than twelve legions of angels?" (Matt. 26:53). Obviously, Christ had the power to open the earth and swallow His opposition, but He didn't. I believe Jesus restrained Himself because He trusted the sovereignty of His Father. In difficult times we, too, need to trust God's sovereignty. That means if He has allowed something difficult and shocking to happen to one of His children, He plans to use it mightily if the child will let Him. God did not cause Judas to be a thief and a betrayer, but He used the fraudulent disciple to complete a very important work in the life of Christ.

Scripture clearly tells us that Satan used Judas, but God ultimately took it over for His good work. If your spouse has betrayed you with infidelity, my heart aches for you. I know my words may be difficult to read; but I believe God can use the betrayal to complete a very important work in your life, too. How? Only you can find out. I've seen good ultimately evolve from the ravages of unfaithfulness several times. I never cease to be amazed at the bad God can use for good.

God doesn't often tell us why He allows wounds to come to us, but He graciously gave me Scripture to explain one reason I experienced what I considered a very painful betrayal. "I want to know Christ and the power of his resurrection and the fellowship of sharing in his sufferings, becoming like him in his death" (Phil. 3:10). I pray continually to be Christlike; but when He allows me to "fellowship" in a few of His sufferings, I tend to whine and carry on.

Few of us will escape betrayal in one way or another, but will we choose to fellowship with Christ in the midst of it? Will we choose to trust the sovereignty of our heavenly Father who allowed it? Betrayal can either hurt and hurt. Or hurt and help. The choice is up to us.

CHAPTER 22

HEARTS BROKEN BY LOSS

*Jesus said to her, "I am the resurrection and the life. He who believes
in me will live, even though he dies."*

(JOHN 11:25)

In recent years God introduced a season of loss in my life that spanned
the most difficult two-year period of my adulthood to date. This painful
season began with the excruciating loss of our son Michael to his birth
mother—a loss so difficult I am still in the process of healing from it.
On the heels of Michael's departure came the news that my mother's
cancer had entered the bones and was incurable. For the ensuing
months we watched helplessly as our tiny "Queen of Everything" suffered terribly.

God moved one of my two best friends, leaving a tremendous void
of laughter and frivolity in my life. My mother's illness continued to steal
more and more of her until God, in His tender mercy, carried her home.
One week later, my other best friend moved to Mississippi. The second
week, I moved my oldest daughter into her college dorm room and
kissed a treasured season of my life good-bye. I've never recorded the
experiences in sequence before. My lower lip is practically quivering, but
I speak to people whose suffering far exceeds anything I've imagined.

I'm learning so many things from God through this season of letting go. I know God's timing purposely corresponded with the writing of this study. Many emotions have swept over me during the last two years; but if you asked which emotion served as the common denominator, I would not hesitate to say grief. In fact, I was somewhat taken aback over the feelings of grief accompanying the moving of my two best friends. The grieving seemed out of place in relation to my other losses, yet oddly unavoidable.

God finally opened my eyes to see that grief was not inappropriate. Each of my experiences represented a death of some kind. With the loss of Michael, I experienced the death of being the mother of three, the mother of a son, a dream, and, overall, the death of a relationship that had practically consumed me for seven years. With the departure of my two best friends, I experienced the death of instant camaraderie, of expected company at women's events, of relationships I had known for many years, and of pure togetherness. Best friendships with long histories are not easy to replace. The death of my mother has been the death of my head cheerleader, of my children's maternal grandmother and best friend, of a daily relationship, of someone who undoubtedly loved me with all her heart. In essence, hers was the death of a relationship impossible to replace. Two weeks later when I drove away from Texas A&M University leaving behind my firstborn, I knew I was facing death to family life as we had known it. I knew that many wonderful times lay ahead and trusted that Amanda and I would always be close, but I knew the nature of my role must change. She's only an hour and a half away, but that's farther than right up the stairs where she's been for all these years!

Life involves change. Change involves loss. Loss involves death of one kind or another. Before we conclude this part of our study, I believe we will discover a new way to personally apply the words of the apostle

Paul in 2 Corinthians 4:11: "For we who are alive are always being given over to death for Jesus' sake, so that his life may be revealed in our mortal body."

Every time we suffer loss, we encounter an opportunity for the loss to bring gain for Jesus' sake by allowing His life to be revealed in us. I hope to prove this hypothesis through a fresh look at one of the old, old stories—the story of Lazarus in John 11.

Jesus had many followers. He had a few disciples, but we don't know of many people who were just His friends. Pure friendship doesn't come easy when your life is ministry. Mary, Martha, and Lazarus were considered Jesus' friends.

When Lazarus became ill, they sent word to Jesus and said, "Lord, the one you love is sick" (John 11:3). Verse 5 tells us that "Jesus loved Martha and her sister and Lazarus." Later in the story, when Jesus came to Lazarus's tomb and wept, the Jews said, "See how he loved him!" (v. 36).

But in John 11 we encounter a strange happening. When Jesus heard His friend was sick, He waited for two long days. What possible reason could Jesus have had for delaying? We don't have to wonder. He told His disciples, "This sickness will not end in death. No, it is for God's glory so that God's Son may be glorified through it" (v. 4).

When the thick-headed disciples failed to understand, Jesus told them, "For your sake I am glad I was not there, so that you may believe" (v. 15). We can safely assume that Jesus didn't just want the disciples to believe. John told us that many Jews had gathered to comfort Martha and Mary.

Jesus' action in waiting two days seems callous, unless we consider how His raising Lazarus from the dead affected those who were there. When Jesus restored Lazarus to life, we read that "many of the Jews who had come to visit Mary, and had seen what Jesus did, put their faith in him" (v. 45).

I'd like to offer three fresh breaths of life for those times when we experience the death of something or someone we cherish.

1. *Christ never allows the hearts of His own to be shattered without excellent reasons and eternal purposes.* Christ dearly loved Mary and Martha, yet He purposely allowed them to suffer a loss. Our Father would never allow our hearts to break for trivial reasons. We may never see the reasons like Mary and Martha did, but could we walk by faith and believe the best of Christ? You see, the most debilitating loss for a Christian is not the loss of a loved one but the loss of faith. Do you see how the loss of faith could turn into a form of bondage?

2. *Christ never allows any illness to end in death for a Christian.* All believers in Christ will rise from the dead. What made Lazarus unique was his return to mortal life. Please don't think me morbid, but I'm not sure Lazarus got the better end of the deal! When I die, I would rather not wake up and do it all over again! Either way, however, death is never the end of anyone's life in Christ. In the midst of this grief encounter, Jesus revealed Himself to Martha in a new and powerful way. He said, "I am the resurrection and the life" (v. 25).

3. *Any kind of "death" is an invitation to resurrection life for the believer.* Thank goodness, the loss of something or someone dear never has to mean the end of abundant, effective, or even joyful life for any Christian. Joy and effectiveness may seem to pause for a while as grief takes its course, but those who allow their broken hearts to be bound by Christ will experience them again. Our Savior is the God of resurrection life, no matter what kind of death has occurred in the life of any believer!

Nothing is more natural than grief after a devastating loss, but those of us in Christ can experience satisfying life again. When our hearts have been shattered by loss, we have an opportunity to welcome a supernatural power to our lives. The power to live again on this earth when we'd really rather die. Perhaps the most profound miracle of all is living through something we thought would kill us. And not just living, but living abundantly and effectively—raised from living death to a new life. A life indeed absent of something or someone dear but filled with the presence of the Resurrection and the Life.

No, my life will never be the same. I no longer have a son. My mom is in heaven. My two best friends have moved. My firstborn is off to college. But the life of a Christian is never about sameness. It's always about change. That's why we must learn to survive and once again thrive when change involves heartbreaking loss. We're being conformed to the image of Christ. When our hearts are hemorrhaging with grief and loss, never forget that Christ binds and compresses them with a nail-scarred hand. Life will never be the same, but I have the invitation from Christ to rise to a new life—a more compassionate life, a wiser life, a more productive life. And, yes, even a better life. Sound impossible? It is without Christ.

I can almost hear Christ calling out a name. Is it yours? By any chance, have you been among the living dead? The stone's been rolled away. Resurrection life awaits you. Will you continue to sit in a dark tomb, or will you walk into the light of resurrection life? Lazarus, come forth!

PART IV

DREAMS SURPASSED AND OBEDIENCE THAT LASTS

You've waded with me in some waters swift and cold. Now it's time to see some of the rewards our loving Master has in store for pilgrims on the freedom road.

I fear that many of us have almost despaired of ever seeing two things: the fulfillment of our childhood dreams and a solution to the wickedness that haunts our hearts. In the chapters to follow, we will explore the satisfaction God desires to bring deep in our hearts. He is leading us to a land of fulfilled dreams and victory over our sin nature. Does that seem almost too good to be true? Actually, He's too good to be false.

At the end of each of these short chapters, take a moment to work on hiding God's Word in your heart. Review the verses you have memorized, and add to your list the source of Benefit 3: To find satisfaction in God.

Why spend money on what is not bread,
   and your labor on what does not satisfy?
Listen, listen to me, and eat what is good,
   and your soul will delight in the richest of fare.
   (Isa. 55:2)

CHAPTER 23

ASHES INSTEAD OF HONOR

Tamar put ashes on her head and tore the ornamented robe she was wearing.
She put her hand on her head and went away, weeping aloud as she went.

(2 SAM. 13:19)

In the Old Testament people covered their heads with ashes as a symbol of mourning. Ashes were a reminder of our mortality. Those who covered themselves in ashes symbolically stated that, without God, they would be nothing more than ashes. Perhaps the reason I have a favorable view of some of the ancient practices is because I am so demonstrative, but I can't help believing that we can all find a little freedom in expression at times.

I make an issue of this point because our society is tending toward a frightening reduction of emotions. Squelching emotions only stores them in explosive containers. God's Word constantly recognizes our emotional side.

Let's look at a heart-wrenching expression of grief in Scripture and discover a few ways we unfortunately can relate. We can assume women in ancient times also put on sackcloth and ashes as they mourned. The

Bible describes in detail only one time, however, when a woman covered herself in ashes.

In 2 Samuel 13:1–22 we read of the tragedy of Tamar and her brother Amnon. Tamar was the beautiful daughter of King David. David of course had many wives and children by several different mothers. Tamar's half brother Amnon was infatuated with her.

Amnon listened to the evil advice of his cousin Jonadab, feigned illness, and asked his father David to send Tamar to care for him. The innocent sister came to feed Amnon, but he grabbed her.

> "Don't, my brother!" she said to him. "Don't force me. Such a thing should not be done in Israel! Don't do this wicked thing. What about me? Where could I get rid of my disgrace? And what about you? You would be like one of the wicked fools in Israel. Please speak to the king; he will not keep me from being married to you." But he refused to listen to her, and since he was stronger than she, he raped her. (2 Sam. 13:12–14)

We've all heard the expression "add insult to injury." Amnon added even greater injury to injury. After he raped Tamar, he "hated her with intense hatred. In fact, he hated her more than he had loved her. Amnon said to her, 'Get up and get out!'" (v. 15). As a final act of insult, "he called his personal servant and said, 'Get this woman out of here and bolt the door after her'" (v. 17).

If we analyze the situation, we see that Amnon felt guilt for his evil actions. Then, as people so often do, he turned his guilt feelings on innocent Tamar. I feel particular sympathy for her because of Amnon's last action. He knew full well that servants talk. He wanted to inflict the maximum pain on Tamar by ruining her reputation.

The virgin daughters of the king wore a robe that indicated their status. Tamar expressed her grief by tearing her richly ornamented robe and putting ashes on her head. When her brother Absalom saw her weeping, he knew what had happened. He "said to her, 'Has that Amnon, your brother, been with you? Be quiet now, my sister; he is your brother. Don't take this thing to heart'" (v. 20).

We also find that David learned of the rape. Don't forget that he was the unwitting accomplice because he sent Tamar to her brother's house. He was furious with Amnon, but he did nothing. My heart aches for Tamar. Betrayed by one brother. Counseled to keep quiet about it by another brother. Ignored by her father. As a result Tamar lived the rest of her days "a desolate woman" (v. 20).

Tamar's father, the king, was highly responsible for her unchanging sense of desolation. He was furious, but he did nothing tangible and positive with his anger. You can rest assured that God is also furious when women are abused and mistreated. The difference is that we can trust Him to do something about it—His way, His time. If we assume Tamar's dignity was never restored, what do you think she might have been like by the time she was forty?

I ask you to consider how much like Tamar we are in this generation. Those of us who have received Christ are literally children of royalty. Every woman who has been renewed in Christ through faith and repentance is spiritually a virgin daughter of the King. The biblical image and intent of womanhood is honor and purity.

Whether or not you have ever been personally and individually victimized, we are living in a time of victimization of women. Satan is actively and progressively pedaling the demoralization of women.

Those of us who have been individually and physically victimized know the desolation Tamar experienced. Many of us were convinced by the enemy that we were no longer fit to have honor and dignity. By the time I learned what a virgin was, I shuddered with the shock that I probably wasn't one. I never had much of a chance. What I'm asking you to recognize is that you also have been hurt and affected by the frightful experiences of women, whether or not you realize it.

Several years ago an article appeared in our local paper exposing a secret network for the victimization of little girls in the Orient. I was devastated for my gender. What's more, so was every other woman who read it, even those who had never been personally violated. Why? Because we've all been innocent little girls at one time or another, and the terror they face is unimaginable. We are all violated by crimes like these. Certainly, many men who read the article were outraged, too. I know that many men clearly recognize the demoralization of women and children.

Satan desires to have women in a stronghold of exploitation, sexploitation, distortion, and desolation. He knows how effective and influential women can be, so he works through society to convince us we are so much less than we are.

If Satan has convinced you to see yourself as anything less than the handpicked child of the King of all kings . . . if you think anything could happen to you that could steal your royal heritage . . . if you think you deserve mistreatment or disrespect, you have something in common with Tamar. I pray that the Holy Spirit will be free to mend the torn coats of the children of royalty. And that He will also restore lost dignity, teach us our true identity, and liberate us to live in purity.

Conclude by reading aloud Psalm 45:13–15.

All glorious is the princess within her chamber;
    her gown is interwoven with gold.
In embroidered garments she is led to the king;
    her virgin companions follow her

and are brought to you.
They are led in with joy and gladness;
    they enter the palace of the king.

That, my dear sister in Christ, is your destiny. And my dear brother in Christ, you are included in verse 16.

Your sons will take the place of your fathers;
    you will make them princes throughout the land.

CHAPTER 24

To Be a Bride

I delight greatly in the LORD;
my soul rejoices in my God.
For he has clothed me with garments of salvation
and arrayed me in a robe of righteousness,
as a bridegroom adorns his head like a priest,
and as a bride adorns herself with her jewels.

(ISA. 61:10)

In this section of our study, we are going to explore some childhood dreams. Since I am female, I know more about girlhood dreams. I think men will be able to see their own version of each of these dreams.

We are studying the tender—and if I may say, romantic—ministry of Christ: "to bestow on them a crown of beauty instead of ashes." Most often the mourner poured the ashes on his or her head as Tamar did. Come with me for an imaginary look back.

Imagine Tamar: grief-stricken, sobbing, ashes on her head. Her body in a heap on the cold floor. Soot covers her beautiful face and smears the rich colors of her torn robe. Her outward appearance echoes the cavernous darkness in her soul. Hopelessness and death well up in her. She is nothing but a tomb.

The door of her room slowly creaks open. A stream of cloudy sunlight pours through the door. A figure of a man takes form within it. Not Absalom. No, she would recognize Absalom anywhere. Her heart jumps with sickening terror, then the figure steps through the door and His visage becomes clear. Tamar has never seen Him before, yet He looks so familiar. Not frightening. And she should be frightened. No man should be entering her chamber. She should run, but she cannot seem to move.

She glances down at the hands that seem paralyzed on her lap, suddenly shamefully aware of her ash-covered appearance. Wretchedness sears her heart. She is certain her violated estate is obvious. She despises herself.

"Tamar," the man speaks gently and with warm familiarity.

Her heart sobs, "She is dead!" A slave of shame has taken her place.

He approaches and takes her face in His hands. No one has ever done that before. The overwhelming intimacy turns her face crimson, not with shame but with vulnerability. His thumbs sweep over her cheeks and wipe the tears from her face. As He takes His hands from her face and places them on her head, her throat aches with fresh cries as she sees the filth on His hands. Her filth. He draws back His hands, and she senses something on her head. Perhaps in His mercy He has hooded her disgrace.

The man offers her His hands, still covered with soot, and she takes them. Suddenly she is standing. Trembling. He leads her to the brass mirror hung on the wall. She turns her face away. He lifts her chin. She gives the mirror only a glance. Her heart is startled. She begins to stare. Her face is creamy white. Her cheeks are blushed with beauty. Her eyes are clear and bright. A crown sits on her head, and a veil flows from its jewels to her shoulders. Her torn coat is gone. A garment of fine white linen graces her neck and adorns her frame. The King's daughter, pure and undefiled. Beauty from ashes.

No, I do not believe in fairy tales. But I do believe in God. He sent His Son for just such a purpose. Whatever the cause of our mourning, Christ can be the lifter of our heads. He can give us beauty instead of ashes. This was not Tamar's story, but it might have been. It can be yours.

I believe practically every little girl has at least four dreams, which are the topics of the next four chapters: (1) to be a bride, (2) to be beautiful, (3) to be fruitful (which we usually define as having children), and (4) to live happily ever after. Boys have dreams that don't differ all that much. They also want a significant relationship and to be considered handsome. Boys desire a legacy, and they certainly want to live happily ever after. Satan wants to destroy our dreams. God wants to surpass them. He gives us dreams so we'll long for His reality. We'll examine all four of our common dreams. We start with the first dream: to someday be a bride.

I can almost sense some contented singles bristling up on me. Could you admit that you had dreams of being a bride when you were a little girl? God instituted marriage so that we could comprehend a greater relationship (Eph. 5:25–33). Only two individuals can make up a marriage. Our union with Christ is common to all believers, but the intimacy of this relationship is expressed between Christ and individual believers. Whether we are male or female, we are the bride of Christ.

I love the term *bride*. Interestingly, God's Word does not refer to us as wives of Christ but as the bride. Let's look back in the context of Isaiah 61. The crown of beauty in its original meaning is an ornamental headdress like a crown or a wedding veil. The original term is derived from the Hebrew word *pa'ar*, meaning "to gleam . . . to explain oneself . . . to beautify" (*Strong's*). The kind of headdress a woman wore explained who she was. Isaiah 61 portrays God blowing away the ashes of mourning and replacing them with a crown, and not just any crown. In this case we are the bride of the Prince of Peace!

To me, the word *bride* indicates lots of things *wife* doesn't. Bride implies newness and freshness. A crisp, beautiful dress. The fragrance of perfume. Richly colored lips. Sparkling eyes. I usually picture youthfulness. Perhaps innocence. I believe all of these things will characterize our relationship with Christ and the ultimate consummation of marriage. Scripture implies that our relationship to Christ, though enduring for an eternity, will remain fresh and new. Yes, I think we will somehow always be brides, somewhat like my mother-in-law. Keith's parents have been married forty-five years, but my father-in-law always refers to his wife as his bride. To me, his tender expression implies a lasting romance. He loves to bring her gifts. They still embrace, kiss, and date!

Let's look at two insightful references to God's people as bride. In Jeremiah 2:2 God spoke to Israel. He said to her, "I remember the devotion of your youth, / how as a bride you loved me / and followed me through the desert." One of the characteristics of a loving bride is her willingness to follow her groom to places that at times may seem like wilderness. Our Bridegroom sometimes leads us to difficult places, but we can trust Him always to have purpose in our stay and never to forsake us.

This year I followed my Bridegroom to a place of aloneness. I've grown closer to Him than ever before, which miraculously makes me closer to my earthly mate. I don't think I'll always be in this place. It's looking less and less like a wilderness now.

Usually the reason our earthly grooms move us to new places is to seek a higher quality of life. I believe the same is true of Christ. All moves He prompts are to offer you a better quality of life.

Certainly we can't think of this topic without considering Revelation 19:4–8. These verses describe the corporate gathering of all believers and Christ at the marriage supper of the Lamb. Verse 7 implies an important responsibility of the bride. It says, "The wedding of the Lamb has come, / and his bride has made herself ready." Notice the qualifier of the bride's actions: she has *made* herself ready. Past tense. We cannot make ourselves ready the moment we see Christ any more than a woman can be prepared to meet her groom at the altar with three minutes' notice. I want to be ready. Don't you? I don't want to be caught with spiritual curlers in my hair!

When I was preparing for my wedding, I often thought about being a wife. Not just any wife. Keith's wife. Mind you, I didn't just get married. I got married to a man! A wedding is not about a lovely ceremony. It's about a long-term relationship. I could not think about being married without thinking about Keith.

Sometimes I thought about how different we were. He is such an outdoorsman. My hair does better in air-conditioning. I also thought about a few similarities. We both like to be in control. We both like to be right. Hm-m-m-m. So much for things in common. But he was the cutest thing I had ever seen, and when he smiled, my heart melted. And, after all, we both enjoyed a hot cup of coffee. In hopes that he thought I was cute, too, I prepared myself as best I could to be darling and make a good cup of coffee. Make fun of us if you want, but twenty years later it's still working! I still send him out the door with a fresh cup of coffee in the morning and put on a little blush when he drives up in the evening.

In complete seriousness, the same is true as we prepare to be eternal brides. We won't just be part of a beautiful ceremony. We will be the bride of Christ. God's Word doesn't imply that we are to make ourselves ready for the wedding, but for the Groom. Thus, we cannot make ourselves ready without thinking about Him—meditating on our similarities (which hopefully are multiplying), thinking about our differences and how we might adjust—simply thinking about how wonderful He is.

In the previous chapter, we read Psalm 45:13–15. The psalm is a wedding song. I purposely avoided showing you the verses preceding this passage so you could end with them now. Remember, an important part of making ourselves ready is studying and knowing our Groom. Verses 1–12 contain intimate descriptions of the Groom. Note the following specific characteristics.

- We cannot help but love Him, for he loves us: "The king is enthralled by your beauty; / honor him, for he is your lord" (v. 11).
- We cannot help but respect Him for His character: "You are the most excellent of men / and your lips have been anointed with grace" (v. 2).
- We stand in complete awe of Him: "In your majesty ride forth victoriously / in behalf of truth, humility and righteousness; / let your right hand display awesome deeds" (v. 4).
- We experience complete joy in Him: "You love righteousness and hate wickedness; / therefore God, your God, has set you above your companions / by anointing you with the oil of joy" (v. 7).

Behold your Groom. He's the One for whom you're preparing. Make yourself ready!

CHAPTER 25

TO BE BEAUTIFUL

How beautiful you are, my darling!
Oh, how beautiful!

(SONG OF SONGS 4:1)

Most people I know who live free have experienced a serious stronghold or hindrance they fought to overcome. They usually appreciate and apply victory more readily because they've experienced the misery of defeat firsthand. I rarely meet people who have come to trust God fully who haven't also painfully confronted the fact that they can't trust themselves.

The enemy is an expert archer. When women are the target, often the bull's-eye is childhood dreams. We grew up believing in Cinderella, yet some of us feel our palace turned out to be a duplex, our prince turned out to be a frog, and the wicked stepmother turned out to be our mother-in-law. Our fairy godmother apparently lost our addresses. Anyway, what we would like to do to her with that wand of hers might not be pretty.

I'm hoping to prove to you that some of your childhood dreams were meant to come true in Christ—in ways far grander than the obvious. In fact, God sometimes allows us to be disappointed so we will set our hopes more fully in Him. Even my friends who preferred baseball to dolls still dreamed of being a bride, being beautiful, having fruitful lives, and living happily ever after. Let's consider the second dream. Almost every little girl dreams of being beautiful. Boys long to be considered strong or handsome. Long into adulthood we harbor hurts if we feel that no one thinks we are.

Watching my daughters go through high school reminded me of the insecurities I felt back then. To feel I looked OK, everything had to be right. No humidity, good hair, lots of makeup, no clumps in the mascara. I worked so hard at trying to look good. Too hard. I believed that nothing about me was naturally beautiful.

How thankful I am for the freedom God has increasingly given me in Christ. I'm in the throes of middle age—a friend says, "Time is a great healer but a lousy beautician." Yet I am happier and more satisfied than I've ever been. The secret? I'm learning to see myself as beautiful to Christ. Don't try stuff on me such as, "You're thin, and your hair goes into all sorts of styles—of course you feel pretty!" Listen here. I had the worst pigeon toes and buck teeth in the free world. My legs looked like knobby sticks with fur on them. Without Christ every woman has intense insecurities. Unless we find our identity in Christ, Christian women are just as prone to insecurities about their appearance as unbelievers. We try to act as if we don't care and that feeling unlovely doesn't hurt, but it does.

Now it's time to go barefooted in the waters of the Bible's most provocative book. The Song of Songs is a love poem filled with terms of endearment. I encourage you to get your Bible and read chapters 2 and 4. In chapter 2 Solomon says of his bride, "Like a lily among thorns / is my darling among the maidens" (v. 2). That sounds pretty contemporary. But how about this tidbit from chapter 4:

How beautiful you are, my darling!
Oh, how beautiful!
Your eyes behind your veil are doves.
Your hair is like a flock of goats
descending from Mount Gilead. (Song 4:1)

If Keith ever looked romantically into my eyes and said, "Your teeth are like a flock of sheep just shorn" (4:2), I'd run for the dental floss.

Look at one of Solomon's most visual comparisons: "I liken you, my darling, to a mare / harnessed to one of the chariots of Pharaoh" (1:9). Men loved wheels then just as much as they do now. Keith is having a blast with the 1969 classic car he got Melissa for her birthday. The other day I complained about being old, and he retorted, "So is Melissa's car, but you're just as good-lookin'!" I didn't know whether to hit him or hug him. The classy men of Solomon's day had chariots led by fine horses. He was telling his beloved that she looked as good as Pharoah's best horse!

The Song of Songs is a wonderful book, isn't it? It makes me laugh, blush, and long for real romance. We're almost shocked to realize God knows about even these kinds of things, much less writes about them! God created love between a man and a woman. The full expression of that love in sexual intimacy was His idea—His gifts to the first man and woman and offered freely with complete blessing to every couple He unites in marriage. But wait a minute. Earthly marriage represents far more.

In Ephesians 5 Paul repeated the words of Genesis 2:24, that in marriage a man and woman become one flesh. He then carried the Old Testament truth to new heights: "This is a profound mystery—but I am talking about Christ and the church" (Eph. 5:32). What is more profound than a man and woman coming together in marriage? Christ and His bride—the church.

God often teaches the unknown through the known. I believe the Song of Songs was written to help us relate to our union with Christ. In the book we can see Christ and His beloved bride—us. Real romance awaits all of us. Single and married alike can celebrate that some dreams will really come true. One of them is perfectly portrayed in this inspired book. Christ is completely taken with you. He sees you as His beloved, His bride. Take another look at several beautifully expressive verses that show Christ's feelings for you:

"I am a rose of Sharon, / a lily of the valleys" (2:1). Notice these are the expressions of the woman. She was not being egotistical. She simply saw herself as her lover saw her. Her mirror was the face of her mate. How do you suppose your life would be different if you were to allow Christ to become your mirror?

"His banner over me is love" (2:4). The word *banner* means "to flaunt, that is, raise a flag; figuratively to be conspicuous" (*Strong's*). Have you ever been pretty sure someone loved you, but you longed for them to show it more? Song of Songs foreshadows the kind of relationship in which Christ's love for each of us will be completely conspicuous. He will flaunt His love for us. Jesus waves His hand over you, signaling to all in sight that you are the one He loves. Hallelujah!

In the eyes of His beloved, which will be you, note how Christ will look:

My lover is radiant and ruddy,
> outstanding among ten thousand.
His head is purest gold;
> his hair is wavy
> and black as a raven.
His eyes are like doves
> by the water streams,

washed in milk,
    mounted like jewels.
His cheeks are like beds of spice
    yielding perfume.
His lips are like lilies
    dripping with myrrh.
His arms are rods of gold
    set with chrysolite.
His body is like polished ivory
    decorated with sapphires.
His legs are pillars of marble
    set on bases of pure gold.
His appearance is like Lebanon,
    choice as its cedars.
His mouth is sweetness itself;
    he is altogether lovely.
This is my lover, this my friend,
    O daughters of Jerusalem. (Song 5:10–16)

Isaiah 53:2 (KJV) described Christ's appearance during His first advent with these words: "There is no beauty that we should desire him." How wonderfully fitting that Christ will be the fullness of splendor and beauty when we see Him. Think of Him coming for His bride. He longs to see her face and hear her voice.

The face of the bride was always veiled in the ancient eastern world. The lifting of the veil from the face was one of the most intimate parts of the wedding night. Isn't that romantic? Song of Songs implies that Christ will long to see the lovely face of His bride, His beloved. And He will not be disappointed. You will be a beautiful bride. The intimacy we will share with Christ is beyond our comprehension. We do not know what form it will take. We simply know that we will experience oneness with Him in complete holiness and purity. A knitting together of two spirits perhaps. Until then, please bask in the assurance that Christ sees you as beautiful and desirable in a pure and holy way that we cannot comprehend.

Single person, if you are in Christ, you have the ultimate relationship ahead of you. If God calls you to a life of singleness, feel special! Save yourself entirely for Him! The King is enthralled by your beauty.

Husband or wife with common frustrations: give your spouse room to be human. Forgive him for not being God. Forgive her for not always saying what you need to hear; the King is enthralled by your beauty.

Until the ultimate relationship arrives, let your mirror image be the face of Christ. To Him, the most beautiful person on earth is the one who makes preparation to meet the Groom. Your bridal portrait is being painted one day at a time. When it is complete, it will be a breathtaking masterpiece.

CHAPTER 26

TO BE FRUITFUL

"Sing, O barren woman,
you who never bore a child;
burst into song, shout for joy,
you who were never in labor;
because more are the children of the desolate woman
than of her who has a husband," says the LORD.

(ISA. 54:1)

The childhood dream we'll discuss next is one Satan also counterfeits to sow shame—the dream of being fruitful. Without a doubt, some of the unhappiest men and women I've ever known have been those who wanted children and were unable to have them. My friends who have suffered this blow have asked themselves questions like, "Why me?" "Why my husband?" "What did I do to deserve this?" "Is this my punishment for sex before marriage?" "Is this my punishment for having an abortion?" "Would I have been such a terrible parent?" "Why do abusive parents have children? I would never abuse a child!" The questions go on and on.

I've witnessed marriages destroyed by the inability to have children. I've also seen some women suffer shame for not really desiring to have children. I want to make several points about fruitfulness and barrenness:

First, barrenness does not imply sinfulness. Luke 1:5–7 offers biblical proof. Elizabeth was barren not because of sin but because God had something special for her.

Hearts entirely surrendered to God can ordinarily be trusted. If a man or woman's heart belongs entirely to God and they do not long to be married or to have children, they are probably called to singleness or childlessness to pursue other purposes for God. Psalm 37:4 could be translated to support this statement. The psalm promises that if we delight ourselves in the Lord He will give us the desires of our hearts.

Hearts not surrendered to God can seldom be trusted. Until we surrender our hopes and dreams to Christ, we really have very little way of knowing what would fulfill us. We've all known people who claimed they'd be "happy" if only . . . they were married, had children, had a big house, or the right job. Most people who are banking on circumstantial contentment find themselves in emotional bankruptcy sooner or later. Unhappy people are not made happy by marriage or children. An unhappy person usually needs a change of heart more than a change of circumstances. I know this from experience.

God created every life to be fruitful and multiply, but this God-given dream represents more than physical offspring. Let's meditate on this for a moment. Why do most people want to have children?

I believe our dreams to have babies represent a desire to have fruitful lives, to invest ourselves in something that matters. Something that makes a difference. I don't believe God allows surrendered hearts to continue to long for things He will not ultimately grant in one way or another. Our disappointment with God is often the result of our small thinking. Let's consider a biblical basis for this belief system.

Isaiah 54:1 counsels a barren woman to sing, "because more are the children of the desolate woman / than of her who has a husband." Let me give you a few examples. My dear friend Johnnie Haines has two fine sons who are her pride and joy. She always longed for but never had a daughter. One day she said to me, "My boys are virtually grown, and I love them so much, but I still wonder from time to time why God never gave me the daughter I longed for, too." But, you see, He did! For ten years she led the women's ministry at a large church in Houston. She mothered numerous young women! The women under her direction are now mature believers who are serving God effectively in their homes, workplaces, and churches.

Dr. Rhonda Kelley is another friend and author of *Life Lessons from Women in the Bible.* God never gave the Kelleys physical offspring, but He has given them more spiritual offspring than any parents I know! Her husband is a seminary president, and she teaches and mentors on the campus. Only heaven will boast the number of offspring Chuck and Rhonda really have. Their loss was glory's gain. I believe both of them would testify that God ultimately did not restrict them from childbearing. Rather, He loosened the restrictions and made them enlarge their tents!

The potential for spiritual offspring in the lives of those physically barren is virtually limitless. If He restricts you from physical offspring, He desires to empower you to bear spiritual offspring. God created you to bear much fruit.

God often applied the physical truths of the Old Testament as spiritual truths in the New Testament. In the Old Testament God promised great numbers of physical descendants. In the New Testament His emphasis is clearly on spiritual offspring. "Therefore go and make disciples of all nations" (Matt. 28:19) is our equivalent to the Old Testament's "Be fruitful and increase in number; fill the earth" (Gen. 1:28). The Book of Isaiah says those who are barren can have more offspring than those who are able to conceive and give birth.

If we live long enough, each of us will be barren. Are we to assume our fruitfulness has ended? Do we exist until death on memories and large doses of fiber? Why, then, does barrenness come to all women around fifty years of age? Were we meant to sit around for the next thirty or forty years and twiddle our arthritic thumbs? God is far too practical for that!

Older women "can train the younger women to love their husbands and children" (Titus 2:4). When older women pour their lives into younger women and their children, they are birthing spiritual offspring! Older women are a necessity in the body of Christ! Older men have a similar commission (2 Tim. 2:2). I don't see the slightest hint that older people should retire from serving God or witnessing to the lost. Quite to the contrary, they have opportunities that far exceed those of younger men and women. God calls us to be fruitful and multiply until He calls us home.

When I was a little girl, I wanted to be a mommy more than anything in the world. Now my children are almost grown. Recently my older daughter and I were enjoying a time of rich fellowship together when she paused and asked, "Mom, when Melissa and I grow up and perhaps even move far away from you and Daddy, will you be OK?"

A lump welled in my throat, but I still answered confidently, "Yes, darling. Most people just need to feel useful. As long as I have Jesus, I will always feel useful—even if I occasionally feel lonely."

I have tried my hardest to keep my children from growing up, but all my efforts have failed. Sometimes I think, "What will I ever do? I was born to be a mommy!" Then I remember God has called me primarily to women's ministry, and I will always have the opportunity to "mother" a few spiritual offspring as long as I'm willing to invest myself.

One of my spiritual daughters has a particularly dry and delightful wit. She is a gifted Bible teacher at only twenty-seven years of age and hardly ever misses an opportunity to affectionately rib me about my age. I introduced her once as a spiritual daughter, and later she said, "Since you led the person to the Lord who, in turn, led me to the Lord, wouldn't that make you my spiritual grandmother?" After I called her a smart aleck, we had a great laugh, and every card or gift I've sent to her since has been signed, "Love, Granny."

If God chose for you to have physical children, prepare yourself! They will grow up! Then it's time to enlarge your tent and invest in spiritual children! If God chooses for you never to have physical children, He's calling you to a far bigger family! God purposely placed the dream of fruitful lives in our hearts. Oh, how I love the paradoxical ways our glorious heavenly Father works. Only He can bring gain from loss. Only He can make us more fruitful in barrenness!

One final thought. Undoubtedly one of the reasons I wanted children was to bear offspring who were the image of my husband. I wanted little Keiths and Keithettes! I didn't want them to look like me. I've always thought Keith was far more beautiful than I. You see, the same is true of our spiritual offspring. Once we fall in love with Christ, we are so taken with His beauty, we want children who look just like Him. That's spiritual parenting in a nutshell: raising spiritual sons and daughters that look just like their Father. What could be more important?

CHAPTER 27

TO LIVE HAPPILY EVER AFTER

Come and share your master's happiness!

(MATT. 25:21)

Each of us has dreams; and, if we trust Christ with all our hearts, nothing can disable God from surpassing our childhood dreams with His divine reality. The suicide of her husband could not keep God from surpassing Kay Arthur's dreams. Her sudden paralysis could not keep God from surpassing Joni Eareckson Tada's dreams. Corrie ten Boom's horrifying stay in a Nazi concentration camp could not keep God from surpassing Corrie's dreams. A world of poverty and suffering could not keep God from surpassing Mother Teresa's dreams.

God surpasses our dreams when we reach past our personal plans and agendas to grab the hand of Christ and walk the path He has chosen for us. He is obligated to keep us dissatisfied until we come to Him and His plan for complete satisfaction. Next our thoughts will center on the fourth dream, which is the stuff of fairy tales: to live happily ever after.

Living happily ever after began with God, not Cinderella. There's no such thing as fairy godmothers, but angels are a different story. No yellow brick road—just streets of gold. No cottages in the forest—just mansions in glory. No crowns on our heads—just crowns at His feet. You may be thinking I'm imagining things, but actually you or I couldn't imagine it in our wildest dreams. When God fulfills 1 Corinthians 2:9 in a willing person's life on this earth, it's just a crude shadow of a greater reality.

We begin our treasure hunt with our theme text, Isaiah 61:1–3. "The Spirit of the Sovereign LORD is on me, / . . . He has sent me / . . . to comfort all who mourn, / and provide for those who grieve in Zion— / to bestow on them a crown of beauty / instead of ashes, / the oil of gladness / instead of mourning, / and a garment of praise / instead of a spirit of despair." I like all these "insteads," don't you? The verse doesn't mean we'll never mourn or feel despair. But Christ will minister His gladness to us once again. He will give us a heart of praise if we let Him; then one day all mourning and despair will be behind us.

Meditate on the word *gladness* for a moment. Certainly, if any group of people in the world should experience gladness, it should be Christians! But what if we pressed the concept a tad further? I'd like to suggest that God also enjoys seeing us—dare I say—happy? Believe it or not, *happy* really is a biblical word, but we are indeed wise to distinguish it from two closely associated words in Scripture—*blessing* and *joy*.

Both blessing and joy come to us through obedience, often in times of persecution and pain. The obvious difference is that blessing and joy are not circumstantial, while happiness is. Please understand, however, this difference doesn't make happiness lesser, just rarer. In fact, I'm here to say that the word *happy* is getting a bad rap, so let's have the joy and blessing of clearing it up!

I fear we may have become so legalistic in many of our Christian circles that we've dropped the word *happy* from our "religious" vocabulary, even when it's appropriate. Allow me to get this off my chest once and for all: Sometimes God just plain makes me HAPPY! There. I said it. Call me immature, but picture me smiling.

God makes me feel happy lots of times. For instance, when I see Melissa bow her head to pray when she's on the free-throw line, then watch that basketball slip out of her hands and go through the net like silk. Doesn't always happen, but when it does, I feel happy in Jesus! Sure I know that people are starving on the other side of the world. I'm deeply concerned for hurting people, and I pray for other nations every single day; but I also enjoy a happy moment in Christ when it comes. Happiness is inappropriate when it's our goal, but it's not inappropriate when it's God's momentary gift. Open it. Enjoy it. And remember it when times get tough.

How realistic is the dream of living happily ever after? See for yourself: "His master replied, 'Well done, good and faithful servant! You have been faithful with a few things; I will put you in charge of many things. Come and share your master's happiness!'" (Matt. 25:21).

There you have it. Christ is happy. He wants you to share His happiness—to live happily ever after. Until then, He gives us a sudden splash of happiness here and there so we can wet our toes in what we'll be swimming in for all of eternity!

The dearest Scriptures this section engraved on my heart are Song of Songs 2:10–12. Allow me to share some thoughts God gave me as I visualized the Scriptures. I deeply appreciate the vulnerability our study this week demanded. Keep letting the truth set you free!

It was her ninetieth birthday. She didn't plan to live this long. She couldn't help it. She just kept waking up. Her youngest son's spacious home bulged with extended family. She acted as surprised by her party as a ninety-year-old can act. She cackled to herself. They obviously thought her growing lack of conversation was evidence of a growing lack of sense. Why would she be surprised? They had thrown her a surprise party for the past five years. She guessed they figured she'd forget. What the party really meant was they were surprised she was still alive. Oh, she did love them, though. Every one of them. Pretty bags and bows crowded the coffee table. Now, what in heaven's name was she going to do with a bunch of gifts? And how many pairs of socks does a woman need? But that cake was looking mighty tasty. The great-grandkids had insisted on putting all ninety candles on the cake.

The youngest great-grandchild grabbed her by the hand. "Come on, Mammie! It's time to blow the candles out." She grinned and asked God to help her keep her teeth in. Time suddenly seemed to freeze. She looked around the room and studied the faces. Life had been good—painful at times, but God had always been faithful. She had been a widow for twenty-three years. Her last years had been pleasant. Her family made sure of that. But she grew less and less able to participate. She found herself mostly just watching life.

The muffled insistence of the impatient five-year-old finally grew clear, "Mammie, come on!" Before she could draw a breath, all the little ones blew out the candles. Only blood relatives would have eaten that cake after the spraying it took. Later she sat at her old vanity as her daughter-in-law tenderly took the pins from her wispy, white hair. She stared in the yellowed mirror. When had she gotten so old? Where had the years gone?

Her daughter-in-law brushed the strands gently, chattering incessantly about the evening. As she helped her with her gown and tucked her in, the old woman felt so weary. Her body hurt just to lie down.

The soft mattress seemed to swallow her frame. She rested her slight weight and stared at the stars out the window. She heard the familiar sound of the ten o'clock train going over the bridge and nearly shivered as she remembered her baptism in those cold waters underneath. She smiled and voiced a good-night prayer to the Savior she had loved since childhood. She didn't say much. "Thank You, Jesus. Thank You." Almost before she could close her eyes, deep sleep overtook her. Suddenly, her slumber was startled by the most beautiful voice she had ever heard, coming from a man standing over her. "Arise, my darling, my beautiful one, and come with me. See! The winter is past; the rains are over and gone . . . the season of singing has come."

Beauty instead of ashes.

CHAPTER 28

UPSIDE DOWN

You turn things upside down,
as if the potter were thought to be like the clay!
Shall what is formed say to him who formed it,
"He did not make me"?
Can the pot say of the potter,
"He knows nothing"?

(ISA. 29:16)

Warning! I don't think this will be your favorite portion of this study. How does liberty in Christ become a reality in life? In a word: obedience! Obedience to God's Word.

James described the relationship between God's Word and freedom:

Do not merely listen to the word, and so deceive yourselves. Do what it says. Anyone who listens to the word but does not do what it says is like a man who looks at his face in a mirror and, after looking at himself, goes away and immediately forgets what he looks like. But the man who looks intently into the perfect law that

gives freedom, and continues to do this, not forgetting
what he has heard, but doing it—he will be blessed in
what he does. (James 1:22–25)

Rightly responding to the Word of God is our ticket on the freedom
train. God's Word is the perfect law that gives freedom. I've addressed
other issues first because sometimes we are in too much bondage to
imagine living an obedient life. Often when I introduce this pivotal part
of the journey to freedom, I see downcast expressions that show our natural desire. We want God to somehow wave a wand over us and magi-
cally remove every hindrance without requiring anything of us.

If God simply waved a wand over us and broke every yoke without
our cooperation, we would soon pick up another. God desires to
change us from the inside out—renewing our minds, starving our self-
destructive tendencies, and teaching us to form new habits.

The rich Book of Isaiah is going to offer us several crucial motivations toward obedience. In Isaiah 29:16 God used the example of a
marred piece of pottery to describe His people's problem:

You turn things upside down,
    as if the potter were thought to be like the clay!
Shall what is formed say to him who formed it,
    "He did not make me"?
Can the pot say of the potter,
    "He knows nothing"? (Isa. 29:16)

Please allow God to engrave this truth on your heart: liberty and
authority always go hand in hand. During the ministry of the prophet
Isaiah, captivity was imminent for the children of Israel because they
had a serious authority problem.

In essence, God was saying, "You've got things turned around. Let's get this straight: Me, God. You, human. Me, Creator. You, creature. Me, Potter. You, clay. You obey . . . not for My good but for yours."

From all early appearances, my adorable youngest daughter came into the world to take over. By the time she was only two years old, she liked to walk ahead of the rest of us so she could appear to have come by herself. She was born authoritative and seemed to assume that she, Keith, and I were all three on the same level. Keith and I expended no small amount of energy underscoring our authority over her, the penalty for rebellion, and the safety and blessing of obedience. We haven't always done it right, but we've done it often! At this particular season, we are reaping a delightful harvest. Melissa is a wonderful teenager. But if I had a dime for every time I said, "Me, parent! You, child!" she would inherit a fortune! Over and over in the Book of Isaiah, God perfectly underscores the same three principles:

1. He has the right to rule.
2. He sets a high price for rebellion.
3. He pours out safety and blessing for obedience.

In chapter 30 Isaiah portrayed the people's unwillingness to obey: "Give us no more visions of what is right! / Tell us pleasant things / prophesy illusions / . . . stop confronting us / with the Holy One of Israel!" (Isa. 30:10–11). God responded:

"Because you have rejected this message, . . .
this sin will become for you
    like a high wall, cracked and bulging,
        that collapses suddenly, in an instant.
It will break in pieces like pottery,
    shattered so mercilessly
that among its pieces not a fragment will be found

for taking coals from a hearth
or scooping water out of a cistern."

This is what the Sovereign LORD, the Holy One of Israel, says:

"In repentance and rest is your salvation,
in quietness and trust is your strength,
but you would have none of it." (Isa. 30:12–15)

Pretty confrontational, isn't it? Think about your own human nature as I consider mine. Without the Holy Spirit controlling your life, do any of these verses sound familiar? I think so too. Later we'll consider how rebelling against God's authority is not just foolish, it is an affront to Almighty God, our Creator and King. For now, however, let's consider rebellion from a strictly selfish point of view. God's children cheated themselves through rebellion.

The word *rebellion* means what you'd probably expect. Words like *defiant* and *disobedient* are accurate synonyms. The Hebrew definition also uses the English synonym *refractory.* I chuckled when I checked my thesaurus for the meaning of *refractory.* It gave *pigheaded.* Webster's defines *pigheaded* as "obstinate, stubborn." This hits me—stubborn, resisting authority.

Let's face it: without God's intervention in our lives, we all tend to be pigheaded. We want to boss ourselves, but bossing ourselves is a ticket to slavery. Each of the following phrases from Isaiah 30:8–21 characterizes rebellion. Several of the characteristics signal impending disaster! In this chapter we will see that a rebellious child of God: (1) doesn't act like a child of God, (2) isn't willing to listen to the Lord's instruction, (3) prefers pleasant illusions over truth, and (4) relies on oppression. In the next chapter we'll examine the last two characteristics: that a rebellious child of God (5) learns to depend on deceit and (6) runs from the real answers God provides.

1. *A rebellious child of God doesn't act like a child of God* (v. 9). *Deceitful* means "not acting like sons . . . giving a false impression of who you are." If you are in covenant relationship with God but not acting like His child, you are living a lie! The world preaches the "be true to yourself" philosophy. Christians can only be true to self when demonstrating that they belong to God.

2. *A rebellious child of God isn't willing to listen to the Lord's instruction* (v. 9). The Hebrew word for "listen" is *shama,* meaning "to give undivided listening attention." Rebellious people don't want to listen. Sometimes we're unwilling to listen to God because we're resistant to being corrected. That's rebellion. The tragedy is that God would never tell us anything to defeat us. He has a one-track mind as far as we are concerned. He wants us to live like the overcomers we are.

The Scripture paints vivid pictures of the overcoming benefits of obedience. Psalm 81 proclaims the promise, "If my people would but listen to me, / . . . how quickly would I subdue their enemies / and turn my hand against their foes!" (Ps. 81:13–14).

3. *A rebellious child of God prefers pleasant illusions over truth* (vv. 10–11). We crave messages that make us feel good. When we are living in rebellion, the last thing we want is to confront the Holy One of Israel. Notice the demand of the people of God in verse 10: "Tell us pleasant things." Who doesn't like to be flattered? If enjoying flattery puts a noose around our necks, then seeking flattery hangs us! Satan could have written the book *Flattery Can Get You Anywhere.*

Paul the apostle correctly warned that, "the time will come when men will not put up with sound doctrine. Instead, to suit their own desires, they will gather around them a great number of teachers to say what their itching ears want to hear" (2 Tim. 4:3). If we strongly prefer certain teachers and preachers over others, we are wise to ask why. If our basis is anything other than balanced biblical teaching, we could be in rebellion while occupying pews every Sunday. Let's make sure we are not looking for people to scratch our itching ears and hide us from the truth.

4. *A rebellious child of God relies on oppression* (v. 12). Here's a shocker. Not only can God's children be oppressed, but we can come to rely on that oppression. The word *relied* in verse 12 is the Hebrew word *batach,* meaning "to attach oneself, to trust, confide in, feel safe." The Hebrew word for *oppression* (*osheq*) indicates oppression by means of fraud or extortion, a thing "deceitfully gotten" (*Strong's*).

We might say this: People who detach themselves from truth inadvertently attach themselves to lies that defraud and extort. God created us to be attached to Him; therefore, He made us with a very real need to be attached. Satan knows he cannot entice us to simply detach from God and His Word and be independent. In reality, there is no such thing as a completely independent human psyche. To entice us, Satan offers us alternate attachments masquerading as fulfillments to our inner needs. Any attachment other than God is a fraud. The word *attachment* in this context differs from healthy relationships with things or people. The key word is *reliance*. Wrong attachment means growing dependent on something other than God.

I grew up in a stronghold of fear. I longed to find a safe place to hide. I desperately wanted someone to take care of me. From the realm of my own painful experience, let me alert you to a toxic emotional cocktail: a relationship made up of someone who has an unhealthy need to be taken care of and someone who has an unhealthy need to caretake. The relationship ended up extorting God-given liberties and proved fraudulent.

Any place we have to hide is not safe. In Christ, we find the freedom to be safely exposed! If only we could begin to understand that God's authority does not imprison; it sets free! Next, we will continue our look at rebellion and the wisdom of obedience.

CHAPTER 29

BROKEN POTTERY

This sin will become for you
like a high wall, cracked and bulging,
that collapses suddenly, in an instant.
It will break in pieces like pottery.

(ISA. 30:13–14)

We continue our list of the marks of rebellion from Isaiah 30:8–21. The fourth characteristic most penetrated my heart. I pray God will expose all fraudulent attachments in our lives and draw us to the light of healthy relationships with both things and people. Let's continue now with the fifth characteristic.

5. *A rebellious child of God depends on deceit* (v. 12). The Hebrew word for "depended" is *sha'an,* "to support oneself, lean against." Any time you've seen someone walk with a cane or a crutch, you've witnessed the word picture drawn in this phrase.

The paired phrases in Isaiah 30:12—"relied on oppression" and "depended on deceit"—particularly strike me. Any time we attach ourselves or seek safety in a fraudulent savior we have to depend on lies to support the habit. Many tragically experience that picture as a reality:

172

A young Christian girl has a harsh, abusive father. She grows up with a fear and distaste for men. Satan supplies a slightly older woman who seems tender and caring. The comforting relationship turns into a physical relationship, so the young woman assumes she must be homosexual. In her heart she knows what she is doing is wrong, but she feels helpless without her new comforter. Soon she starts socializing with other women who are practicing homosexuality, because they will support her new habit with the lies she needs to continue. She avoids the Bible and chooses books that advocate homosexuality. She drops all relationships except those that support the fraudulent attachment with lies.

Scary, isn't it? I used an obvious scenario to make my point, but Satan uses countless unhealthy attachments to things or people. Interestingly, the lost world characterizes Christians as emotionally needy people who use religion and faith as a crutch. How wrong they are. The biggest crutch of all is deceit. Satan's lies keep us walking in our chains.

6. *A rebellious child of God runs from the real answers* (vv. 15–17). God said, "In repentance and rest is your salvation," but the people said, "No, we will flee on horses." (vv. 15–16). Have you experienced a season in your life when you knew what would rescue you but you ran from it? Like me, you may rank these memories among your greatest regrets. Virtually everyone has run from the real answers at one time or another.

In Isaiah 30:15, the word *salvation* is not used in a strictly eternal sense. The word represents being saved or delivered from any kind of calamity or attack. God presented the truth in the form of an equation:

Repentance + Rest = Salvation

Eternal salvation requires that we repent of our sins and depend on the work of Christ. Our need of deliverance does not end, however, once we become Christians. We still need lots of help avoiding snares and pitfalls. The same equation applies: "In repentance and rest is your salvation!"

The word *returning* more accurately translates the Hebrew rendered here as *repentance. Strong's* says *shuwbah* actually means "returning." The word *repentance* used elsewhere in God's Word usually means "turning from sin," but often we omit the next step! Acts 3:19 reflects the two-fold step: "Repent, then, and turn to God, so that your sins may be wiped out, that times of refreshing may come from the Lord." If we only turn from our sins but do not turn to God, we lack the power to over-come the temptation the next time it arises! The word *returning* in Isaiah 30:15 (KJV) encompasses both repenting and returning to God!

Now let's look at the second variable in the equation: "In repentance [or *returning*, KJV] and rest is your salvation."

The word *rest* probably means what you think it does. The Hebrew word is *nachath. Strong's* dictionary gives a definition that tickles me. It says the word means "lighting down." I can picture my grandmother in our kitchen in Arkansas with a flyswatter in her hand and a most seri-ous expression on her face. "Whatcha doin', Nanny?" I'd ask. "I'm wait-ing for that filthy fly to light down somewhere so I can smack it."

In just a moment I'd hear, "ka-WHACK!" Then she would say, "Take that, you little nuisance!" Somehow, we often believe we are like that fly. We think if we light down for a second, God's going to whack us. Untrue. We're not flies, and Nanny wasn't God! God desires for us to rest in Him, to light down on His truth and be set on who He is.

In returning to God and resting confidently in His promises and power, we will continually find salvation. I love the Hebrew meaning of the word *salvation. Yasha* means "to be open, wide, or free . . . It is the opposite of *tsarar,* to cramp." *Yasha* draws the picture of a spacious place in which to move. I have personally experienced the wide-open freedom of obedience to Christ! I've also known the miserable, pinned-in feeling of rebellion.

We all know that God wants us to return and rest, but many of us have tried this equation: repent plus be determined to do better on my own strength. This formula has often been my downfall.

Another equation can be found in Isaiah 30:15: "in quietness + trust = your strength." Strength in this verse means "implying victory." I deeply desire to be a victor, don't you? Consider two primary elements involved in victory: quietness and trust. The word for "quietness" is *shaqat,* meaning "to lie quietly, be undisturbed, . . . to calm." Have you sometimes experienced defeat because you refused to calm yourself in the presence of God and trust Him?

The exact Hebrew word translated "trust" in this verse appears only once in the Old Testament. The word *bitchah* means "there is nothing more that one can do." Once we've obeyed God, we can do nothing more. We then wait on Him to bring the victory, knowing that the consequences of our obedience are His problem and not ours. Our human nature is to run when we're in trouble, but we've learned two very important precepts from Isaiah 30:15:

1. To flee from God's salvation is rebellion.

2. To flee from God's strength is to flee from victory.

As we approach our conclusion, remember all six characteristics of rebellion:

1. A rebellious child of God doesn't act like a child of God (Isa. 30:9).

2. A rebellious child of God isn't willing to listen to the Lord's instruction (Isa. 30:9).

3. A rebellious child of God prefers pleasant illusions over truth (Isa. 30:10–11).
4. A rebellious child of God relies on oppression (Isa. 30:12).
5. A rebellious child of God depends on deceit (Isa. 30:12).
6. A rebellious child of God runs from the real answers (Isa. 30:15–17).

Which of the characteristics have been your tendencies in your history with God? Which are present struggles for you? Spend some time in prayer with the list. Confess any tendencies toward rebellion or areas of rebellion based on the six characteristics we've noted. Then review the equations. Don't respond to your confession with how you are going to do better. Run to the Father and rest in Him.

God wants to respond to you. His response is already recorded in Isaiah 30:18. He "longs to be gracious to you; / he rises to show you compassion." We can picture God being merciful and forgiving when we accidentally get ourselves into a mess, but we almost cannot imagine how God can be compassionate when we're outright rebellious.

Oh, what a disservice we do when we try to humanize God by imagining Him as the best of humanity rather than all-together God! God's compassion demands that He reach out to us even in our rebellion, but His righteousness demands that He bring painful chastisement if we don't grab His reaching hand and return to Him wholeheartedly.

Remember Isaiah 30:12–14. If we continue in rebellion, rejecting God's Word, relying on oppression, and depending on deceit, the walls of protection around our lives will crumble like pottery broken to pieces. Those who are Christians will not lose salvation, but we stand to lose a significant amount of protection. The bottom line of these two lessons is this: Clay that insists on acting like the Potter will inevitably end up in pieces. Let's not wait until we're in pieces to return and trust.

CHAPTER 30

GOD'S RIGHT TO RULE

I am God, and there is no other;
I am God, and there is none like me.

(ISA. 46:9)

🌰

We are focusing on obedience: the crucial key that ignites the liberty of Christ and makes it a reality in life. The liberty of Christ was ours the moment we received Him as our Savior; but if this internal gift is not released externally through obedience, we may never experience it. Let's see how this works.

Only the Lord possesses true liberty. "The Lord is the Spirit, and where the Spirit of the Lord is, there is freedom" (2 Cor. 3:17). Jesus spoke of this truth often. Notice the word *received* in the following Scriptures:

- "Yet to all who received him, to those who believed in his name, he gave the right to become children of God" (John 1:12).
- "For you did not receive a spirit that makes you a slave again to fear, but you received the Spirit of sonship. And by him we cry, '*Abba*, Father'" (Rom. 8:15).
- "We have not received the spirit of the world but the Spirit who is from God, that we may understand what God has freely given us" (1 Cor. 2:12).

Note the clear teaching of this divine reception in John 14:15–17.

> If you love me, you will obey what I command. And
> I will ask the Father, and he will give you another
> Counselor to be with you forever—the Spirit of truth.
> The world cannot accept him, because it neither sees
> him nor knows him. But you know him, for he lives
> with you and will be in you.

When we receive Christ as our Savior, we literally receive Christ! His Spirit takes up residence in us. Romans 8:9 says: "If anyone does not have the Spirit of Christ, he does not belong to Christ."

When we receive Christ as Savior, we receive His liberating Spirit, but we must understand that the freedom never leaves the bounds of His Spirit. Therefore, our liberation is expressed as a reality only in the places of our lives where the free Spirit of God is released. We are free when, and only when, He is in control.

Reflect again on the words of 2 Corinthians 3:17: "Now the Lord is the Spirit, and where the Spirit of the Lord is, there is freedom." Freedom and lordship are inseparable partners in the believer's life. When we read that freedom can be found anywhere the Spirit of the Lord is, we can take it literally.

Freedom becomes reality when we yield to the authority of God. We are as filled with the Spirit as we are yielded to His lordship. Although the Spirit of the Lord is always in us, He floods only the parts of our lives where He is in authority. Freedom flows where the Spirit of the Lord floods.

This point brings up an interesting question. Have you ever noticed that you can experience freedom in one part of your life and remain in bondage in another? Sometimes we allow God to have full authority in one area while refusing Him in another.

How, then, can we be fully liberated? Can we study God's Word until we finally experience freedom? Can we pray ourselves into freedom? Can we rebuke the enemy so thoroughly that we experience freedom? No. Until we choose to withhold no part of our lives from His authority, we will not experience full freedom. The answer to liberty is withholding no part of our lives from His authority.

Again, allow me to stress that obedient lives are not perfect lives. Obedience does not mean sinlessness but confession and repentance when we sin. Obedience is not arriving at a perpetual state of godliness but perpetually following hard after God. Obedience is not living miserably by a set of laws, but inviting the Spirit of God to flow freely through us. Obedience is learning to love and treasure God's Word and see it as our safety.

Do you know Christ's ultimate purpose in His earthly life? He continually proclaimed that purpose.

- In Gethsemane he prayed "may your will be done" (Matt. 26:42).
- "My food," he said, "is to do the will of him who sent me and to finish his work" (John 4:34).
- "I have come down from heaven not to do my will but to do the will of him who sent me" (John 6:38).

The only begotten Son of the Father came to do the will of His Father. Even the Father and the Son had a Potter/clay relationship. Christ obeyed the Potter. As an earthen vessel, Jesus had to trust His Father's will completely. Although rejection, suffering, and shame were part of His experience, Christ accepted His God-given ministry at every difficult turn because He trusted His Father's heart.

I believe Christ's unrelenting obedience to the Father came not only out of love but from two additional motivations as well: He was committed to God's right to rule and was convinced that God's rule is right. Let's consider God's right to rule, and in our next lesson we will research the rightness of God's rule.

We've already seen one of the clearest messages of the Book of Isaiah: obedience is a ticket to freedom, and rebellion is a ticket to slavery. Not coincidentally, the Book of Isaiah also has as much to say about God's right to rule and the rightness of His rule. In chapters 40, 45, and 46, Isaiah powerfully addresses God's supremacy over creation, idols, and humanity. The chapters also contain personal proclamations of God's absolute uniqueness. I encourage you to do an exercise in personal Bible study. Read from Isaiah these passages: 40:12–28; 45:5–25; 46:1–13. Then write down or underline the statements that show God's superiority over creation, idols, or humanity, and His absolute uniqueness. Here is one example in each of the categories:

- *Creation:* He measures the waters in His hand (Isa. 40:12).
- *Idols:* Idols themselves are man-made (Isa. 40:19).
- *Humanity:* No human can understand or instruct Him (Isa. 40:13).
- *God's Absolute Uniqueness:* "Who is my equal?" (Isa. 40:25).

As I read over these passages, I am sobered and humbled once again. Sometimes what we need to cure our fat egos is a strong dose of God. Long before a certain visionary "discovered" the earth was round, God sat enthroned above the circle of the earth. Long before men were so "enlightened," God formed the light and the darkness. Long before the first billion dollars was invested in exploring space, God's own hands stretched out the heavens. Long before there was a "beginning," God had already planned the end. Like Peter on the mount of transfiguration, we're so caught up in the tabernacles we want to build that we sometimes miss a fresh revelation of God's glory right before our eyes.

We make life so much more complicated when we think life is "all about me." The rest of the world never cooperates. No one else got the memo. When we see ourselves as the center of the universe, we live in constant frustration because the rest of creation refuses to revolve around us.

Life vastly simplifies, and satisfaction greatly amplifies when we begin to realize our awesome roles. God is God. From our perspective, it's all about Him. Thank goodness, He is the center of the universe. So how can we live with such a God-centered mentality? Freely! Because from God's perspective, it's all about us. We seek to please Him. He seeks to perfect us—and life works. Not without pain, but with purpose.

Without the Potter, clay is just dirt. "The LORD God formed the man from the dust of the ground and breathed into his nostrils the breath of life, and the man became a living being" (Gen. 2:7).

I am God, and there is no other;
I am God, and there is none like me. (Isa. 46:9)

CHAPTER 31

GOD'S RULE IS RIGHT

But my salvation will last forever,
my righteousness will never fail.

(ISA. 51:6b)

❧

I have a nightmare—having to obey an unrighteous authority. In case you think obedience comes easy for me, let me clear up a few things. Submission and subservience are to me as easy as cuddling a litter of baby porcupines. A child who has been forced into things she didn't want to do usually grows up never wanting to be told what to do again—by anyone.

Until my mother's dying day, every time I asserted myself about anything, she reminded me of the time our family doctor told me I couldn't go swimming because I had an ear infection. Mom said I squinted my eyes, looked as mean as I could, and said, "Oh, yeah? Well, you're not the boss of me!" Unfortunately, the doctor was the president of our small-town country club. He retorted, "No, but I'm the boss of that swimming pool, and I'd better not catch you in it." I promptly began to lobby for a pool in our backyard so I could boss myself.

The problem is, God did not design us to boss ourselves. He formed our psyches to require authority, so we'd live in the safety of His careful rule. Satan tries to draw us away from God's authority by making us think we can be our own producer and director. The apostle Paul addressed the impossibility of mastering our own lives and destinies in Romans 6:16:

> Don't you know that when you offer yourselves to someone to obey him as slaves, you are slaves to the one whom you obey—whether you are slaves to sin, which leads to death, or to obedience, which leads to righteousness?

We have exactly two options: we can be slaves to a loving God or slaves to sin. Door number three only exists on *Let's Make a Deal*. We need not be distressed that the verse characterizes us as slaves. Because we are creatures, we are going to be mastered; the question becomes, Who will be our master? As important as our previous lesson was to me, God's right to rule is not my primary motivation for pursuing the obedient life. I resist obeying someone strictly on the basis of his or her position. This will probably shock you, but I probably would have chanced eternity in hell rather than bend my knee to any ruler just because he was in charge.

My primary motivation for pursuing the obedient life is an absolute belief that the One who has a right to rule is also the One whose rule is right. I try to obey God because with all my heart I believe He is always good, always right, and loves me in ways I cannot comprehend.

You can't fully appreciate my emotions as I prepare to write these next three words: I trust God. After a lifetime of trust problems, I can't understand how such a miracle of grace has come to me, but it has. This may seem silly, but I love Him so much that sometimes I can't wait for Him to ask me to do something a little difficult, because I want to obey Him. I not only love God and trust Him; I love trusting Him. It is a constant reminder of a perpetual miracle in my life.

What about obeying other humans? I've slowly come to trust God's sovereignty enough to believe that anyone I must obey on this earth had better be careful with me, or they have God to answer to!

Now that I've been transparent with you, it's your turn. Do you also have authority problems? If so, how have you become aware of them? How about God's authority? How convinced are you that you can trust Him? Our text encourages us to trust and obey. If you feel like you're barely beginning a life of trust, possibly you will take a step of faith and obey so you can learn to build trust.

Isaiah 51 begins with the command "Listen to me." Again and again God appears to be trying to get His reader's full attention.

> Listen to me, you who pursue righteousness
> and who seek the LORD:
> Look to the rock from which you were cut
> and to the quarry from which you were hewn;
> look to Abraham, your father,
> and to Sarah, who gave you birth. (Isa. 51:1–2)

In Galatians we see that these verses apply to Gentile Christians as well as Jews: "If you belong to Christ, then you are Abraham's seed, and heirs according to the promise" (Gal. 3:29). If we look to the rock from which we were hewn, we can . . .

- believe God can do the impossible (Gen. 18:14).
- admit the futility of taking matters into our own hands (Gen. 16).
- believe God still loves and can use us even when we detour—if we agree to return to His path (Gen. 17).
- believe God could still call us righteous based on our faith in Him, even if our righteous acts are like filthy rags (Gen. 15:6; Isa. 64:6).
- believe that blessing ultimately follows obedience (Gen. 22:18).

Because the Lord is so compassionate, He can work wonders with the ruins, deserts, and wastelands of His children's lives.

The LORD will surely comfort Zion
and will look with compassion on all her ruins;
he will make her deserts like Eden,
her wastelands like the garden of the LORD. (Isa. 51:3)

Have you felt like the waves of the sea were pounding against you and you were drowning in a relentless tide? Isaiah reminds you that God can do for you what He did for Moses. He "made a road in the depths of the sea / so that the redeemed might cross over" (Isa. 51:10b).

Have you ever felt like a cowering prisoner? I have! Have you ever felt like you would never be released? I love the words of Isaiah 51:14: "The cowering prisoners will soon be set free." Believe it and claim it! Obey and see that you can trust! Do not allow the enemy another success at using your past record against you. God said He is doing a new thing:

Forget the former things;
do not dwell on the past.
See, I am doing a new thing!
Now it springs up; do you not perceive it?
I am making a way in the desert
and streams in the wasteland. (Isa. 43:18–19)

I want to shout hallelujah! Yes, fellow sojourner, God has the right to rule. But better yet, God's rule is right! He cannot ask anything wrong of us, nor can He mislead us. He knows every authority problem we have. He knows the times our trust has been betrayed. Like a father cupping his rebellious child's face in his strong hands, He says, "Listen to me . . . Hear me . . . I, even I, am he who comforts you . . . I am the LORD your God" (Isa. 51:1, 7, 12, 15). Essentially, God is saying to us, "I am for you, Child! Not against you! When will you cease resisting Me?"

CHAPTER 32

GOD'S DAILY RULE

O LORD, be gracious to us;
we long for you.
Be our strength every morning,
our salvation in time of distress.

(ISA. 33:2)

Last year my sweet daddy had a stroke, and I rode with him in the ambulance. The paramedics were wonderful and, although I appreciate them, we didn't trade phone numbers or plan to have lunch! Sometimes we tend to approach God in the same way. He gets us through an emergency. We appreciate Him, but we don't necessarily stay in close touch once the crisis passes. It is not during crisis points that we develop an appreciation for God's presence. Pure appreciation for His presence emerges from the daily walk—perhaps in the mundane more than the miraculous.

A profound change occurred in my daily approach to God when I realized God wanted me to walk with Him. For years I asked God to walk with me. Talk about the clay trying to spin the Potter! I wanted to take my feet of clay and walk where my heart led and count on the Potter to bless my sweet-if-selfish little heart. My clay feet got scorched walking through some terrible fires sparked by the misguided passion of my own heart. Finally I realized God's blessing would come when I did what He said. For safety and the pure enjoyment of God, we are so wise to learn to walk with God instead of begging Him to walk with us. Walking with God in pursuit of daily obedience is the sure means of fulfilling each of His wonderful plans.

Imagine going to heaven and standing by God as He lovingly shows you His plan for your life. It begins with the day you are born. Once you received Christ as Savior, every day that follows is outlined in red. You see footprints walking through each day of your life. On many of the days, two sets of footprints appear. You inquire: "Father, are those my footprints every day, and is the second set of prints when You joined me?"

He answers, "No, My precious Child. The consistent footprints are Mine. The second set of footprints are when you joined Me."

"Where were You going, Father?"

"To the destiny I planned for you, hoping you'd follow."

"But, Father, where are my footprints all those times?"

"Sometimes you went back to look at old resentments and habits. Sometimes, you chose your own path. Other times, your footprints appear on another person's calendar because you liked their plan better. Sometimes, you simply stopped because you would not let go of something you could not take with you."

"But, Father, we ended up OK even if I didn't walk with You every day, didn't we?"

He holds you close and smiles, "Yes, Child, we ended up OK. But, you see, OK was never what I had in mind for you."

Does the scenario seem far-fetched? Actually, it's quite biblical. The Scripture frequently tells us why we should walk God's way instead of ours: "God . . . always leads us in triumphal procession in Christ" (2 Cor. 2:14).

Remember, walking consistently does not mean walking perfectly. It means we may stumble, but we will not fall! Let's see what God has to say to us through the prophet Isaiah about the daily-ness of God. In Isaiah 33:2–6 we see the first three of five results of a daily walk with God.

1. *God offers us the daily treasure of His strength.* "Be our strength every morning, / our salvation in time of distress" (Isa. 33:2). Psalm 84:5 proclaims, "Blessed are those whose strength is in you, / who have set their hearts on pilgrimage." How often do we remind ourselves that we're on a journey leading to a glorious heavenly city? We may go from trial to trial, but according to Psalm 84:7, we also go "from strength to strength."

2. *God offers us the daily treasure of His sure foundation.* "He will be the sure foundation for your times" (Isa. 33:6). Obedient lives flow from obedient days, and victorious lives flow from victorious days. Likewise, constructive lives flow from constructive days, built on the sure foundation of Jesus Christ. The King James Version uses the English word *stability* for *sure foundation* in Isaiah 33:6. I love the thought of God's being our stability, don't you? When was the last time you felt that everything in your life was quaking except your stability in Christ? Words to a familiar hymn ring out in my soul: "On Christ the Solid Rock, I stand; / All other ground is sinking sand, / All other ground is sinking sand." God's benefits include the daily treasures of His strength and a sure foundation.

3. *God offers us the daily treasure of wisdom and knowledge.* "He will be . . . a rich store of salvation and wisdom and knowledge" (Isa. 33:6). When we rub shoulders with Christ day-to-day, His wisdom and knowledge rub off on us little by little. Wisdom is the application of knowledge—knowing what to do with what you know. God wants to guide us daily in His own wisdom and knowledge. Remember, He's the One with the plan. Psalm 119:105 paints such a beautiful word picture for us. His Word "is a lamp to my feet," meaning a guide for the steps I'm taking

right now. His Word is also "a light for my path," meaning a guide for my immediate future. God's Word sheds light on our "present" path and on our immediate future so we'll know what steps to take, but for further instruction we'll have to walk today and check again! If you're like me, you might not keep checking with Him if you knew the whole plan.

Let's continue with results 4 and 5 from Isaiah 50.

4. *God offers us the daily treasure of a fresh morning word.* "He wakens me morning by morning, / wakens my ear to listen like one being taught" (Isa. 50:4). I believe God awakens us in the morning with a supernatural capacity to hear from Him. At the beginning of the day, we haven't gone the wrong way yet.

5. *God offers us the daily treasure of victory* (Isa. 50:7–8). We cannot escape the warfare of the Christian life. Satan doesn't take time off for good behavior. What wonderful words from the prophet:

Because the Sovereign LORD helps me,
    I will not be disgraced.
Therefore have I set my face like flint,
    and I know I will not be put to shame.
He who vindicates me is near.
    Who then will bring charges against me?
Let us face each other!
Who is my accuser?
    Let him confront me! (Isa. 50:7–8)

Every day can bring trouble, but every day we have a blessed Troubleshooter. Satan seeks to disgrace us, accuse us, and condemn us. We must daily set our faces like flint on the face of Christ and follow Him step by step to victory. Let's conclude with a look at Isaiah 50:10–11:

Who among you fears the LORD
>and obeys the word of his servant?
Let him who walks in the dark,
>who has no light,
trust in the name of the LORD
>and rely on his God.
But now, all you who light fires
>and provide yourselves with flaming torches,
go, walk in the light of your fires
>and of the torches you have set ablaze.
This is what you shall receive from my hand:
>You will lie down in torment.

No matter how long we've walked with God, we will still have days that seem dark. In those times God tells us to trust in His name and rely on who He is. Job 23:10 continues to be a blessing to me when I don't know what to do: "But he knows the way that I take." When you feel you've lost your way, take heart! He knows the way that you take. Stand still, cry out, and bid Him to come to you! He'll lead you on from there, and miraculously, when once again you see the light, you'll be able to see the footprints you made in the dark. Never will He hold your hand more tightly than when He is leading you through the dark.

What is your biggest temptation when you don't feel that God is illuminating your way clearly? Isaiah 50:11 describes mine perfectly. I tend to want to light my own fire and walk by the illumination of my own torch. Yes, you and I will still veer periodically from the path, no matter how obediently we want to walk, because we're pilgrims with feet of clay. The beauty of God's light is this: it will always lead us right back to the path. No matter how long the detour has been, the return is only a shortcut away. "Save me, for I am yours" (Ps. 119:94).

PART V

UNFAILING LOVE

You've come such a long way on this journey. I hope you're meeting the Master on every page.

Remember the wedding feast in Cana of Galilee? The master of the banquet made a statement about Jesus that always touches my heart. It just describes Him so well. "Everyone brings out the choice wine first and then the cheaper wine after the guests have had too much to drink; but you have saved the best till now" (John 2:10). Jesus always seems to have something greater waiting up around the bend. I would never claim divine inspiration, but Christ has been true to Himself once more. I believe He has greater things just ahead.

What do we need when our mountains shake? When our hills are removed (Isa. 54:10)? Babies die without it. Children must have it. Youth plead for it. Adults search for it. We'll only find real freedom in the love that will not fail or go away. The key to peace can only be found in such a love. Come along as we consider God's unfailing love

Memorize the promise of Benefit 4: To experience God's peace.

You will keep in perfect peace
>   him whose mind is steadfast,
>   because he trusts in you. (Isa. 26:3)

191

CHAPTER 33

FINDING UNFAILING LOVE

"Though the mountains be shaken
and the hills be removed,
yet my unfailing love for you will not be shaken
nor my covenant of peace be removed,"
says the LORD, who has compassion on you.

(ISA. 54:10)

I am coming out of a year of unparalleled transition. Nothing seems untouched. Relationships, circumstances, surroundings—everything has changed. I held on for dear life to anything standing still. One morning on my way to work, I made the same stop I had made for eighteen months: my favorite little coffee shop. I pranced in and made my usual order: "a banana nut bagel with plain cream cheese, please." The server looked at me cheerfully and said, "We're not carrying that kind any more. Is there something else I can get you today?"

I stood stunned with my eyebrows pinned like two barrettes to my hairline. I must have been in shock for some time because the person behind me finally bumped me out of the way, providing all I needed to burst into tears. As I walked out to the car, I looked up and inquired, "Could I have one thing around this place I can count on!"

As I got in the car, I sensed the Father speak His Word to my heart. "Beth, I will never leave you, nor will I ever forsake you."

We are about to study the lifesaving love of God. The word *compassion* in Isaiah 54:10 comes from the Hebrew word *racham*, meaning "to soothe; to cherish; to love deeply like parents; to be compassionate, be tender . . . This verb usually refers to a strong love which is rooted in some kind of natural bond, often from a superior one to an inferior." Now for my favorite part of the definition: "Small babies evoke this feeling."

I have never experienced a more overwhelming, inexpressible feeling than the one my two little infants birthed in me. My babies brought out a capacity to love I had never experienced before, and yet I had also never been so totally vulnerable.

I once heard a Christian child psychologist explain the necessity of some conflict and power struggle with teenagers. He explained that a certain amount of difficulty must naturally arise as children begin to become young adults, or parents would never be able to "help them" out of the nest and on to independence. He commented, "If the bond we had with them as infants did not change, we would never be able to let them go."

Now look back at the definition of compassion. All our lives God retains the strong feelings toward us that infants evoke in their parents because He never has to let us go! He's not rearing us to leave home! God is rearing us to come home!

I love Psalm 136. You may remember the passage because every one of the twenty-six verses begins with a line like "Give thanks to the LORD, for he is good" or "Give thanks to the God of gods." Then every verse concludes with the refrain: "His love endures forever." The psalm celebrates God as Creator, Conqueror, and Compassionate One. Of utmost importance to captives seeking complete freedom is this: God's works change, but His love stays steady and strong. The moment we think we've grasped His ways and figured out His methods, they will change.

Kings will rise and fall, but His love endures forever. Riches will come, and riches will go. But His love endures forever. Sometimes we'll be healed from physical afflictions, and sometimes we won't. But His love endures forever. The heavens and earth will pass away. But His love endures forever.

The apostle Paul penned the same truth when he proclaimed, "I am convinced that neither death nor life, neither angels nor demons, neither the present nor the future, nor any powers, neither height nor depth, nor anything else in all creation, will be able to separate us from the love of God that is in Christ Jesus our Lord" (Rom. 8:38–39).

Do you realize that we have just uncovered the answer to our greatest psychological need? Look what the Word of God says about the emotional needs of all human beings: "What a man desires is unfailing love" (Prov. 19:22). This verse is putting that which we long for most into a capsule phrase for us. Please don't miss this! Every human being longs for unfailing love. Lavish love. Focused love. Radical love. Love we can count on. The taxicab driver, the plumber, the stockbroker, the runway model, the actress, the streetwalker, the drug pusher, the schoolteacher, the computer programmer, the rocket scientist, the doctor, the lawyer, the president, and the custodian all yearn for the same thing: unfailing love.

Proverbs 20:6 suggests something important about unfailing love: "Many a man claims to have unfailing love, / but a faithful man who can find?" Paul described *agape* love as a supernatural love that only God fully possesses and only God can give. It's the New Testament word for God-love just like *chesed* is the Old Testament word for God-love. The only way we can love with *agape* is to pour everything else from our hearts and ask God to make them pitchers of His *agape*. Before we can even begin to give God-love away, we've got to fully accept it. God loves you with perfect love, and "perfect love drives out fear, because fear has to do with punishment. The one who fears is not made perfect in love" (1 John 4:18).

Have you ever feared that someone would cease loving you? Not only have I feared it; I've experienced it! God has carefully and graciously allowed some of my fears to come true so that I would discover that I would not disintegrate. God taught me to survive on His unfailing love. It wasn't fun, but it was transforming!

The only thing I absolutely could not survive is the loss of God's love, and that is a loss I will never have to try. His love endures forever. That's what He meant by perfect love driving out fear. The Word of God uses the phrase *unfailing love* thirty-two times, and not once is it attributed to humans. Every single use of the phrase refers to God and God alone. As rich as is the love that others can extend, only God's love is unfailing.

In his marvelous book *Holiness, Truth, and the Presence of God,* Francis Frangipane wrote, "There are many aspects to the nature of Christ. He is the Good Shepherd, our Deliverer and our Healer. We perceive God through the filter of our need of Him. And thus He has ordained, for He Himself is our one answer to a thousand needs."[1]

How gloriously true! But God is not only the answer to a thousand needs, He is the answer to a thousand wants. He is the fulfillment of our chief desire in all of life. For whether or not we've ever recognized it, what we desire is unfailing love. Oh, God, awake our souls to see—You are what we want, not just what we need. Yes, our life's protection, but also our heart's affection. Yes, our soul's salvation, but also our heart's exhilaration. Unfailing love—a love that will not let us go!

CHAPTER 34

THE FREEDOM OF
UNFAILING LOVE

Let them give thanks to the LORD for his unfailing love
and his wonderful deeds for men,
for he breaks down gates of bronze
and cuts through bars of iron.

(PS. 107:15–16)

Not long ago I tried a little experiment as I spoke to a group of women on the subject of God's love. I asked them to look eye to eye with the person beside them and say, "God loves me so much." Almost instinctively they turned to one another and said, "God loves you so much." I stopped them, brought the switch in words to their attention, and asked why they were struggling with my request. We readily accept God's love for others but struggle with the belief that He loves us equally, radically, completely, and unfailingly.

One reason I used to struggle with this truth was that I knew my own sins and weaknesses—all the reasons He shouldn't love me. Surely everyone else wasn't the mess deep inside that I was! In retrospect, I am glad I didn't go to the other extreme. Some people can be so full of self-righteousness that they seem convinced God loves them best of all.

Why do we have such difficulty believing that God could love with the same unfailing love those we perceive as good and those we perceive as bad? Because we relentlessly insist on trying to humanize God. We tend to love people according to how they act, and we keep trying to re-create God in our image.

Now we turn our attention to God's outlook on the heart of the foolishly rebellious. Psalm 107 serves as a warning to our wandering hearts:

> Some sat in darkness and the deepest gloom,
>   prisoners suffering in iron chains,
> for they had rebelled against the words of God
>   and despised the counsel of the Most High.
>   (Ps. 107:10–11)

Verse 12 comes across like a brisk slap in the face: "So [God] subjected them to bitter labor." We think of Satan imprisoning his victims, but we don't like to think of God subjecting rebellious humans to suffering.

In the next verse we see the purpose of the Lord's discipline: "Then they cried to the LORD in their trouble" (v. 13). Once God's people cried out to Him, "he saved them from their distress" so they could once again praise Him.

Verse 20 gives us another wonderful piece of the puzzle: "He sent forth his word and healed them; / he rescued them from the grave." When God heals any affliction, He does it by sending forth His Word.

Few people have grateful hearts like captives who have been freed and the afflicted who have been healed. Notice God's directive to them:

"Tell of his works with songs of joy" (v. 22). What an appropriate psalm for our study! Our hearts will never be healthy unless we learn to accept and abide in God's unfailing love. I'd like to draw two points from the psalm to encourage us toward our goal.

1. *God's unfailing love extends to the most rebellious captives and most afflicted fools.* Psalm 107 is refreshingly clear: God's unfailing love motivates wonderful deeds for the worst of men and women who cry out in their troubles. The Hebrew word for "wonderful" is *pala*, meaning "extraordinary, miraculous, marvelous, astonishing." These kinds of adjectives seem like they would be limited to God's good children, don't they? Yet, God's Word tells us that He does extraordinary, miraculous, marvelous, and astonishing things for the worst of the worst who cry out to Him. Why? Because He loves them with an unfailing love.

One of the works I'm convinced God wants to accomplish in this study is broadening our spiritual vision as we look at His love. You see, we don't only see God's unfailing love through broken chains and healed afflictions. His unfailing love also appears in His unwillingness to allow rebellion to go unnoticed and undisciplined. I see several ways God dealt with the rebellious so they would cry out:

- *He allowed them to sit "in darkness and the deepest gloom"* (v. 10). Our bulging prisons prove that rebellion can lead to literal incarceration. It can as easily lead to emotional cells of darkness and gloom. Although certainly not all depression is a result of rebellion, willfulness can lead to depression. I think depression is especially likely if the rebel was formerly close to God. Now that I know the indescribable joy of intimacy with God, living outside His fellowship would depress me. I am thankful that God allows darkness to follow rebellion. Sometimes He uses darkness to lead us to the light!

- *"He subjected them to bitter labor"* (v. 12). Rebellion can begin with fun and games, but eventually it leads to hard work. God allows rebellion to become a heavy burden after a while.

- *He allowed them to stumble* (v. 12). No doubt each of us can think of a few ways God allows the rebellious to stumble. When I was a teenager, I could have accepted the little truth I knew, but I didn't. I not only stumbled; I crashed and burned! And I am so thankful. Had I never fallen, I don't know that I would have cried out for help.

- *He allowed "no one to help"* (v. 12). How I thank Jesus for His unfailing love to make sure others "failed" in their attempts to help me! Sounds strange, doesn't it? I believe most of us would never acknowledge God as God alone if we didn't experience crises when no one else could help.

- *He allowed some to suffer affliction* (v. 17). Once again, certainly not all physical affliction is caused by rebellion, but rebellion can result in physical affliction. I can think of a time in college when I rebelled against God; I lost my appetite and became physically ill. I wasn't the first one in history to become sin-sick.

Glance back at all of these ways God can respond to rebellion. Hebrews 12:5–11 demonstrates that all of these responses are evidences of God's unfailing love rather than His wrathful condemnation.

My son, do not make light of the Lord's discipline,
  and do not lose heart when he rebukes you,
because the Lord disciplines those he loves,
  and he punishes everyone he accepts as a son.

No discipline seems pleasant at the time, but painful. Later on, however, it produces a harvest of righteousness and peace for those who have been trained by it. (Heb. 12:5–6, 11)

You see, God loves us enough to make us ultimatealy miserable in our rebellion! We see a second point to encourage us.

2. *God strives with His captive children until they are free.* The worst possible result of our disobedience would be God giving up on us. In Psalm 107 God's own children rebelled. Over and over He disciplined them; but He never forsook them, hallelujah!

One of the most common occurrences in the lives of those sent to prison is the subsequent serving of divorce papers by the spouse. Few prisoners have people on the outside standing by them throughout lengthy incarcerations. Most people would just as soon forget prisoners existed. They are the unpeople of our society. The same trend appears in less tangible terms among Christians. The best of our churches tend to welcome those captive (to alcohol, drugs, homosexuality, promiscuity, and so forth) at first; but if they don't "fix" pretty quickly, they will probably soon be despised. We like success stories—powerful testimonies. A captive in our midst wears out her welcome if she doesn't get with it and change.

In gracious contrast God stands by us until we are free. He never forsakes us. God is the only One who is not repelled by the depth and length of our needs. Although God never excuses our sin and rebellion, He is fully aware of what drives our actions. When I was growing up, I had no idea why I was making some poor decisions, but God knew. Even though my rebellion was still sin, God's heart was full of compassion. Through loving chastisement, He continued to strive with me and waited patiently for me to leave my prison.

No matter how long we struggle, God is not giving up on us. Even if we've drained all the human resources around us dry, He is our inexhaustible well of living water. He may allow the life of a captive to grow more and more difficult, so she will be more desperate to do what freedom in Christ requires—but He will never divorce her. He woos and

He waits. The measures God takes to woo us to liberty may be excruciating at times, but they are often more powerful evidences of His unfailing love than all the obvious blessings we could expound. Few truly know the unfailing love of God like the captive set free. "Let them give thanks to the LORD for his unfailing love / . . . and tell of his works with songs of joy" (Ps. 107:21–22). Beloved, if He has become God alone to you, you have a powerful story to tell. Start talking.

CHAPTER 35

THE FULLNESS OF UNFAILING LOVE

Satisfy us in the morning with your unfailing love,
that we may sing for joy and be glad all our days.

(PS. 90:14)

Where would I be without the love of God? Everything I possess of any worth is a direct product of God's love. I would like to focus with you on one of the most wonderful works of God's *chesed* or *agape* in my life: the love that met my cavernous needs.

Let's consider the account in John's Gospel of Jesus' meeting with the woman at the well. From this encounter we can observe several realities:

- Our insatiable need or craving for too much of anything is symptomatic of unmet needs or what we call "empty places."
- Salvation does not equal satisfaction. (You can be saved and still be dissatisfied.)
- Satisfaction comes only when every empty place is filled with the fullness of Christ.
- While salvation comes to us as a gift of God, we find satisfaction in Him as we deliberately surrender all parts of our lives to Him.

I'm going to tell you a big secret: Christians who are supposed to be fully satisfied with Jesus often still harbor an unidentifiable emptiness or need. Our unwillingness to be truthful about our lack of satisfaction in the Christian life keeps us from asking the right questions: Why do I find the Christian life lacking? How can I be more satisfied? Because we don't ask questions inside the circle of believers, the enemy tempts us to look outside for godless answers.

Remember that finding satisfaction in God is one of the five benefits of our covenant relationship with Christ. Finding satisfaction and fullness in Christ was never meant to be a secret treasure that only a few could find. Satisfaction is a blessed by-product of our relationship with God, and it is meant for every believer.

Peter expressed God's intention clearly: "His divine power has given us everything we need for life and godliness through our knowledge of him who called us by his own glory and goodness" (2 Pet. 1:3). Either Christ can satisfy us and meet our deepest needs, or God's Word is deceptive. In the days before I began to enjoy the fullness of Christ, I somehow knew God's Word was true and that the problem rested with me; but, for the life of me, I couldn't figure out what the problem was. I served Him. I even had a love for Him, however immature; but I still fought an emptiness that kept me looking for love and acceptance in all the wrong places.

Never once in my youth did I hear clear teaching about the Spirit-filled life. Perhaps this is the reason I refuse to shut up about it now. Let's boil a few things down to the basics.

John 4:24 tells us that God's essence or state of existence is spirit. Don't get the idea that the word *spirit* implies invisible. God definitely has a visible, however glorious and indescribable, form; but we do not presently have eyes that can behold the spirit world. Just as surely as God is spirit, God is love (1 John 4:16). Love is not only something God does; love is something God is. God would have to stop being in order to stop loving. Again, our temptation is to humanize God, because we are limited to understanding love as a verb. With God, love is first a noun. It's what and who He is.

We know from 1 John 4:13–15 and Romans 8:9 that, in the form of the Holy Spirit, God takes up residence in the lives of all who receive His Son as Savior. God can no more cease being love than He can cease being spirit; therefore, when the Spirit of God moves into our lives, the love of God comes, too. Remember the promise of 2 Corinthians 3:17: "Where the Spirit of the Lord is, there is freedom."

See how it all fits together? Wherever God is welcomed, His Spirit is loosed. Wherever the Spirit is loosed, so is His love. And wherever you find His loving Spirit, you find freedom. How is the Spirit of God loosed? Through confessing or agreeing with His Word. We will focus on this last element later, but I wanted you to see all the pieces fit together.

My point is this: only the places we allow the love of God to fully penetrate will be satisfied and, therefore, liberated. Nothing expresses this truth better than the divinely inspired words of the apostle Paul:

> For this reason I kneel before the Father, from whom his whole family in heaven and on earth derives its name. I pray that out of his glorious riches he may strengthen you with power through his Spirit in your inner being, so that Christ may dwell in your hearts through faith. And I pray that you, being rooted and established in love, may have power, together with all the saints, to grasp how wide and long and high and deep is the love of Christ, and to know this love that surpasses knowledge—that you may be filled to the measure of all the fullness of God.

Now to him who is able to do immeasurably more than all we ask or imagine, according to his power that is at work within us, to him be glory in the church and in Christ Jesus throughout all generations, for ever and ever! Amen. (Eph. 3:14–21)

In this passage the apostle taught what God deeply desires for us:

1. *To be rooted and established in love* (v. 17). Whose love? His love. The Greek word for "rooted" is *rhizoo*, meaning "to be rooted, strengthened with roots, firmly fixed, constant." A plant or tree is as strong as its roots are deep. The deeper you and I are rooted in the unfailing love of God, the less we sway when the winds of life blow harshly.

2. *To have the power to grasp the colossal love of Christ* (v. 18). The word for "grasp" is *katalambano*, meaning "to lay hold of, seize with eagerness, suddenness . . . an allusion to the public games, to obtain the prize with the idea of eager and strenuous exertion." God longs for us to eagerly lay hold of the depth, length, breadth, and height of Christ's love.

We study so many other things, but how about exerting some energy on grasping the love of Christ? Later we'll discover a few reasons why seeking to accept, grasp, and abide fully in God's love is energy so well spent. Look back at the definition for a moment and note the English synonym *suddenness*. I love this part of the definition because I've experienced times when I seemed suddenly to grab hold of the enormity of Christ's love for a moment.

I remember a time when I was experiencing a deep hurt in my heart. Keith and I usually walk together in the evening, but this particular night he wasn't home. All I felt like doing was sobbing, but I decided to throw on the headphones, play some good worship music, and walk out on the neighborhood golf course all by myself. The night was pitch black, and no one appeared to be on the course but me. The more the music rang through my soul, the more the tears of my wounds turned to tears of worship. Finally, I stopped walking, lifted both my hands in praise, and worshiped Him. Flashes of distant lightning began to burst in the sky like fireworks on the Fourth of July. The more I sang, the more the Spirit of God seemed to dance through the flashes of lightning. I haven't had many experiences like this one, but I believe God allowed me a sudden, flashing grasp of His amazing love.

Can you think of a time when you were suddenly awash with the magnitude of God's love for you personally? If not, ask Him to make you more aware. God's love is demonstrative. Ask Him to widen your spiritual vision so that you can behold unexpected evidences of His amazing love.

3. *To know Christ's love that surpasses knowledge* (v. 19). Look closely at the words *know* and *knowledge*. Those of us who speak English would assume those two words were the same, but the Greek language is more specific. The word *know* in this verse is *ginosko,* meaning to "come to know . . . in a judicial sense, to know by trial . . . to learn, find out . . . in the sense of to perceive . . . it could be said that *ginosko* means to believe." Now let's see how it differs from the word *knowledge* used at the end of the phrase. *Knowledge* in this passage comes from the Greek word *gnosis,* meaning "present and fragmentary knowledge as contrasted with epignosis, clear and exact knowledge." The apostle Paul meant for us to come to know and learn by experience Christ's love that surpasses all present and fragmentary knowledge. Paul prayed for us to perceive a depth of love that surpasses any kind of limited knowledge our minds could now grasp. Christ longs for you to know—by trial through walking with Him daily—a love you cannot begin to comprehend.

4. *To be filled to the measure of all the fullness of God* (v. 19). Now watch this all come together. The word *filled* is the Greek word *pleroo,* meaning "to make full, fill, particularly to fill a vessel or hollow place."

Remember those empty places? They probably cause us more havoc than almost anything in our lives! They grow from hardships, injustices, losses, and unmet needs, not to mention the hand of God, who carves out places only He can fill. When you received Christ, God's Spirit took up residence inside of you. Through the filling of the Holy Spirit, He desires to permeate every inch of your life and fill up every hollow place with the fullness of His love.

Remember our greatest desire according to Proverbs 19:22? God has what you need. He alone has unfailing love, and He wants to flood your life with it. The fullness of God is not a one-time occurrence like our salvation. Every day of our lives—to live victoriously—we must learn to pour out our hearts to God, confess sin daily so nothing will hinder Him, acknowledge every hollow place, and invite Him to fill us fully! Then we need to continue to fan the flame of His love by reading Scripture, listening to edifying music, and praying often. We also need to avoid things that obviously quench His Spirit. When you make a daily practice of inviting His love to fill your hollow places and make sure you are not hindering the process, God will begin to satisfy you more than a double cheeseburger!

I practice what I'm "preaching" here almost every day. I begin the day with God's Word. Somewhere in the midst of my morning time with God, I ask Him to satisfy all my longings and fill all my hollow places with His lavish, unfailing love. This frees me from craving the approval of others and requiring others to fill my "cup." Then, if someone takes the time to demonstrate love to me, that's the overflow! I am free to appreciate it and enjoy it, but I didn't emotionally require it!

See how the love of God brings freedom? Not only am I freed; I am able to free others from having to boost me up emotionally all the time. Hallelujah! Where the Spirit of the Lord's lavish love is, there is freedom!! Try it and see!

If we're not experiencing satisfaction in God, a hindrance exists, and we want to identify it and ask God to remove it. Ordinarily, the primary hindrance to satisfaction in our lives is refusing Him access to our empty places.

CHAPTER 36

FAILURE TO BELIEVE
GOD'S UNFAILING LOVE

*For God so loved the world that he gave his one and only Son, that whoever
believes in him shall not perish but have eternal life.*

(JOHN 3:16)

I believe Christ's bride, the church made up of all believers, is ill. She is
pale and frail. Not because of judgment. Not because of neglect. Not
because she doesn't have plenty to eat and drink. The meat of God's
Word and the drink of His Spirit are there for her taking. Not because
of warfare. She's bruised by the enemy, but he's not the one who is making her sick. He's just taking advantage of the opportunity. Her malady
comes from within. Christ's bride is ill with unbelief. We don't recognize
the illness because most of us have suffered with it all our lives.

Several years ago I slowly began noticing my energy level was lower
than usual. About the time I became convinced something was wrong,
I'd have a little burst of energy and decide I was imagining things.
Finally, I got a blood test. I told a friend later in the day how mad I was
at myself for spending the money on the test. "I feel fine! Occasionally
I'm a little tired, that's all. I wish I hadn't gone to the expense."

That evening the doctor called. He immediately put me to bed for two weeks with a fierce case of mononucleosis.

I kept asking him if he was certain. "I don't feel that bad. I'm just tired!" A few months later, I could not believe how good I felt. I finally realized that I had been sick for so long, I had forgotten how wellness felt!

I believe that the church suffers from a strength-sapping case of unbelief; but we've had the ailment so long, we don't know how good authentic belief feels. The healthiest Christians you will ever meet are not those with perfect physiques but those who take a daily dose of God's Word and choose to believe it works!

When I began to research and pray about this study, God kept repeating a word over and over to my heart: *unbelief.* Unbelief! I kept sensing Him saying, "My people are suffering from unbelief!" At the time I felt that this word was a separate message from the material He was beginning to give me for *Breaking Free.* Finally, I got a clue! Belief is an absolute prerequisite to breaking free! Early in our study we talked about removing the boulder of overall unbelief; now I want to talk to you about a specific, debilitating area of unbelief.

I continue to see this statement in my mail: "I have such trouble really believing and accepting how much God loves me." So I began to ask God, "Lord, why do we have so much trouble believing and accepting Your love for us?" I offered God multiple-choice answers to my own question: "Is it our backgrounds? Our childhood hurts? The unsound teachings we've received? The unloving people who surround us?" I would have gone on and on except that He seemed to interrupt me— and He had the gall not to choose one of my multiple-choice answers.

As clearly as a bell, God spoke to my heart through His Spirit and said, "The answer to your question is the sin of unbelief." The thought never crossed my mind. Since then, it's never left my mind. Humor me for a moment. Suppose I heard God correctly. (I have certainly misread Him before!) Why do you think not believing God personally and lavishly loves us could be a sin?

Let me answer with an illustration. For several reasons, I am absolutely positive Keith loves me. He tells me several times a day. He shows me in all sorts of ways. He tells me he thinks about me often during the day. I know this is true because he calls me at least once or twice at work every day. He testifies of his love for me to others. Often someone will tell me they've seen Keith; then they'll remark, "He sure seems to love his wife."

A buddy of his said, "I'll tell you something, Keith. My wife is a great cook." Keith looked back at him, thought of my cooking, and wasn't sure what to say! Finally, he responded, "Well, my cook is a great wife!" We've laughed about it ever since!

Keith shows his love for me by telling me when he thinks I'm wrong. He loves me enough to stop me from saying or doing something foolish. If you're married and your spouse is not as loving, please don't despair! Let me remind you that God graciously delivered Keith and me from filing for divorce several times. Don't give up! God can work miracles! I've just stated a few reasons I'm convinced someone loves me so I can introduce evidence of God's lavish love. Here's my list.

1. *God* tells *us He loves us.*

> But it was because the LORD loved you and kept the
> oath he swore to your forefathers that he brought you
> out with a mighty hand and redeemed you from the
> land of slavery, from the power of Pharaoh king of
> Egypt. (Deut. 7:8)

You are forgiving and good, O Lord,
   abounding in love to all who call to you. (Psalm 86:5)

If they violate my decrees
   and fail to keep my commands,
I will punish their sin with the rod,
   their iniquity with flogging;
but I will not take my love from him,
   nor will I ever betray my faithfulness. (Ps. 89:31–33)

God's Word is full of His proclamations of love for you! He made sure to inscribe His love in His Word so you would never have to wait for a phone call. You can hear God tell you He loves you every single time you open the Word. When you're feeling unlovely, soak yourself in the proclamations of God's unfailing love for you!

2. *God* demonstrates *His love for us.* Perhaps you are loved by someone who is not very demonstrative. Many people have difficulty showing affection, but remember that God is not one of us. Innate in the nature of both *chesed* (Hebrew word for God's love) and *agape* (Greek word for God's love) is the demonstration of affection. Because God is love, He cannot keep from showing His love—even if He sometimes demonstrates it through discipline. He loves us through blessing, answered prayer, loving chastisement, constant care, intervention, and much more.

3. *God* thinks *about us constantly.* In John 17:24, Jesus said, "Father, I want those you have given me to be with me where I am." I think heaven will be heaven because He will be there, but He thinks it will be heaven because you will be there. A line from a song expresses it so well, "When He was on the Cross, I was on His mind." No matter what time of night you roll over in the bed and become conscious, you will catch God in the middle of a thought about you.

213

4. *God* testifies *to others how He loves us.* Does this happen to be a new thought for you? According to John 17:23, look how much God has loved you: "You sent me and have loved them even as you have loved me." Christ wants the whole world to know that God loves you and me just as God loves Him! God is proud to love you!

Why do we have such trouble believing and accepting the love of God? The question hits much harder this time, doesn't it? You see, unbelief regarding the love of God is the ultimate slap in His face. The world came into being from the foundation of God's love. God nailed down His love for us on the cross. Can you imagine the grief of our unbelief after all He's done? You may say, "But I just can't make myself feel like God loves me." Belief is not a feeling. It's a choice. We may live many days when we don't feel loved or lovely; but in spite of our emotions, we can choose to take God at His Word.

You may say, "But you don't know what I've been through!" Please hear my heart. I am completely compassionate, because I've also been hurt by people who were supposed to love me; but let me say this: no one has ever done more to show you that you were unloved than God has done to show you that you are loved.

If need be, make a list of ways you've become convinced no one could truly love you; then make a corresponding list of ways the God of all creation has told you differently. No list could compare to God's. Believer, let's get on our way to genuinely believing lives. Church, let's rise up from our sickbed of unbelief. How do we begin? We begin by repenting of our unbelief. Then we cry out with the man in Mark 9:24: "Help me overcome my unbelief!"

CHAPTER 37

THE FRUIT OF UNFAILING LOVE

Sow for yourselves righteousness,
reap the fruit of unfailing love,
and break up your unplowed ground;
for it is time to seek the LORD,
until He comes
and showers righteousness on you.

(HOS. 10:12)

Those who believe God loves differ from all others. Look at the way God's love impacted the lives of key figures in Scripture. I hope you'll find these reasons inviting enough to want to be among those who choose to take God at His loving Word.

Moses penned his conviction that in His unfailing love God would lead His people to His "holy dwelling" (Exod. 15:13). David wrote that "The LORD'S unfailing love / surrounds the man who trusts in him" (Ps. 32:10). After the destruction of Jerusalem, Jeremiah recognized that "though he brings grief, he will show compassion, / so great is his unfailing love" (Lam. 3:32). The apostle Paul wrote, "Because of his great love for us, God, who is rich in mercy, made us alive with Christ even when we were dead in transgressions" (Eph. 2:4–5).

Ephesians 5:1–2 articulates the effect of God's love on His children: "As dearly loved children . . . live a life of love, just as Christ loved us." God calls us to act like the dearly loved children we are. Give this admonition some thought. To gain insight, let's draw a parallel between God's children and the children of earthly parents. We don't need a degree in childhood development to imagine how differently children feel and behave based on whether they believe they are truly loved.

In my own family experience, God has taught me two things:

1. God is the only One who can love anyone to wholeness.

2. Even almighty God refuses to make anyone accept his love.

We can draw a number of similarities between earthly parents and God, but we must recognize an important difference. Sometimes earthly parents are unloving or unable to express love appropriately. God, however, is not human. We cannot create His love in our image!

God loves perfectly. His love is both vocal and demonstrative. He balances blessing and discipline. God's love is unfailing, so any time we perceive He does not love us, our perceptions are wrong. Anything we perceive about God that does not match up with either the truth of Scripture or the portrayal of His character in Scripture is a lie.

When we realize we've been believing a lie, our bonds lose their grip. At those times we might pray something like: "I may not feel loved or lovable, but Your Word says You love me so much that You gave Your Son for me. I don't know why I continue to feel unloved, but at this moment I choose to believe the truth of Your Word. I rebuke the enemy's attempts to make me doubt Your love. I also pray for forgiveness for the sin of unbelief. Help me overcome my unbelief."

Long-term liberation comes from accompanying God on a trek to (1) identify the problem, (2) demolish the stronghold, and (3) continue to walk in truth. The first step takes one moment. The second and third steps represent a process, because getting to know the Healer is more important than the healing. Let's spend the remainder of our lesson examining the fruit of God's unfailing love by analyzing the child described in Ephesians 5:1–2 who knows he is dearly loved.

1. *The child of God who trusts God's love possesses security in God's leadership.* Exodus 15:13 says, "In your unfailing love you will lead / the people you have redeemed." God promises us that we are not left to wander around aimlessly until we enter heaven. According to Jeremiah 29:11, He knows the plans He has for us. He leads those He has redeemed so they will fulfill His wonderful plan. What a comfort to know that the places God chooses to lead us always flow out of His unfailing love.

2. *The child of God who trusts God's love possesses security in salvation.* God never will cease loving. I love psalms like Psalm 13, where David boldly asks God, "How long, O LORD? Will you forget me forever? / How long will you hide your face from me?" (v. 1). We can pour our frustration from our hearts with courage because we know the father will not reject us.

3. *The child of God who trusts God's love possesses security in God's mercy.* In Psalm 51:1, King David cried out, "Have mercy on me, O God, / according to your unfailing love." Please receive this truth: God cannot be unbiased toward you. He cannot set His love for you aside and make an objective decision. Once you become God's covenant child, He cannot see you through anything less than a loving Father's eyes.

4. *The child of God who trusts God's love possesses security in His comfort.* Psalm 119:76 says, "May your unfailing love be my comfort, / according to your promise." So, what is our comfort in death? The unfailing love of God. What is our comfort in life? Sometimes harder than death—the unfailing love of God.

5. *The child of God who trusts God's love possesses security in His defense.* In Psalm 143:12, King David said, "In your unfailing love, silence my enemies; / destroy all my foes, / for I am your servant." When your heart belongs to God, those who are against you are against God. He takes personally any wrongs that are done to you. God upholds your cause (Lam. 3:59). Do you realize that if our hearts are humble and right before God, we can hand over to Him all the conflicts and foes that rise up against us?

Our list could go on and on. In fact, I encourage you to look up every verse containing the words *unfailing love,* meditate on them, and believe them!

PART VI

FREEDOM AND SPLENDOR

We draw near the grand climax of our journey. Not the end, but the beginning of a grander, fuller walk with God. Benefit 5 points us to the wonderful hallmark of our destination: The land where we become a display of His splendor. The country whose inhabitants share a common trait—all enjoy the presence of the King.

Can you imagine it? Living fully the life God intends. What could be a greater portrait of genuine freedom? To be truly free is to

- know God and believe Him,
- glorify God,
- find satisfaction in God,
- experience God's peace, and
- enjoy God's presence.

Memorize the great promise of Benefit 5:

When you pass through the waters,
     I will be with you;
and when you pass through the rivers,
     they will not sweep over you.

When you walk through the fire,
   you will not be burned;
   the flames will not set you ablaze.

For I am the LORD, your God,
   the Holy One of Israel, your Savior;
I give Egypt for your ransom,
      Cush and Seba in your stead. (Isa. 43:2–3)

CHAPTER 38

A VIEW FROM THE OLD

You will keep in perfect peace
him whose mind is steadfast,
because he trusts in you.

(ISA. 26:3)

Freedom from strongholds is serious business. In-depth study and deliberate application of truth are not just helpful but absolute necessities for those who choose liberty. We win freedom on the battlefield of the mind.

Notice in Isaiah 26:3 the inclusion of trust in the life of the one who possesses a steadfast mind. Only a trusting heart will approach God honestly with the secret struggles of the mind. When we offer a trusting heart and an honest, open mind to God, renewal is on its way. Through the power of the Holy Spirit, I pray we will be able to accomplish three primary goals in this section of our study.

1. Research the concept of the steadfast mind from Scripture.
2. Illustrate with a five-step process how to develop a steadfast mind.
3. Learn to apply the five-step process to virtually any stronghold.

Resist the temptation to take any shortcuts! I believe these chapters will be a supernatural turning point for all who take advantage of what they learn. Pause and ask God to give you deep insight into His Word.

Few biblical subjects are more controversial than spiritual warfare and the battlefield of the mind. Many events and passages of Scripture demonstrate that Satan deals directly with the human mind. In the parable of the soils, Jesus said Satan comes and takes away the Word sown in some people (Mark 4:15). In the story of Ananias and Sapphira, Peter said Satan had filled their hearts to lie to the Holy Spirit. Paul warned that Satan seeks to lead believers' minds astray (2 Cor. 11:3). Clearly Satan engages us at the point of our thought lives.

We must use Scripture to win on the battlefield called the mind. In this chapter we are going to dig into the Hebrew meanings in Isaiah 26:3. In the next we will examine the Greek meanings in 2 Corinthians 10:3–5. Carefully read Isaiah's words again:

You will keep in perfect peace
him whose mind is steadfast,
because he trusts in you. (Isa. 26:3)

Phrase 1: "You will keep." Satan is cunning. Our knowledge alone will not keep us protected. What you and I need is a watchman sitting guard on the walls of our mind. Here is the good news: we have One who is willing and able—if we will also set our minds on Him. In Isaiah 26:3, the Hebrew word for "keep" is *nasar,* meaning "to guard, protect, keep; used to denote guarding a vineyard . . . and a fortress. Those who performed this function were called 'watchmen.'" Psalm 139 makes it clear that God knows us completely. Thus He is the perfect candidate for watchman over our minds. No wonder the psalm ends with the words: "Search me, O God, and know my heart; / test me and know my anxious thoughts. / See if there is any offensive way in me" (vv. 23–24).

What we're talking about is serious business. Romans 1:28–32 teaches that surrendering our thought lives to God is not just a means to more consistent victory; it is the safeguard against finally being given over to a depraved mind. We can persist so long in our willful wrong thinking that God can give us over to our desires.

Phrase 2: "in perfect peace." Before we determine what this phrase means, let's set the record straight concerning what it doesn't mean. Isaiah 26:3 doesn't say God will give us perfect minds if we are steadfast in Him. He says He will give us perfect peace in our imperfect minds. The Hebrew term translated "perfect peace" may be familiar to you. *Shalom* means "to be safe, be complete . . . As an adjective it means well, peaceful, whole, secure . . . friendly, healthy, sound . . . Though *shalom* can mean the absence of strife, it usually signifies much more. It essentially denotes a satisfied condition, a state of peacefulness, a sense of well being. It is used of a prosperous relationship between two or more parties."

God is faithful to His Word. If you remain steadfast in Him, a two-fold prosperity is inevitable. Both the kingdom of God and you will be built up. Just as surely as the kingdom of God prospers when we are steadfast in Him, so our own hearts and minds benefit.

Phrase 3: "him whose mind is steadfast." The Hebrew word for "mind" is *yetser.* The word sounds like what my siblings and I were expected to say every time our dad, the Army major, told us to do something. The mind is certainly where we decide if we're going to say "yes, sir" or "no, sir" every time our heavenly Father tells us to do something! *Yetser* means "frame, pattern, image; conception, imagination, thought; device . . . it is what is formed in the mind (i.e., plans and purposes)." Look carefully at the word frame in the Hebrew definition of *yetser.* The implication of the word should be understood more in terms of a picture frame than our physical frame or body. In essence, our minds work to frame every circumstance, temptation, and experience we have. We see events from our own perspective and context.

Have you noticed how two people can look at the same experience so differently? They put the event in different frames and act accordingly. Our reaction depends on how we have framed the event.

Recall a crisis in your home. Perhaps a number of people were affected, but you probably noticed how different the reactions and responses were. You see, each person's mind worked differently to frame the same situation. Often we cause ourselves more pain by the way we frame events than the events themselves cause. Let's pretend we've already won the battle over our thought lives. How could you frame that particular situation differently?

The original definition of the word *steadfast* will help us determine whether or not we're on the right track. *Samak* means "to sustain . . . to be braced . . . to lean upon." One part of the definition draws a wonderful word picture to help us visualize the steadfast life in God: "to lay (one's hand on)." When temptations and troubling thoughts come, steadfast believers choose to lay their hands on God's Word and know that it's the truth.

When I first discovered this definition, I thought of a time when I had been hurt by someone close to me. The pain in my heart felt like a searing hot iron. My thoughts were troubled. I knew that the only way to battle the lies of the evil one was to lay a firm hold on truth. I found that during the day, I could read or quote Scripture when my thoughts began to defeat me, but nighttime seemed an altogether different challenge. My worst attacks came at night.

At the risk of being labeled a lunatic (I've been called worse), I'll tell you what I did during the most intense part of the battle. When I got into bed at night, I turned to Scripture that spoke truth to my circumstances. I would literally lay my head on my open Bible until I fell asleep. The Holy Spirit never failed to bring my mind comfort and relief. Had my action not been mixed with faith, it would have served little purpose, but because I believed God would spiritually accomplish what my posture simply symbolized, the enemy was not able to defeat me.

Let's conclude with a brief look at the final phrase in Isaiah 26:3.

Phrase 4: "because he trusts in you." The Hebrew word for "trust" is *batach*, meaning "to attach oneself . . . to confide in, feel safe, be confident, secure." Picture a small child with her mother or father. I want to trust God like that child trusts her mom or dad.

As we conclude this chapter, let's ponder an important fact: Those who have never given their hearts fully to God are not likely to offer Him the deepest, darkest crevices of their minds. Would you consider concluding with a prayer asking for a deeper trust so that you are more likely to have an open mind in which God can work? Remember, His plan is "not to harm you" but "to prosper you" (Jer. 29:11). Invite Him to be the watchman on the wall of your mind.

CHAPTER 39

A VIEW FROM THE NEW

For though we live in the world, we do not wage war as the world does. The weapons we fight with are not the weapons of the world. On the contrary, they have divine power to demolish strongholds. We demolish arguments and every pretension that sets itself up against the knowledge of God, and we take captive every thought to make it obedient to Christ.

(2 COR. 10:3–5)

In our previous chapter we researched the steadfast mind from the Old Testament perspective in Isaiah 26:3. Let's compare this wonderful Old Testament passage with the New Testament perspective in 2 Corinthians. While the prophet Isaiah's words exude refreshment and security, the apostle Paul's words pack a serious punch. God inspired both men to essentially make the same point. Paul simply made his point with a pair of boxing gloves. Now we will research what he had to say in 2 Corinthians 10:3–5.

Phrase 1: "divine power to demolish strongholds" (v. 4). The Greek word for "demolish" is *kathairesis,* meaning "demolition, destruction of a fortress." The original word for "stronghold" comes from the word *echo,* meaning "to hold fast." The derivative, *ochuroma,* means "a stronghold, fortification, fortress. Used metaphorically of any strong points or arguments in which one trusts." You might think of the term this way: a stronghold is anything we hold on to that ends up holding us.

Now let's consider what Paul meant by demolishing strongholds. The word *demolish* implies a kind of destruction requiring tremendous power; to be exact, divine power. Much of the reason believers have remained in a yoke of slavery is because we swat at our strongholds like they are mosquitoes. Strongholds are like concrete fortresses we've constructed around our lives block by block, ordinarily over the course of years. We created them, whether or not we were aware, for protection and comfort. Remember the shelters in Gideon's day? Inevitably, however, these fortresses become prisons. At some point we realize we no longer control them. They control us.

Human effort is useless in demolishing strongholds. No amount of discipline or determination will do it. Satanic strongholds require divine demolition. Discipline and determination are often important factors in opening your life to the supernatural power of God, but only He can provide the divine dynamite needed to destroy a stronghold.

Last year I had the privilege of tracing the apostle Paul's travels in Greece and Rome. As I stood on the grounds of ancient Corinth facing the ruins of what was once a thriving city, I saw a fortress in the distance on top of the tallest mountain. I asked the guide to identify the structure. She responded, "It's an ancient stronghold. Virtually every ancient Greek city had a stronghold or a fortress on top of the highest peak in the vicinity. In times of war, it was considered practically impenetrable and unapproachable. It was the place of hiding for the governors of the cities in times of insecurity."

I was astonished. I was looking at the very stronghold the apostle Paul used as an analogy when he wrote these words to the people of Corinth. As I stared at the imposing fortress that still stood proudly at the top of the mountain after centuries had eroded the buildings below,

I realized why the opposing army gave up. Sadly, we have too often done the same thing. My prayer is that each of us will say, "No more!"

Remember, Satan's power comes from his ability to bluff. Once we learn the truth and how to use it, he loses his hold. Look back at the last statement the guide made to me. She described a stronghold as the place of hiding . . . in times of insecurity.

Think about a stronghold you've experienced. What part did insecurity play?

Without a doubt, insecurity played a major role in the strongholds the enemy built in my life. An important part of learning to live in victory has been discerning the heart rumblings of insecurity. I have learned to dramatically increase my prayer life and time in God's Word during times when my security is threatened.

A primary example occurred with the loss of my precious mom. I knew that even during my time of mourning, I would be unwise to neglect God's Word or avoid my prayer time. Even if all I did was cry, at least I was drawing close enough to God that Satan couldn't build a wedge between us. I haven't always responded rightly at times of insecurity; but when I have, Satan has failed to gain an advantage.

Phrase 2: "We demolish arguments and every pretension" (v. 5). The Greek word for "arguments" is *logismos,* meaning "a reckoning, calculation, consideration, reflection. In the Classical Greek writers, [*logismos* was] used of the consideration and reflection preceding and determining conduct." These arguments are our rationalizations for the strongholds we continue to possess in our lives. We maintain excuses for not surrendering areas of our lives to the authority of Christ. You've had them. I've had them. Never forget that Satan persists where a stronghold exists. He supplies an endless list of rationalizations for the things we do and refuse to do.

Can you think of an excuse or rationalization that no longer has power over you? If so, never forget that the same God who came to your aid before will come to your aid again! You may feel your present obstacles are larger, but I assure you God doesn't. He is all-powerful.

Now, let's look at the other primary word in this phrase: *pretension.* The Greek word *hupsoma* means "something made high, elevated, a high place . . . figuratively of a proud adversary, a lofty tower or fortress built up proudly by the enemy. Pride." I believe we can draw three conclusions about strongholds based on this definition:

1. Every stronghold is related to something we have exalted to a higher position than God in our lives.

2. Every stronghold pretends to bring something we feel we must have: aid, comfort, the relief of stress, or protection.

3. Every stronghold in the life of a believer is a tremendous source of pride for the enemy. Let that make you mad and determine to stop giving him satisfaction.

Often, the enemy will stir pride in us to keep strongholds from being broken. Humility is a necessary part of the mind-set for someone ready to be free. I have a friend who works with alcoholics through a Christ-centered twelve-step ministry. He always emphasizes that the crucial step toward sobriety is humility. His words remind us that in the body of Christ, the proud are never the free.

Phrase 3: "that sets itself up against the knowledge of God" (v. 5). The Greek word for the phrase "sets itself up" is *epairo,* meaning "to hoist up as a sail . . . to lift up the eyes, meaning to look upon." I want to make a point that will be emphasized in a later chapter: Satan's goal is to be worshiped. This is what he's always wanted.

Satan's desire to be worshiped fuels his rebellion against God. If Satan can't get people to worship him directly, he accomplishes his goal by tempting people to worship something or someone other than God.

God created us to worship. We all worship something. According to the definition of *epairo,* the focus of our worship can be determined by the gaze of our eyes—what or who is the object of our primary focus. Don't miss this: whatever we worship, we will also obey. Look at the first part of the definition: "to hoist up as a sail." What purpose does the sail on a vessel serve?

Arguments and sails serve both to propel and to determine the direction of the vessel. I hope you're seeing biblical proof of something you've already known experientially: strongholds affect behaviors! The enemy cannot enter a believer. We are sealed by the Holy Spirit of God (Eph. 1:13–14). The enemy cannot make us do anything. He can only lead us to do things. Strongholds are the cords of the yoke by which Satan attempts to lead us.

Hosea 11:4 says of God, "I led them with cords of human kindness, / with ties of love." As I reflect on my history with God and how He is singlehandedly responsible for my liberty, I am almost moved to tears over this verse. Satan, the ultimate counterfeiter, also desires to lead us. God leads us "with cords of human kindness" and "ties of love." Satan presses the yoke on our necks as he leads us with cords of falsehood and ties of lies.

Look at the last part of this phrase: "against the knowledge of God." Again we're reminded why knowing the truth is the key to liberty (John 8:32). If we don't know God's Word (His knowledge expressed to us), we can hardly recognize what is setting itself up against the knowledge of God. The more we know God's Word, the quicker we recognize Satan's attempts to cover it by hoisting his sail over it.

Phrase 4: "we take captive every thought" (v. 5). For now, I just want to research the meaning of the phrase. We will spend time later on how we captivate our thoughts to Christ or, as the prophet Isaiah conceptualized it, how we practice the "steadfast mind." The phrase "we take captive" comes from the Greek word *aichmalotizo,* meaning "a prisoner, captive, to lead captive . . . By implication, to subdue, bring into subjection." The verb tense in this phrase implies a repeated and continuous action.

We're all looking for a quick fix, but God is after lasting change—lifestyle Christianity. To possess a steadfast mind is to practice a steadfast mind. You and I have been controlled and held prisoner by destructive, negative, and misleading thoughts for too long. Through the divine power of the Holy Spirit, we can take our thoughts prisoner instead!

Phrase 5: "to make it obedient to Christ" (v. 5). God wants us to be victors. We don't become victors by conquering the enemy. We become victors through surrender to Christ. We don't become victors by our independence from the enemy. We become victors by our dependence on God.

The road to freedom seems to be a paradox. To experience victory and freedom we need to become captives. We need to develop minds captive to Christ. In this life, we are most free whose minds are captivated by Christ. Victorious lives flow from victorious thoughts. Thinking victorious thoughts comes from setting our focus on a victorious God.

This complicated lesson concludes rather simply: We can be led astray by the cords of an evil yoke, or we can be led to victory by the cords of divine love. We have important work to do in the chapters to come. Remember, this war is for freedom, and the battlefield is the mind. Before you begin the next chapter, please spend a little extra time allowing God to cleanse your heart and clear your mind. Joshua's exhortation to the children of Israel applies to us beautifully today: "Consecrate yourselves, for tomorrow the LORD will do amazing things among you" (Josh. 3:5). The wonders God wants to do in all our tomorrows are prepared for in our todays.

CHAPTER 40

TEARING DOWN THE
HIGH PLACES

Your enemies will cower before you,
and you will trample down their high places.

(DEUT. 33:29)

We researched the Old Testament concept of the steadfast mind and the New Testament concept of the captive mind. Gathering information, however, would do us little good if we didn't learn to apply it. For the next three chapters, we will study a five-step process. The following illustrations picture the journey from captivity to our thoughts to taking our thoughts captive to Christ. Before we go through each step individually, take a moment to study the following illustrations so you can begin to conceptualize the goal.

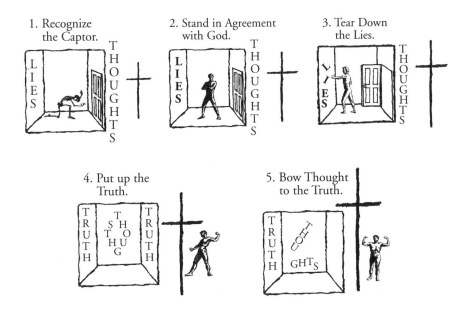

1. Recognize the Captor.

2. Stand in Agreement with God.

3. Tear Down the Lies.

4. Put up the Truth.

5. Bow Thought to the Truth.

The process we are going to study can apply to absolutely anything or anyone who is captivating our thoughts. Imagine how being the victim of rape could captivate your mind and nearly destroy you. Deep compassion floods my heart as I realize that many readers of this statement know from personal experience. If we don't surrender our minds to Christ, the loss of a loved one also can take us from appropriate grief and mourning to a lifetime of agonizing captivity. Remember, Satan fights dirty. He jumps on anything that could keep you from centering your thoughts on Christ.

Not all captivating thoughts come from painful experiences. Our thoughts can be held captive to someone or something that builds up our egos or satisfies our fleshly appetites. Simply put, captivating thoughts are controlling thoughts—things you find yourself meditating on too often.

Taking thoughts captive to Christ doesn't mean we never have the thought again. It means we learn to "think the thought" as it relates to

Christ and who we are in Him. I will always have thoughts of my precious mother; but when I relate the thoughts to Christ, they will cause me less and less despair. They will not control me. With the power of the Holy Spirit, I will control them. Seems impossible or too hard to attain? Don't give in. Stay with me throughout this process and believe God will do a miraculous work in your heart and mind. Let's begin to study each illustration that will teach us how to go from overcome to overcomer.

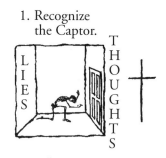

1. Recognize the Captor.

This drawing illustrates the imprisoned believer held captive by controlling thoughts. The cross shows she knows Christ but that something has grown between her and her Lord. That something has grown so large, in fact, that it has become the captor, and the believer has become the prisoner. The controlling thoughts have become a high place.

Have you noticed that no small disobedience exists? Disregarding God's commands always bears bitter fruit sooner or later. Some of Israel's kings who otherwise followed God's ways still failed to tear down the high places. Ultimately, the oversight took its toll. A kingdom resulted in which God's own people sacrificed their children on the altar of pagan gods.

We can compare our strongholds to the high places in ancient Israel. Anything we exalt over God in our thoughts or imaginations is an idol.

Idolatry is not only a terrible affront to God; it is also an open invitation to disaster. Never forget the ever-increasing nature of sin (Rom. 6:19). I don't believe I'm being overly dramatic when I say that we can either tear down our strongholds with the mighty power of God or they will eventually tear us down.

Please keep in mind that we don't have to love something or someone to idolize or exalt it in our minds. We can easily idolize something we hate. I'll never forget realizing that a person I felt I couldn't forgive had become an idol to me through my unforgiveness. Humanly speaking, I didn't even like the person, yet Satan had seized my imagination until the whole situation stole my focus and therefore became idolatrous to me.

Now take a look at the next illustration:

2. Stand in Agreement
with God.

In our second illustration the believer has come to her feet. She is not yet free from the captive, controlling thoughts; but something important has occurred: she has confessed her sin. In 1 John 1:9 the word *confess* means more than simply admitting our sin to God. The Greek word is *homologeo*. The first part of the word, *homo*, means "the same," and the second part, *logeo*, means "to speak." Confession means coming to the point of saying the same thing God says about any specific matter.

For the believer the first step of freedom from any stronghold is agreeing with God concerning the personal sin involved. Please understand, the object itself of our imaginations is not always sin. The sin may lie solely in the exaltation of it in our own minds. For example, nothing could be more reflective of the heart of God than a mother's love for her child. However, if she has passed the bounds of healthy affection to overprotection, obsession, and idolatry, she has constructed a stronghold.

Let's take the same relationship one painful step further. Nothing could be more natural than a mother grieving the loss of a child. However, if ten years later the mother is still completely consumed with the loss and bitterness that have eclipsed all comfort and healing, she has wedged a stronghold between appropriate grief and gradual restoration. The enemy will capitalize on normal emotions of love or loss to swell them out of healthy proportion. They can consume our very lives if we're not aware of his schemes. Loving is never sin. However, obsession that flows from putting something in the place of God is sin. Likewise, grief is never sin, but disallowing God to minister comfort and healing to you over the passage of much time is.

Virtually anything that cheats you of what God has for you could be considered sin. I say this with compassion, but I must say it, because some of us may not be recognizing how Satan has taken advantage of normal, healthy emotions. We easily view adultery, robbery, or murder as sin, but we often don't realize that sin can also be anything we allow to grow between us and the completing work of God. So the first step in freedom is agreeing with God's Word about your personal stronghold or high place. As you can see in the illustration, the believer is still not fully liberated from captivity; but she is no longer bowing down to the enemy in her thought life.

As we conclude this lesson, consider these questions.

- If you are aware of a stronghold or high place presently existing in your life, have you come to a place of agreeing with God's Word and confessing all sin involved?

- If you are aware of a stronghold in your life that you've never agreed with God about and confessed all sin involved, would you be willing to do so now?
- If you are not aware of any stronghold in your life, can you remember a time in the past when Christ led you to freedom through honesty and confession of the sin involved?

The divine power of God is available to all of us who will agree to apply it. Once you learn how to use God's Word and live in His Spirit, "Your enemies will cower before you, / and you will trample down their high places" (Deut. 33:29).

CHAPTER 41

DEPROGRAMMING AND REPROGRAMMING

But encourage one another daily, as long as it is called Today, so that none of you may be hardened by sin's deceitfulness.

(HEB. 3:13)

We're now ready to move to the third illustration:

3. Tear Down
the Lies.

Illustration 3 shows that an important turning point has occurred. Once we are willing to see the sin involved in the stronghold and agree with God through confession, we begin to see the lies surrounding us. Tearing down the lies wallpapering our minds causes the prison door to swing open.

Satan does not have the power or authority to lock believers in a prison of oppression, but he works overtime to talk us into staying. He woos us into prison cells with all the lures he has perfected, but he cannot lock the doors. Unfortunately, Satan doesn't require a written invitation. Failure to post a "keep away" sign through Bible study and prayer can be invitation by default.

Look at Illustration 3 again. Picture the captivity of our thought life like a prison cell wallpapered in lies. Demolition of strongholds really begins when we expose and tear down the lies fueling our strongholds. We cannot repeat this fact enough: deception is the glue that holds a stronghold together. By the time a stronghold exists, our minds are covered with lies.

Where do these lies originate? John 8:43–45 tells us that Satan is the father of lies and "when he lies, he speaks his native language." Satan has to use lies because he is a totally defeated foe. Lies are all he has. That's why he has to be so adept at using them.

Now think about a stronghold you've battled or may be battling. Picture yourself in Illustration 3. Imagine you have agreed with God about the stronghold and confessed the sin involved. God then began to open your eyes to the lies plastered like graffiti on the walls of your mind. The illustration pictures you recognizing these lies that are wallpapered all over the prison cell and receiving the divine strength to rip them down.

As you picture yourself with eyes open to the lies, I want you to think what several of them were. I'll share a few of my own as a springboard for yours. The most powerful stronghold of my young life came from childhood victimization. As if the experiences themselves were not traumatic enough, I also believed many lies:

- I am worthless.
- All men will hurt you.

- When men hurt you, you can do nothing about it.
- You can't say no.
- I am not as good as my friends.
- If people knew what was happening to me, I would make them sick.
- I can never tell what has happened to me, or I'll be destroyed.
- I am the only one this has ever happened to, and it's all my fault.

And that's just one wall! I could have gone on and on with all the lies I believed.

Satan became far more sophisticated in my adult life. One yoke he put around my neck involved someone who came to me for help. Satan twisted the truth to make me believe I was responsible for helping this person. The enemy counterfeited God's concepts of mercy, compassion, and acceptance. The Holy Spirit signaled me not to get involved in the situation, but I chose what I thought was my religious duty over obedience. When I suggested we go to others for help, the response would always be: "I don't want anyone else involved." It was a trap set by the enemy. The person was certainly worth helping, but I was not the one to help. The problem was out of my league. I learned that if you don't listen to God and obey in the early stages, the longer you wait, the less discernment and strength you have.

Listen! Not every person who comes to you for help has been sent by God! We must learn to discern the schemes of the evil one. God used the encounter to teach me more than a college degree could have, but the lessons were excruciating.

A stronghold could be anything from compulsive eating to paranoia, from bitterness to obsessive love. No matter what it may be, all strongholds have one thing in common: Satan is fueling the mental tank with deception to keep the stronghold running.

I want to say something with tenderness and much compassion. If you know a stronghold exists somewhere in your life, but you cannot identify the lies, you are still a captive. If you've not yet recognized the lies that are keeping you glued to the prison cell, please ask God to drop the scales from your eyes and help you see! "Then you will know the truth, and the truth will set you free" (John 8:32).

Now, let's concentrate on our next illustration:

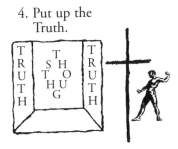

4. Put up the
Truth.

Hallelujah! Our captive has escaped the prison of her controlling thoughts and is very close to controlling them instead.

What has happened to set her free? First, she was forgiven for all sins involved in her stronghold the moment she agreed with God and confessed (Illus. 2). Because she fully cooperated with God, her eyes were opened to mind-binding lies, and she sought the divine strength necessary to tear them down (Illus. 3). Excellent progress, but thankfully she realized more needed to be done to make liberty in Christ a reality in life.

She didn't just tear down the wallpaper of lies on her prison walls, she determined to put up the truth in their place. Give this next statement your full attention: the walls of your mind will never stay bare. Never. Once we tear down lies, we must rewallpaper with truth, or the enemy will happily supply a new roll of his own. Different pattern maybe—a more updated look—but the same deceptive manufacturer.

I cannot emphasize this step enough. Illustration 4 represents our only means of both deprogramming and reprogramming our way out of captivity. Truth is the only way out. Say John 8:32 out loud until it sticks to your ribs: "Then you will know the truth, and the truth will set you free." Take it very literally.

We possess the mind of Christ (1 Cor. 2:16), but we still have the full capacity to think with the mind of the flesh. We are mentally bilingual, you might say. My older daughter is almost fluent in Spanish, but she still thinks mostly in English because she practices it more. The same concept is true of you and me. We will think with the mental language we practice most. In Romans 7 the apostle Paul portrayed the struggle with the two "languages." Look at the words of the apostle:

> So I find this law at work: When I want to do good, evil is right there with me. For in my inner being I delight in God's law; but I see another law at work in the members of my body, waging war against the law of my mind and making me a prisoner of the law of sin at work within my members. (Rom. 7:21–23)

How much can you relate to Paul's struggle? If you would answer "totally," count me right in there with you! However, I've learned to think far more victoriously. Here's what I've learned: God will not release us from anything that has enslaved us until we've come to the mind of Christ in the matter. Take the bondage of unforgiveness, for example. When we want to be free of the burden of not forgiving, we want God simply to take that person out of our minds. We want Him to wave a magic wand so we'll never think about the person again. That's not how God works. He wants to transform and renew our minds (Rom. 12:2) so we can think the thoughts of Christ about the person we are to forgive.

We will not be free until we adopt the mind of Christ in the matter that has enslaved us. If a believer has allowed Satan to build a stronghold through an adulterous relationship and she finally repents and desires to be free, her mind will not be released until she has torn down the lies and reprogrammed with the truth. She would probably beg God simply to remove the person from her mind. God knows that little would be accomplished by doing that, and she would be vulnerable to a similar attack again. Rather than drop the person from her mind, He wants her to begin to think the thoughts of Christ toward the situation and the person.

This process of applying God's truth to the matter is what brings the cross between the former captive and her thoughts. Once the mind of Christ has taken over, the power of the stronghold is broken and the person and situation will finally begin to evacuate the premises.

I am so proud of you. Hang in there, my friend. Liberty in Christ is about to become a reality in life! Next we're going to learn specific ways to accomplish this rewallpapering of the mind.

TAKING THOUGHTS
CAPTIVE

The mind of sinful man is death, but the mind controlled
by the Spirit is life and peace.

(R O M .   8 : 6)

God's goal for our thought lives is that we learn to think with the mind of Christ. Rarely will God release us from captivating or controlling thoughts by suddenly dropping them from our minds. God rarely performs lobotomies. If we simply forgot the object of our stronghold, we might also forget to praise Him for deliverance. The richest testimonies come from people whom Christ has made whole and who still remember what it was like to be broken.

In my travels, staggering numbers of women confess being involved in affairs. Often I am relieved to hear them say that they have repented and walked away in obedience to God. Just as often, however, they will say, "He's out of my life, but I can't seem to get him out of my mind." I can see their sincerity. God has forgiven the sin, but the mental stronghold is still overwhelming. Just as many women come to me wanting to forgive people who have hurt them. They cry, "I'll think I've forgiven, but it still keeps coming up in my mind."

When I began research for this book, I knew a key existed somewhere to help us be victors on the battlefield of the mind. I believe the key is right there in 2 Corinthians 10:5. Before we can get controlling thoughts out of our minds, they must become Christ-controlled thoughts while still in our minds. That is what taking every thought captive to make it obedient to Christ means. This process begins in Illustration 4 as we rewallpaper the mind with truth—specific truth. If we're going to walk out of the prison of controlling thoughts, we are going to have to rewallpaper with God's Word. Please allow me to share a few practices that God used profoundly in renewing my mind and providing subsequent freedom from some strongholds.

1. *Search God's Word for Scriptures that speak the mind of God to your specific stronghold.* Use a Bible concordance or a topical Bible tool. If you're new to the study of Scripture, ask a pastor or Bible study teacher to help you get started. Whatever it takes, compile a list of Scriptures. Don't just look for one or two, and don't just look for those Scriptures that rebuke. Also find Scriptures that speak God's unfailing love and forgiveness to you.

2. *Write these Scriptures on note cards.* The best way to keep them compiled is on spiral-bound note cards. I call these my Truth Cards; with them I use Scriptures not only defensively to tear down existing strongholds, but offensively so Satan can't put up new ones.

3. *Take these Truth Cards wherever you go until the power of the stronghold is broken.* Be prepared to fight for your freedom with some radical choices. Expect the battle to heat up when you start tearing down the lies. In the heat of a battle to be free, I can remember a time when I took my spiral Truth Cards into the grocery store with me! I put them in the baby seat and every aisle or two I flipped to the next card!

Our cupboard was filled with the strangest concoction of stuff you've ever seen, but I'm free today!

4. *Avoid as many forms of deception as possible.* Until you are less vulnerable, flood your mind with truth and with materials that line up with truth. When we're not coming out of a stronghold, we still need to be careful about what we program into our minds, but we must exercise radical caution when we're escaping. God's Word is your truth serum. The more you use it, the clearer your mind will become.

Now let's consider our final illustration:

5. Bow Thought
to the Truth.

Glance back to the complete, five-part illustration on page 233. Contrast the first and last pictures. For a moment, don't look at the three in between. Take time to note every detail that has changed positions.

Now read 2 Corinthians 10:3–5. Do you see what has happened? The figure in our illustration has gone from captive to captor. Now glance at illustrations 2, 3, and 4. Think through the process: How did she go from captive to captor?

The final question becomes, How did the believer get her thoughts to bow to the truth? By believing, speaking, and applying truth as a lifestyle. This step is something we live, not just something we do. The verb tense of the phrase "take captive every thought" is a present active participle that expresses continuous or repeated action. Our thoughts of Illustration 4 are like a well-trained dog. We can't just shout, "Sit!" and expect the dog to stay there for a week. We've worked a long time to get that dog to sit; but it's still not going to sit forever. We don't achieve victory once and never have to bother with that thought problem again. Our thought life is something we'll work on for the rest of our lives in our desire to be godly. But take heart in two important facts:

1. *Working on our thought lives is the only thing that will keep them from working on us.* Either our thoughts have control of us through the power of the enemy, or we have control of them through the power of God. Neutral doesn't exist among the mental gears. That doesn't mean rest doesn't exist. No rest compares to the relief of thoughts that are captive to Christ.

2. *Staying at work on our thought lives is the very essence of godliness.* Godliness is not perfection. If you are striving daily to give God your heart and mind and are sensitive to sin in your thought life, I'd call you godly. But I could never call myself that. Maybe that's how it should be.

Here's a rule of thumb for the thought life that will be a catalyst to victory in all parts of life: starve the flesh and feed the spirit. These phrases were pivotal for me, and I hope they will be to you. For every day that the believer in Illustration 5 practices this principle, victory will be the rule and defeat the exception in her life.

When we do not make the deliberate choice to think according to the Spirit, we "default" to the flesh. You've noticed we never have to choose to be self-centered. I default into self-centeredness automatically unless I deliberately submit to the authority of Christ and the fullness of His free Spirit.

Pray for God to give you a heightened awareness of the way you're thinking. Become alert to times you're thinking according to the flesh. Think about the feeling it is sowing in your heart. I often hear people say, "I can't change the way I feel." No, but we can change the way we think, and that will change the way we feel. Every day and in every situation, we have the invitation to think according to the Spirit or according to the flesh. If we want to think according to the Spirit, however, we have to learn to feed the Spirit and starve the flesh.

The less we feed the Spirit of God within us with things that energize Him to fill us, the more His presence "shrinks" within us. Praise God, the opposite is also true. The more we feed the Spirit of God within us and yield to His control, the more His presence will fill and satiate us with life and peace.

Remember our desire for certain things or people to leave our minds once we've repented? Starving the flesh and feeding the Spirit is the process by which people or things out of God's will finally depart our thoughts. Let's use our two examples from the beginning of this lesson.

If someone has repented of an ungodly relationship and walked away from it physically, the first thing she must do is tear down the lies and put up the truth. She must begin to meditate on truth that speaks to her specific challenge. She needs to fill her mind with things that feed the Spirit and avoid situations that feed the flesh. (If the person is at the same workplace, I strongly suggest a change in departments or a change in employment—yes, it's that important!) Over time, the person formerly filling her thoughts will fill them less and less until, finally, the thoughts are neglected and starved to death. This process takes perseverance! Many people give up before the old thoughts give out! This process works! Give God your complete cooperation and time to renew your mind. You will be victorious, and Satan will be defeated.

CHAPTER 43

A PLANTING OF THE LORD

They will be called oaks of righteousness,
a planting of the LORD
for the display of his splendor.

(ISA. 61:3)

I can hardly believe we are approaching the last miles of our journey together. I pray we will conclude with a vivid picture of freedom. We've been learning to actively demonstrate the agape love Christ wants from us. Jesus clearly stated God's absolute priority commandment for you and me: "Love the Lord your God with all your heart and with all your soul and with all your mind and with all your strength" (Mark 12:30). Consider the four areas Jesus named (heart, mind, soul, and strength). We actively love God with all our hearts when we surrender to His authority, because we know and rely on the love God has for us (1 John 4:16).

In my opinion, loving God with all our minds is the most difficult of the four areas. Everything we studied in the last few chapters reflects loving God with our minds. Surrendering the inmost places of our thought lives to God and asking Him daily to take control are ways we love God with all our minds.

The challenge of loving God with all our strength touches my heart right now, because I have so recently watched someone I love slowly diminish in all areas of physical strength. In this portion of God's priority command I believe He is saying, "Love Me with whatever physical strength you have. Offer Me your temple for My full habitation in weakness or in strength, in living or in dying." I watched my weak and dying mother as she tried to move her lips to sing hymns with me in her last hours. In those last hours, she loved God with all her strength until He finally came and lifted her burden for her. We love God with all our strength when we give Him all we have, however little, however much.

Throughout this study, you have been actively living out Mark 12:28–30. This journey has required the full participation of your heart, soul, mind, and strength. This has been an exercise in loving God. How I pray that all the freshly exposed portions of your heart, soul, mind, and strength have granted you a new and increased capacity to love God. If you love Him more today than you did when you began, then this difficult road has been worth traveling. I can't think of anything more appropriate than repeating Isaiah 61:1–4. Hopefully you know these verses well by now.

Throughout these final chapters, we will highlight the last sentence of Isaiah 61:3. The entire goal of our journey is wrapped up in this solitary statement. Christ came to set the captives free so they could be called "a planting of the LORD / for the display of his splendor."

First look at the phrase, "They will be called." The Hebrew word for "called" is *qara*, meaning "to cry out, call aloud, roar; to proclaim . . . to be named; to read aloud." Probably the part of the definition truest to our context is the act of being named. I've been called a lot of things in my life, and I can't think of one I wouldn't gladly trade for being called a display of God's splendor!

Perhaps most significant is *who* will be doing the calling or naming. Who will look on the captives set free and call us displays of His splendor? I believe God will. Our heavenly Father celebrates your willingness to be victorious through His might. "He will rejoice over you with singing" (Zeph. 3:17), so put on your dancing shoes and celebrate! He who is mighty to save is delivering you!

If you're like me, you may be pretty excited about being called a "display of his splendor," but you may not be all that thrilled about being called a tree. Yet captives set free will be called "oaks of righteousness, / a planting of the LORD" (Isa. 61:3). The Hebrew word for "righteousness" is *tsedheq*, reflecting "honesty, integrity, liberation. It is righteous conduct that issues from a new heart."

No matter what our strongholds have been, God can plant us deeply in His love, grow us by the water of His Word, and call us "oaks of righteousness." We can be called persons of honesty, integrity, and liberation. As you can see from the definition, these results come only to those who have allowed God to create in each of them a new and clean heart.

Being a tree isn't so bad when you've been planted by the Lord for the express purpose of displaying His splendor! Let's consider what God means by "displays of his splendor." In the original language, the words *display* and *splendor* in Isaiah 61:3 are the same Hebrew word: *pa'ar* means "to embellish, beautify, adorn; to glorify, be glorified; to bring honor, give honor; to boast." To display God's splendor is to radiate His beauty. Can you imagine such a high and wonderful calling? We're called to be the radiance of God's beauty on this earth.

Like Moses, whose face shone with the glory of God in Exodus 34, the life of a captive set free radiates the splendor of God. Is it any

251

wonder? Any captive who has victoriously made freedom in Christ a reality in life has spent more than a little time in the presence of God. Psalm 45:11 could be appropriately spoken of any captive who has been set free: "The king is enthralled by your beauty; / honor him, for he is your lord."

Look at the last English synonym in the definition of *pa'ar*. To be a display of God's splendor is to be someone God can boast about! My friend, if you've agreed to go the extra mile with God and do whatever freedom requires, He is proud of you! God always loves us lavishly, but imagine God being proud of us and having the privilege of boasting about us.

Imagine Christ, your Bridegroom, boasting about how beautiful you are because of the time you've spent gazing on "the beauty of the LORD" (Ps. 27:4). I don't know about you, but my heart is leaping at the thought! I am secure in God's love for me, even when I'm not very beautiful, but the idea of giving Him something to boast about elates me! You see, the more we gaze on the beauty of the Lord as we seek Him in His temple, the more our lives absorb and radiate His splendor. God's ultimate goal is to display our portraits and say, "Doesn't she look like my Son? A remarkable likeness, wouldn't you say?" That's what it means to be a "display of his splendor." A living and visible portrait of the beauty of God.

For the remainder of our journey, we will discuss lives God can boast about. This is your destiny.

CHAPTER 44

THE DISPLAY OF HIS RENOWN

Yes, LORD, walking in the way of your laws,
we wait for you;
your name and renown
are the desire of our hearts.

(ISA. 26:8)

We are exploring qualities God can boast about—elements in earthly lives that display His splendor. Second Peter 1:3–4 tells us that "His divine power has given us everything we need for life and godliness." We fulfill the high calling to display His splendor when we reach up and fully receive the benefits He bowed low to give us.

Christ gave His life so you could be free. Free to live the reality of 1 Corinthians 2:9. Free to become displays of God's splendor. Free to enjoy the five benefits of your covenant relationship with God.

1. To know God and believe Him
2. To glorify God
3. To find satisfaction in God
4. To experience God's peace

5. To enjoy God's presence

One of the most important truths I hope we've learned is that any benefit missing in our lives is an indicator of a stronghold, an area of defeat. As we approach the conclusion of our journey, we're going to look at each of the benefits one more time. This time, however, we're going to see them fully applied and actively exhibiting the display of His splendor. Let's find out what each benefit looks like at its most beautiful moment.

Isaiah 43:9 states the primary purpose of a witness: "Let them bring in their witnesses to prove they were right, / so that others may hear and say, 'It is true.'" We are never more beautiful portrayals of mortals who know and believe God than when others can look at our lives, hear our testimonies, and say, "It is true." That's what it means to be living proof! If you bask in knowing God and dare to believe Him, whether or not you are aware of the effectiveness of your testimony, someone has seen truth through your witness. Isaiah 43:10 proclaims, "'You are my witnesses,' declares the LORD, / 'and my servant whom I have chosen, / so that you may know and believe me / and understand that I am he.'"

Now watch the portrait of belief in Isaiah 43:9–10 evolve into a radiant display of God's splendor. Isaiah 26:8 tells us that God's "name and renown" is the desire of the hearts of those "walking in the way" of His laws. What do you suppose Isaiah meant by God's name being the desire of their hearts?

The Hebrew word for "name" is *shem*. The Jewish designation as "Semites" comes from this word. God chose Israel to be called by His name. The "Semites" or Israelites were literally a people of God's name. *Shem* means "the idea of definite and conspicuous position . . . a mark or memorial of individuality. By implication, honor, authority, character" (*Strong's*). Thus, the Israelites were called forth as a nation to show the definite and conspicuous position of the one true God in their lives.

They were called to be a mark of His individuality and were to show His honor, authority, and character.

The name you and I are called most in reference to our spiritual beliefs is Christian. We are a people of Christ's name. God has called us to show the definite and conspicuous position of His one and only Son in our lives.

Isaiah also said God's *renown* was the desire of their hearts. The concept of God's renown means growth in the acceptance of God's name. We could restate the verse accurately this way: Your name and Your fame are the desire of our hearts. Stay with me here!

In the very next verse, Isaiah wrote, "My soul yearns for you in the night; / in the morning my spirit longs for you" (26:9). Without a doubt, the more you know God, the more you want to know God. The more time you spend with Him, the more you will yearn for Him. I think of Psalm 63:2: "I have seen you in the sanctuary / and beheld your power and your glory." You see, the yearning described in Isaiah 26:8–9 and Psalm 63 comes from the heart and soul of a person who has truly known God. People who know God well want God well-known. No one has to force a person who is intimately acquainted with God to be a living witness. Those who truly know His name (and all it implies) always want His fame.

As I ask you the following question, please trust my heart toward you because I do not have a hint of judgment or condemnation no matter what your answer: Do you presently have a yearning for the presence of God? I'm not talking about guilt feelings or even conviction of sin when He's not your priority. I'm referring to a yearning for God that draws you over and over into His presence. A yearning that makes only a few days without time in prayer and His Word seem like an eternity.

Your original motivation for reading this study may have been to find deliverance, but I am praying that you've found more of the

Deliverer! God can use any motivation to get us into His Word and prayer, but He wants to refine our motivations until they become the desire for Him.

My motivation for Bible study and prayer could still be all about me. Fix my circumstances, Lord. Use me powerfully, Lord. Direct me in obvious ways today, Lord. Make a way for me, Lord. Make me successful, Lord. Not one of those prayers is wrong. But if my motivation for my relationship with God is what He can do for me, a lust for His power may grow but a yearning for His presence will not. God deeply desires to hear our petitions, but His greatest joy is to hear them flow from the mouths of those who want Him more than anything else He could give.

The last thing I want you to feel is guilt, if knowing God is not your chief motivation for prayer and study. Creating awareness is my goal. Awareness is always the first step to freedom. This very awareness is exactly what motivated me in my late twenties to begin asking God to give me a heart to love Him and know Him more than anything in life. I do not have the words or the space to explain the transformation that has taken place through this petition. To this day, it is the most often repeated request I make of God on my own behalf. More than anything on earth, I pray to know Him.

Do you see what has happened in my heart as a result of changing to a God-centered motivation for study and prayer? It is not enough for me to know Him and believe Him. I want everyone else to know Him, too! I don't often use myself as a good example, but I want you to see that God is faithful to turn Isaiah 43:10 into 26:8 for anyone! Once you really know His name, you'll want His fame! What He has made known to you, you will want to make re-known to everyone else. That's the heart's desire of seeking God's renown!

Knowing God and believing Him displays His splendor most when our soul's desire is for others to know and believe Him, too. Be careful what you assume, however. You may be thinking that you lack a yearning for God because you don't have the courage to knock on the doors of strangers and evangelize. Although I have a great respect for knocking on doors and giving out tracts, these are not the only or even the most effective ways we can seek to make God known. Here are just a few of the ways we can share our love for Christ:

- Invite people to Bible study. I'll never forget the letter I received from a group who had studied *A Woman's Heart: God's Dwelling Place*. At the last meeting, the leader asked, "Does anyone have anything to say before we end our journey together?" A woman who had finished every lesson of that study said, "Yes, I'd like to pray to receive Christ."
- Invite people to church. Keep the goal in mind, however: We're not seeking the renown of our church. We are seeking God's renown!
- Invite people to Christian concerts or plays.
- Visit with friends or neighbors over coffee or get a little exercise group together to provide opportunities for casual conversation in which Christ can be seen as part of your life.
- Support home and foreign missions through prayer and financial giving.

Oh, God, may we allow You the joy of boasting over us with these words: My name and My renown were the desire of their hearts.

CHAPTER 45

THE DISPLAY OF HIS GLORY

"No weapon forged against you will prevail,
and you will refute every tongue that accuses you.
This is the heritage of the servants of the LORD,
and this is their vindication from me," declares the LORD.

(ISA. 54:17)

As we walk our last couple of miles together, let's slow our pace and reflect on five displays of God's splendor. We first met these displays as the five benefits God bestows on His children: to know and believe Him, to glorify Him, to find satisfaction in Him, to experience His peace, and to enjoy His presence. Let's imagine these as both displays of His splendor and as landscape portraits propped on easels toward the end of our journey. They help us remember what complete liberty looks like. Each represents lives God can boast about.

Benefit 2 is to glorify God. We defined God's glory as the way He makes Himself known or shows Himself mighty. Therefore, when God seeks to glorify Himself through an individual, He proves who He is by causing the believer to be and do what is otherwise impossible.

A wonderful example of persons living beyond their human responses appears in 2 Corinthians 4:8–9. Paul described their condition this way: "We are hard pressed on every side, but not crushed; perplexed, but not in despair; persecuted, but not abandoned; struck down, but not destroyed."

The verses that sandwich Paul's testimony demonstrate why God often insists on pushing us beyond our human limitations.

> But we have this treasure in jars of clay to show that
> this all-surpassing power is from God and not from us . . .
> We always carry around in our body the death of Jesus, so
> that the life of Jesus may also be revealed in our body.
> (2 Cor. 4:7, 10)

Any time we glorify God we are displays of His splendor, but right now I want to paint a portrait of a life that truly withholds nothing from God. A life through which God does something only He can do. We're going to view the ultimate captive set free! I have purposely waited until now to look back at the first account in all of Scripture recording the adventures of captives set free. Let's go back to the land of Egypt and hear the groans of the Israelites, the children of God, held fast in a cruel captivity:

> The Israelites groaned in their slavery and cried out,
> and their cry for help because of their slavery went up to
> God. God heard their groaning and he remembered his
> covenant with Abraham, with Isaac and with Jacob. So
> God looked on the Israelites and was concerned about
> them. (Exod. 2:23–25)

> I have indeed seen the misery of my people in
> Egypt. I have heard them crying out because of their

slave drivers, and I am concerned about their suffering.
So I have come down to rescue them from the hand of
the Egyptians. (Exod. 3:7–8)

Virtually every time you see God described as remembering something
or someone, He moves to act in their behalf as you see in Exodus 3:8. He
remembered, so He came down to rescue them. How does this scene apply
to us? God knows our suffering from the first pang. He desires, however,
to hear us cry out specifically for His help. God never misses a single groan
or cry of His children. He always has a rescue mission planned. When the
time is right, God will move in behalf of His children.

When God set about to rescue Israel, however, His plan was unique.
Exodus tells us that God instituted the Passover. Every Jewish family
slaughtered a Passover lamb and smeared its blood on the doorpost.
Then the death angel passed through Egypt, killing the firstborn of
every family but passing over the homes marked with the blood.

If you are tenderhearted as I am, this scene may be hard to imagine,
but keep in mind that our God knew what deliverance of His children
would cost. He would one day lay down the life of His own firstborn so
that any captive, Jew or Gentile, could be free. While God set His plan
in motion, He demanded preparation from His people. I believe the
same is true for us. God sent Christ to set the captives free, but
undoubtedly He demands our attention and preparation. He wants us
never to forget that blood was shed by the Lamb of God so we could be
delivered. We have no door of escape unless the doorpost has been
painted with the blood of Christ.

If God simply delivered His people, then and now, that would be
more than we could imagine, but there's more to the story. "The
Israelites did as Moses instructed and asked the Egyptians for articles of
silver and gold and for clothing. The LORD had made the Egyptians

favorably disposed toward the people, and they gave them what they asked for; so they plundered the Egyptians" (Exod. 12:35–36).

The Hebrew word for "plunder" is *nasal,* meaning "to snatch away" (*Strong's*). When God delivers His children, they never have to escape by the skin of their teeth! The Israelites were impoverished slaves, but when God delivered them, they left with the riches of the Egyptians. We can draw a wonderful parallel from this event. In the classic *Streams in the Desert,* Mrs. Charles E. Cowman expressed this wonderful phenomenon better than I can:

> The gospel is so arranged and the gift of God so great that you may take the very enemies that fight you and the forces that are arrayed against you and make them steps up to the very gates of heaven and into the presence of God . . . God wants of every one of His children, to be more than conqueror . . . You know when one army is more than conqueror it is likely to drive the other from the field, to get all the ammunition, the food and supplies, and to take possession of the whole . . . There are spoils to be taken!
>
> Beloved, have you got them? When you went into that terrible valley of suffering did you come out of it with spoils? When that injury struck you and you thought everything was gone, did you so trust in God that you came out richer than you went in? To be more than conqueror is to take the spoils from the enemy and appropriate them to yourself. What he had arranged for your overthrow, take and appropriate for yourself.[1]

What about you? Did you come out of your Egypt, your time of slavery, with plunder from the enemy? Did you give the enemy an offensive blow by allowing God to bring you out of your captivity twice the person you were when you went in? Way back in Abraham's day God had promised, "I will punish the nation they serve as slaves, and afterward they will come out with great possessions" (Gen. 15:14).

Don't forget! What God appropriated to the nation of Israel in a tangible sense, we can almost always see applied to New Testament believers in a spiritual sense. He wants to bring us out of our times of captivity with possessions!

You don't have to escape from captivity with nothing to show for it. After all the enemy has put you through, take your plunder. Let God bring you forth from your time of slavery with gold, silver, and costly stones. Stronger than ever because in your weakness God was strong. More of a threat to the kingdom of darkness than Satan ever dreamed you'd be. Don't just reclaim surrendered ground. God wants to enlarge your borders and teach you to possess land you never knew existed. Make the enemy pay for scheming against you so hatefully. Snatch the plunder!

Oh, how I pray that you are already aware of plunder you stole from the enemy after God delivered you from a time of slavery. Let God have your failures. Surrender to Him your most dreadful times of slavery. Your most humiliating defeats. God and God alone can use them to make you twice the warrior you ever dreamed you'd be. Let there be plunder!

There's more! Let's see this plunder become a display of God's splendor. When God commanded the delivered Israelites to build a tabernacle and its furnishings, from where do you suppose the gold and silver came? If you answered the plunder of the Egyptians, you are right on target. The Israelites reinvested the plunder by offering it back to God. A God who can take a few simple fish and loaves and multiply them to feed thousands. A God of awesome returns. How can a person reinvest the plunder she or he brings out of captivity? Have you already had an opportunity to offer your plunder to God as a reinvestment and see Him bring greater returns?

While I was still a sinner, Christ died for me. He heard the groans of my self-imposed slavery, and the God of the universe looked on my ugliness and called this captive free. And was there plunder? You are staring it in the face right this moment. This book, for whatever it's worth, is nothing but plunder. Every line is what God allowed me to take from my seasons in Egypt's humiliation. I deserved to be placed on a shelf and simply live out my time patiently until the glory of heaven. Instead, God chose to use the very things Satan had used to defeat me to teach me. How could I not pour my life back into God? He is the only reason I have survived—let alone thrived.

You become a display of His splendor every time you take the plunder of Egypt and offer it back to God for His magnificent glory. If you have repented and escaped from Egypt, don't hang your head another minute. God will force the enemy to give up plunder to you; but if your head is not lifted up in expectation, you might not catch it.

I want to share one final word of testimony with you. Some days I don't feel like being vulnerable or transparent, no matter who it would help. Some days I want to forget I've ever been to Egypt. Some days I just want to act like I've always done it right. Some days I don't want to give; I want to take. And some days I just want everybody out of my personal business. My times in Egypt are painful for me to remember. Embarrassing for me to admit. Leaving nothing for others to admire. Some days I think I just can't do it. But each morning the Holy Spirit woos me once again to the place where I meet with God. The God of grace bows low and meets with me. In the simplicity of my prayer time, I am suddenly confronted by the majesty of my Redeemer. The One who is responsible for any good in me. My past sins are forgiven and fresh mercies fall like manna from heaven. And once again, my heart is moved, and I surrender all. Morning after morning.

CHAPTER 46

THE DISPLAY OF SATISFACTION AND PEACE

The LORD will guide you always;
he will satisfy your needs in a sun-scorched land
and will strengthen your frame.
You will be like a well-watered garden,
like a spring whose waters never fail.

(ISA. 58:11)

Now we're going to look at Benefits 3 and 4. Our goal is to see these two benefits at the summit of their beauty—as displays of God's splendor.

1. *The Display of Satisfaction Found in God*

We simply must find satisfaction in God (Benefit 3) because dissatisfaction or emptiness waves a red flag to the enemy. The empty places in our lives become the enemy's playground. Picture a spacious, green golf course. The flags tell the golfer where the holes are. Something similar happens to us in the unseen. None of us have reached adulthood without some holes in our lives. Some have more than others due to hurts and traumas, but we all have holes. You can be sure the enemy has flagged every hole as a target. We spend untold energies in anger and bitterness over why those holes exist and who is to blame. Healing begins when we recognize how vulnerable those empty places make us, tally the cost of filling them with useless things, and seek wholeness in Christ alone. In my opinion, wholeness in Christ is that state of being when every hole has been filled by Christ.

No one can take away the holes that my childhood traumas left. The damage cannot be undone; it must be healed. The holes can't be taken away, but they can be filled. As we take our last look at satisfaction in Christ, our goal is to see satisfaction at its greatest beauty. We want to see a picture of a satisfied person fully displaying God's splendor. Isaiah 58 paints the portrait perfectly. Let's step up to the easel and take a look.

Is not this the kind of fasting I have chosen:
to loose the chains of injustice
    and untie the cords of the yoke,
to set the oppressed free
    and break every yoke? (Isa. 58:6)

The LORD will guide you always;
    he will satisfy your needs in a sun-scorched land
    and will strengthen your frame.
You will be like a well-watered garden,
    like a spring whose waters never fail. (Isa. 58:11)

God inspired the prophet Isaiah to pen what might be considered a play on words. The Holy Spirit expressed a beautiful paradox in these verses. Careful meditation brings two themes to the surface—themes that seem to be virtually opposite concepts.

• *Theme 1* (v. 6): "The kind of fasting [God] has chosen."

• *Theme 2* (v. 11): "[The Lord] will satisfy your needs in a sun-scorched land."

While fasting speaks of emptiness, satisfaction speaks of fullness. How does God bring both concepts together? He promises that those who empty themselves of other pleasures will have themselves filled by something only He can give.

Now look at the words of verse 10: "If you spend yourselves in behalf of the hungry / and satisfy the needs of the oppressed, / then your light will rise in the darkness, / and your night will become like the noonday." If we pour out our lives to satisfy the needs of the oppressed, God will be faithful to satisfy our needs.

Let's reflect on this unique kind of fasting God has chosen. Usually we think of fasting as avoiding food for the purpose of prayer. The emptiness of our stomachs reminds us to pray. Although New Testament Scripture often speaks of fasting from food for the purpose of prayer, Isaiah 58 speaks of a fasting I believe God may honor most of all. I've spent some time on this question, and I don't think it's an easy one to answer. What is God proposing we fast from? What do we have to give up or fast from to reach out to the oppressed?

God took me to the other side of the world to supply a few answers to these questions. In my two-week stay in India, these verses came to my mind more than any others. If you're looking for a fun little mission trip, keep India out of your travel plans. You never get away from its suffering. Pain follows you down the streets in the form of orphaned, filthy beggars. It penetrates your hotel room with the eerie sound of Hindu music played to appease three hundred million gods. Agony stings your eyes as you stare at the sea of poverty. It wretches in your throat when you smell the rotting flesh blocks away from the leper colony. When I returned, people asked me if I had a good time. No. I didn't have a good time. I had a profound time. I will never be the same. I can't forget what I saw.

What kind of fast did God require of me as He sent me to minister one-on-one to the oppressed? A fast from comfort. A fast from my pretty little world. A fast from rose-colored glasses. In Houston the freeways loop around the inner city to keep me from facing the poor. I can live days on end in my own neighborhood and choose to deal only with pretty problems that smell better. I can choose to fast from poverty and oppression. But if I do, I'll never have a heart like God's.

One of the purposes of a fast is for the emptiness to prompt us to a spiritual response. The emptiness in the people of India brought back vivid memories of my own at one time. So many things tore at my heart. The faces most engraved on my heart are those of the women. Heads covered. Meek. Many to the point of seeming shamed. I stood in a village with raw sewage running only a few feet from me and spoke to four women through an interpreter. I wasn't planning to. The Spirit just came over me. I touched their faces and told them they were so beautiful. I told them that God saw them with great dignity and honor. Like princesses. Within a few moments four women turned into many. I still can't think about it without crying. They wept, held on to me, and were willing to do anything to receive such a Savior. They knew their circumstances might never change, but one day they would lay down this life and wake up in the splendor of God's presence. Do you know what God used to provoke a bond between those women and me? An acute memory of my own former emptiness and oppression.

We don't have to go to the other side of the world to reach out to the oppressed. Oh, how I pray we each will discover glorious satisfaction in Christ; but when it's the real thing, we must find a place to pour the overflow of our lives. Captives truly set free are the most compassionate people in the world. They don't see others as less than themselves, because they've lived a little of their own lives in the gutter too.

Our motivations for reaching out and serving others aren't always pure. My dear friend Kathy Troccoli, who ministers full-time, asked a critical question: "Am I ministering out of my need or out of the overflow of my own relationship with God?" We would be wise to ask ourselves the same question. Do we crave the affirmation of those we serve and do they help us feel important? Or do we serve because Jesus has so filled our hearts that we must find a place to pour the overflow? A ministry to the truly oppressed helps purify our serving motives. You see, they don't have much to give back. The satisfied soul is never a more beautiful display of God's splendor than when willing to empty self for the lives of others.

We've looked at the display of satisfaction in God. Now let's turn to another showcase.

2. *The Display of God's Peace*

The fourth benefit of our covenant relationship is to experience God's peace. What might the peace of God in the soul of a person look like at its most beautiful moment? When does peace become an eye-catching display of God's splendor?

In the beginning of our journey we considered Isaiah 48:18. There we saw that the key to peace is submitting to God's authority. Isaiah suggests that we have "peace like a river" when we pay attention to God's commands. Therefore, the key to peace in each of our lives is submitting to God's authority through obedience.

Obedience to God's authority doesn't come easily for any of us. I heard one of the preachers I admire say that the life of the disciple requires a "long obedience in the same direction." Isn't that a great expression of truth? So are we saddled with nothing but sacrifices in this long obedience in the same direction? Hardly. Let's take a look at peace at its most beautiful moment.

Isaiah painted a wonderful relationship between peace and joy:

How beautiful on the mountains
  are the feet of those who bring good news,
who proclaim peace,
  who bring good tidings,
  who proclaim salvation,
who say to Zion,
  "Your God reigns!"
Listen! Your watchmen lift up their voices;
  together they shout for joy.
When the LORD returns to Zion,
  they will see it with their own eyes.
Burst into songs of joy together,
  you ruins of Jerusalem,
for the LORD has comforted his people,
  he has redeemed Jerusalem. (Isa. 52:7–9)

Don't stop there! Take a look forward at Isaiah 58:13–14.

"If you keep your feet from breaking the Sabbath
  and from doing as you please on my holy day,
if you call the Sabbath a delight
  and the LORD's holy day honorable,
and if you honor it by not going your own way
  and not doing as you please or speaking idle words,
then you will find your joy in the LORD,
  and I will cause you to ride on the heights of the land
  and to feast on the inheritance of your father Jacob."
The mouth of the LORD has spoken.

How did Isaiah say they would find joy in the Lord? Obedience to God often entails not going our own way, not doing as we please, and not even speaking as we please. But, if peace is the fruit of righteousness (Isa. 32:17), then joy is the wine from the fruit! Joy will ultimately flow from obedience, and few things display God's splendor any more appealingly than joy!

Think I'm stretching the analogy a bit? Check out John 15: "I am the true vine, and my Father is the gardener. . . . If a man remains in me and I in him, he will bear much fruit; . . . This is to my Father's glory, that you bear much fruit, . . . If you obey my commands, you will remain in my love, . . . I have told you this so that my joy may be in you and that your joy may be complete" (John 15:1, 5, 8, 10–11).

Put Isaiah 32:17 next to John 15, and here's what you get: Peace is the fruit of righteousness which, in essence, is obedience to God's commands—the product of abiding in the vine. The wine which flows from the ripened fruit is joy!

Paul declared that "the kingdom of God is not a matter of eating and drinking, but of righteousness, peace and joy in the Holy Spirit, because anyone who serves Christ in this way is pleasing to God and approved by men" (Rom. 14:17–18).

The wine of joy will eventually flow from the fruit of peace produced by righteousness. "Weeping may endure for a night, but joy cometh in the morning" (Ps. 30:5, KJV). God will look on you in the full harvest of your obedience, and perhaps He'll say something like my grandmother used to say when I was all dressed up (buck teeth and all): "Girl, you sho is purty." Or maybe He'll say, "You sure are a display of My splendor."

CHAPTER 47

THE DISPLAY OF HIS PRESENCE

The LORD is the stronghold of my life—
of whom shall I be afraid?

(PS. 27:1)

🌰

I never fail to cry as I begin to write the final chapter of any Bible study journey, but I'm at full sob now. Each of the journeys God has allowed me to take through His Word has meant the world to me. This one, however, has been in a league all its own. *Breaking Free* has been the most difficult book I've ever written. God wanted this one to come from a fresh heart that only true brokenness can bring. Hurts and losses occurred during the writing of this study that could not have been coincidental. I have no idea how this book will be received. I don't even know if it's good. But I know it's real. And God is good.

I feel a little like I did after I returned from India. I can't say this trip has been fun, but I won't soon forget it. Never will I be able to express my gratitude to you for sticking with this journey. Oh, how I pray God will engrave His truth on your heart forever. Anything at all that has been accomplished with this book has been from God.

The Book of Isaiah is so rich that I could not imagine how I would ever choose a final passage for our journey. I believe God has chosen one for us: the best possible place in Isaiah to bid one another Godspeed. We'll conclude our journey with a last look at the fifth benefit of our covenant relationship in its fullest display of His splendor. Read the familiar words of Isaiah 40:28–31 and savor every word.

Do you not know?
　　Have you not heard?
The LORD is the everlasting God,
　　the Creator of the ends of the earth.
He will not grow tired or weary,
　　and his understanding no one can fathom.
He gives strength to the weary
　　and increases the power of the weak.
Even youths grow tired and weary,
　　and young men stumble and fall;
but those who hope in the LORD
　　will renew their strength.
They will soar on wings like eagles;
　　they will run and not grow weary,
　　they will walk and not be faint. (Isa. 40:28–31)

I'm praying for three goals to be accomplished as we part:
1. I'm praying that if you are not yet free, you will cooperate with God fully until you are.
2. I'm praying that you will know how to maintain your freedom.
3. I'm praying that you'll always know how to get back to the freedom trail if you ever lose your way.

Sometimes I get tired of fighting the good fight, don't you? How can we muster the energy to hang in there and keep fighting for our liberty? Even the youth grow tired and weary, and young men stumble and fall. If you're like me, you're neither young nor male! We could be in big trouble! So what's a soul to do?

I believe Isaiah 40:28–31 tells us exactly what to do when we get weary in the walk. Notice whose strength the Lord will renew: "those who hope in the LORD." The Hebrew word for "hope" (KJV, "wait upon") is *qawah,* meaning "to bind together (by twisting) . . . to be gathered together, be joined." If we want to keep a renewed strength to face our daily challenges or regain a strength that has faded, God's Word tells us to draw so close to the presence of God we're practically twisted to Him!

The thought of fighting our way through life is exhausting. Can you think of anything more arduous than waking up to win every day? I could probably do it about four days a week. The other three days I'd want to push snooze and go back to sleep. There's got to be a better way.

I believe Isaiah 40:31 is telling us to wrap ourselves so tightly around God that we automatically go where He's going, and the only way He's going is to victory (2 Cor. 2:14). God doesn't want our goal to be to win. He wants our goal to be to win Christ. Consider Paul's familiar words in Philippians 3:8–9. The King James Version uses the words "that I may win Christ." No one had more to say about warfare and fighting the good fight than the apostle Paul; yet his primary goal was not to win, but to win Christ. The next phrase explains what the apostle meant by winning Christ. It says, "and be found in him."

Being "found in Christ" is the very same idea as "hope in the LORD" in Isaiah 40:31. Both concepts describe binding self to God. When my children were little, they used to hold on to my waist and wrap their legs around one of mine. I'd whistle, go about my business, and say, "I wonder what Amanda (or Melissa) is doing right now?" They would laugh hysterically. My heart never failed to be overwhelmed with love, because I realized that their favorite game was to hang onto me! My muscles might ache afterward, but it was worth it.

To "hope in the Lord" is to do with God what my children did with me! To wrap ourselves around Him as tightly as we can. Why does Isaiah 40:31 present the concept of binding ourselves to God in context with being weary and faint? Think about the illustration of the game my children and I played. Who did most of the work? I did! What was their part in the game? Binding themselves to me and hanging on tight. Do you see the parallel? When we start feeling weary, we're probably taking on too much of the battle ourselves.

When we're most exhausted, we're expending more energy fighting the enemy than we are seeking God's presence. More than you seek to win, seek Christ! More than you seek to defeat the enemy, seek his foe! More than you seek victory, seek the Victor! You'll never be more beautiful to God than when He can look down and see you hanging on to Him for dear life!

We have shared some awesome moments through these chapters, but now it's time for us to go our separate ways with God. I'll miss you, and you may miss me, too; but please never confuse missing my companionship with needing my companionship. You don't need me. You need God. Cling only to Him, the One who will lead you on until He leads you home—where once and for all, you'll be free at last.

I feel a little like I did when I left my Amanda at college for the first time. Humor me for a moment, and allow me to say a few motherly things before we go. Remember, we never find freedom from bondage in independence. We find it by taking the same handcuffs that bound us to sin and binding ourselves to the wrist of Christ. When you're imprisoned in the will of God, your cell becomes the Holy of Holies. Never forget, there is only one Stronghold that frees when it binds.

I am so proud of you, I can hardly stand it. Far more important, God is so proud of you. You are someone God wants to boast about. For just a moment, I don't want you to think about how far you have to go. I just want you to think about how far you've come. Just rest for a few minutes. No transparency required. No vulnerability. No telling on yourself. No looking in. Just look up. For a moment, sit back and let me pray Psalm 32:7 over you: May God be your hiding place; may He protect you from trouble, and may He incline your spiritual ears to listen carefully while He surrounds you with songs of deliverance. I come down to my knees in your honor and in God's. You, my fellow sojourner, are a display of His splendor. I am humbled beyond description for the privilege of walking this road with you.

Nothing could be more appropriate than concluding with Isaiah 61:1–4. Read or quote the verses, and allow God to bring back to your memory the torrents of truth we've studied.

May this prayer God wrote on my heart bring summation to our journey and provide a fitting farewell.

A HEALING CAPTIVE

O, God, Who frees the captive
Do not liberate this carnal slave for freedom's sake
For I will surely wing my flight to another thorny land.
Break, instead, each evil bond
And rub my swollen wrists,
Then take me prisoner to Your will,
Enslaved in Your safekeeping.
O, God, Who ushers light into the darkness,
Do not release me to the light
To only see myself.
Cast the light of my liberation upon Your face

And be Thou my vision.
Do not hand me over
To the quest of greater knowledge.
Make Your Word a lamp unto my feet
And a light unto my path,
And lead me to Your dwelling.

O, God, Who lifts the grieving head,
Blow away the ashes
But let Your gentle hand upon my brow
Be my only crown of beauty.
Comfort me so deeply,
My Healer,
That I seek no other comfort.

O, God, Who loves the human soul
Too much to let it go,
So thoroughly impose Yourself
Into the heaps and depths of my life
That nothing remains undisturbed.
Plow this life, Lord,
Until everything You overturn
Becomes a fertile soil,
Then plant me, O God
In the vast plain of Your love.
Grow me, strengthen me,
And do not lift Your pressing hand
Until it can boastfully unveil
A display of Your splendor.

I love you.
Beth

DISCUSSION QUESTIONS

WELCOME TO A JOURNEY TO FREEDOM

1. What issues hold believers captive and hinder the abundant life God intends?
2. Do you believe Christians can be oppressed by the devil? Why or why not?
3. What kinds of shelters do people build to protect themselves?
4. How do shelters turn into strongholds?

CHAPTER 1: FROM KINGS TO CAPTIVITY

1. What do you think Isaiah would have been like as a friend?
2. What do you think caused Uzziah's attack of pride that led to his downfall?
3. How does pride raise its ugly head in your life?
4. Why do you suppose Jotham did not tear down the high places?
5. What could possibly lead a father to sacrifice his own son in the fire?
6. How would you describe Hezekiah's legacy to his children and grandchildren?

CHAPTER 2: THE REIGN OF CHRIST

1. Why do we need more than any human leader can supply on our road to freedom?
2. How has Christ "spoken tenderly" to you after a time of chastening?

3. What does the statement "God always cares more for our freedom than we do" mean to you?

4. In what ways do you see Jesus having fulfilled the promises of Isaiah 61:1–4?

CHAPTER 3: TO KNOW GOD AND BELIEVE HIM

1. Are you experiencing the benefits of your covenant relationship with God through Christ?

2. What has contributed most to your level of trust in God?

3. What gives you the most problem when it comes to believing God?

4. What practical steps could you take to increase your trust in God?

CHAPTER 4: TO GLORIFY GOD

1. How has God made Himself known to you?

2. What does it mean that Christ is the radiance of God's glory?

3. What does giving glory to God mean to you?

4. How does a Christian develop a life that glorifies God?

5. How can a person know if his or her life is glorifying God?

CHAPTER 5: TO FIND SATISFACTION IN GOD

1. How do you react to the statement that many Christians are not satisfied with Christ?

2. What have you sought that turned out to be unsatisfying?

3. What is the difference between salvation from sin and satisfaction of soul?

4. What are the symptoms of an unsatisfied soul?

CHAPTER 6: TO EXPERIENCE GOD'S PEACE

1. Is God's peace an infrequent surprise or the ongoing rule of your life?

2. At what point does a Christian receive the peace of God?

3. What part does authority play in God's peace?

4. What part of the phrase "peace like a river" means most to you?

CHAPTER 7: TO ENJOY GOD'S PRESENCE

1. Which is more constant, the presence of God or the evidence of His presence?
2. Is your enjoyment in God's presence increasing or decreasing?
3. What is the most satisfying part of your relationship with God?

CHAPTER 8: THE OBSTACLE OF UNBELIEF

1. What has God done in your life to prepare the road for His visit as king?
2. What is the difference between believing in God and believing God?
3. How has God proved Himself worthy of your confidence?
4. How has the study of Scripture affected your faith?

CHAPTER 9: THE OBSTACLE OF PRIDE

1. To what degree would you say that God's name and renown is the desire of your heart?
2. In what ways is pride a dangerous enemy?
3. How do you feel toward someone who exhibits pride in his or her life? How do you feel toward one who demonstrates humility?
4. What does it take to humble yourself before God?

CHAPTER 10: THE OBSTACLE OF IDOLATRY

1. Why does God create a nagging sense of dissatisfaction in every person?
2. Why does the Bible call seeking satisfaction in anything but God the sin of idolatry?
3. What forms have idols taken in your personal experience?

CHAPTER 11: THE OBSTACLE OF PRAYERLESSNESS

1. How would you paraphrase Philippians 4:6–7 into a formula for anxiety?
2. What is the difference between superficial and "meaty" prayer lives?
3. Why is prayer a key to peace?
4. How has prayer brought peace to you in a time of great stress?

CHAPTER 12: THE OBSTACLE OF LEGALISM

1. What is so appealing about legalism? Why do people continue to return to legalism?

2. Which condition do you find the greatest temptation: (1) regulations to replace relationships, (2) microscopes to replace mirrors, or (3) performance to replace passion?

3. How has legalism squeezed the joy out of your salvation?

4. Which of the five obstacles you have studied gives you the greatest problems? Which gives you the least?

CHAPTER 13: TOURING THE ANCIENT RUINS

1. Without dishonoring your family, can you identify any ancient ruins that have been in your family for generations?

2. What are the right reasons for looking back at ancient ruins in a family?

3. What are the wrong reasons?

4. Why are generational strongholds so difficult for us to identify?

5. What do you have in your lineage that you need to put in the trophy case? In the trash can?

CHAPTER 14: THE ANCIENT BOUNDARY STONE

1. What was an ancient boundary stone?

2. What always results when someone moves a boundary stone?

3. How does bondage promote sin?

4. How does parental sin impact multiple generations?

5. What does it take for someone to break the cycle of parental sin?

CHAPTER 15: THAT ANCIENT SERPENT

1. How does Satan's knowledge of generational sin influence how he tempts individuals?

2. What have you seen in yourself that you disliked in a parent or grandparent?

3. Why is forgiveness so important to breaking yokes of generational sin?

4. How do the sins of the fathers increase the vulnerability of the children?

CHAPTER 16: SURVEYING THE ANCIENT RUINS

1. What does Ezekiel 18 teach about the relationship between the fathers' sins and the children?
2. If Christians do not literally die for our sins, what kinds of deaths can our sins bring about?
3. What four steps did the son in Ezekiel 18 take to be free of parental sin?
4. How can we forsake parental sin without dishonoring the parent?
5. What is the difference between rebuilding and preserving ancient ruins?

CHAPTER 17: THE ANCIENT OF DAYS

1. What are the agendas of God and of Satan in the life of a believer?
2. In what ways does God's designation as the "Ancient of Days" encourage you?
3. What practical actions can you take to be the one person determined to build a faithful generation?
4. What is your desire for your children and grandchildren?
5. In what ways are you allowing the next generation to see authenticity in your life?

CHAPTER 18: STRAIGHT TO THE HEART

1. What does a broken heart feel like?
2. How do you respond to the knowledge that God gave His son specifically for your broken heart?
3. In what ways do people become self-protective in response to a broken heart?
4. What is different about Christ's way of healing a broken heart as opposed to the natural human response to protect self?

CHAPTER 19: HEARTS BROKEN IN CHILDHOOD

1. How could one person cause another person to sin?
2. How does abuse of a child both prove heartbreaking and promote sin?
3. How does Christ's love for children cause Him to relate to the problem of child abuse?

281

4. How can Christ use the pain of a turbulent childhood for our good?

5. How do you feel about the way Christ relates to the problem of child abuse?

CHAPTER 20: HEARTS MENDED BY TRUTH

1. Why might those who have fallen victim to abuse be more likely to find progressive rather than instantaneous healing?

2. What is Christ's attitude toward children? Toward abuse of children?

3. Why might Matthew 18:6–10 refer to childhood victimization?

4. How do you feel about forgiving those who have offended or hurt you?

CHAPTER 21: HEARTS BROKEN BY BETRAYAL

1. When our hearts have been broken, what are some destructive ways we are tempted to react?

2. Why are people sometimes intimidated by the depth of our need? Why is Christ never intimidated by our need?

3. How do you suppose Jesus felt over the betrayal by Judas?

4. Why did Christ consider only Judas's actions betrayal?

5. What is the difference between betrayal motivated by selfishness and betrayal motivated by evil?

CHAPTER 22: HEARTS BROKEN BY LOSS

1. How does grief feel to you?

2. What is the purpose of grieving?

3. Why did Jesus delay His coming to heal Lazarus?

4. How can those in Christ experience a satisfying life again after loss?

CHAPTER 23: ASHES INSTEAD OF HONOR

1. How do people in your culture give expression to their grief?

2. In what ways does modern society victimize women?

3. How did you first come to realize that you are a virgin daughter or son of the King?

CHAPTER 24: TO BE A BRIDE

1. How do you respond to the "fairy tale" ending to the story of Tamar?
2. How does the term *bride* differ from the term *wife?*
3. What does it mean to you to be the bride of Christ?
4. How can we make ourselves ready for the Bridegroom?

CHAPTER 25: TO BE BEAUTIFUL

1. Why do you think people are so insecure about their appearance?
2. How does the love reflected in the Song of Songs compare to your relationship to Christ?
3. How do you feel about the love Christ displays for you?
4. How is the childhood dream to be beautiful fulfilled in Christ?

CHAPTER 26: TO BE FRUITFUL

1. How does it feel to want something desperately and not be permitted to have it?
2. Why do you suppose people often relate barrenness to sinfulness?
3. How can you invest yourself in rearing spiritual children?

CHAPTER 27: TO LIVE HAPPILY EVER AFTER

1. Why do some people refuse to give up on their dreams while others do?
2. How has God brought happiness from pain in your life?
3. Why do you suppose we discount the importance of happiness in spiritual circles?

CHAPTER 28: UPSIDE DOWN

1. Why is obedience so necessary to freedom in Christ?
2. How have you experienced gaining freedom in one area only to have bondage appear in another area of your life?
3. How are we today like the rebellious Israelites in Isaiah 30?
4. Which of the characteristics of a rebellious child of God have you experienced?

CHAPTER 29: BROKEN POTTERY

1. How can a rebellious child of God come to rely on deceit?

2. Why do rebellious children of God run from the real answers?

3. Which do you find more difficult, returning to God or resting in Him?

4. Which of the characteristics of rebellion have been your tendencies?

CHAPTER 30: GOD'S RIGHT TO RULE

1. When do we experience freedom in Christ?

2. What is the difference between working our way to freedom and withholding no part of our lives from God's authority?

3. How does believing in God's right to rule affect your obedience?

4. How does believing that God's rule is right affect your obedience?

5. How does seeing God as the center of your universe make a difference in your life?

CHAPTER 31: GOD'S RULE IS RIGHT

1. How do you react to having to obey an unrighteous authority?

2. Why do we want so desperately to be our own boss? Is it even possible?

3. What influences have caused your trust in God to increase?

4. Do you have authority problems? How have you become aware of them?

CHAPTER 32: GOD'S DAILY RULE

1. Why do we struggle so much with the "daily-ness" of obedience to God?

2. Which of the five benefits of a daily walk with God means the most to you?

3. How important to you is a fresh morning word?

4. What is your biggest temptation when you don't feel that God is illuminating your way clearly?

CHAPTER 33: FINDING UNFAILING LOVE

1. What risk do we run when we base our relationship with God on His works?
2. What is our deepest psychological need?
3. How does Christ meet that need?
4. How have you learned that God is the answer not only to your needs but also to your wants?

CHAPTER 34: THE FREEDOM OF UNFAILING LOVE

1. Why do you think we have such a difficult time believing that God really loves us?
2. How does God love all people in spite of their behavior?
3. How does God's love relate to His sometimes severe discipline?
4. How can rebellion lead to prisons?
5. What does God do to see that His captive children find freedom?

CHAPTER 35: THE FULLNESS OF UNFAILING LOVE

1. Why can we find genuine satisfaction only in God?
2. How do we find satisfaction in God?
3. How does "Spirit-filled" compare to "Spirit-satisfied"?
4. How is the Spirit of God loosed in our lives?

CHAPTER 36: FAILURE TO BELIEVE GOD'S UNFAILING LOVE

1. How can unbelief make the church ill?
2. Why do Christians have difficulty believing God?
3. How does God tell us He loves us?
4. In what ways does God demonstrate His love for us?

CHAPTER 37: THE FRUIT OF UNFAILING LOVE

1. Why is it unique for someone to believe that God loves?
2. Why does believing that God loves cause our bonds to lose their strength?

3. What has added most to your awareness of security in God's leadership?

4. What means most to you: God's salvation, mercy, comfort, or defense? Why?

CHAPTER 38: A VIEW FROM THE OLD

1. Why do you think freedom requires in-depth study and deliberate application of truth?

2. Why is learning to apply a process to freedom much better than simply obtaining freedom from a stronghold?

3. What evidence do you have in your life that shows God is the watchman over your mind?

4. How is perfect peace in our imperfect minds different than having a perfect mind?

5. What difference does the way you frame events make in your life?

CHAPTER 39: A VIEW FROM THE NEW

1. Can you describe a stronghold you have struggled with in your life?

2. How did the stronghold gain strength in your life?

3. What part does insecurity play in strongholds?

4. What kind of excuses have you made for not surrendering some area of your life to the authority of Christ?

CHAPTER 40: TEARING DOWN THE HIGH PLACES

1. What sort of things have tried to keep you from centering your mind on Christ?

2. What does learning to "think a troublesome thought" as it relates to Christ mean to you?

3. Why is idolatry an open invitation to disaster?

4. How can unforgiveness cause a person to become an idol?

5. Do you tend to think of confession as admitting you have done something shameful or as coming to say the same thing God says about an issue?

CHAPTER 41: DEPROGRAMMING AND REPROGRAMMING

1. What led you to be able to see a particular sin involved in a stronghold in your life?

2. What are some of the lies that you have begun to identify that surround a stronghold in your life?

3. What is the meaning of the statement, "Deception is the glue that holds a stronghold together"?

4. Have you experienced difficulty with the lie that you are responsible to help every person who has a need?

5. Why is identifying the lies that surround a stronghold an absolute necessity to a life of freedom?

CHAPTER 42: TAKING THOUGHTS CAPTIVE

1. Why does God generally refuse to take away a temptation or a controlling thought?

2. How can you develop a list of specific truths to offset satanic lies that support a stronghold?

3. What value do you see in recording your specific truths on "Truth Cards"?

4. Why must we be especially vigilant to avoid sources of deception when we are fighting a spiritual battle?

5. Do you believe that working on our thought lives is the only thing that will keep them from working on us? If so, why?

CHAPTER 43: A PLANTING OF THE LORD

1. In what ways has doing this study been an exercise in loving God with all your heart, soul, mind, and strength?

2. What would you trade for being called a display of God's splendor?

3. How do you feel when you think of God's "[rejoicing] over you with singing"? When you think of Him being proud of you?

CHAPTER 44: THE DISPLAY OF HIS RENOWN

1. What beauty have you seen when you could look at the testimony of a friend's life and see God's truth displayed?
2. Why do "people who know God well want God well-known"?
3. Do you presently have a yearning for the presence of God?
4. How can you grow in the yearning to know God?
5. What is the difference between a lust for God's power and a yearning for His presence?

CHAPTER 45: THE DISPLAY OF HIS GLORY

1. How could your struggle to break free become the steps to the very gates of heaven?
2. What specific spoils have you taken away from your struggles against the enemy and to do the will of God?
3. How can you reinvest the plunder from your past struggles to bring gain for the kingdom of God?

CHAPTER 46: THE DISPLAY OF SATISFACTION AND PEACE

1. Why do unhealed old wounds serve as flags showing the enemy our areas of vulnerability?
2. In what way can a satisfied believer display God's splendor in a way that no other can?
3. What would God have us fast from so we can reach out to the oppressed?
4. What might the peace of God in the soul of a person look like at its most beautiful moment?

CHAPTER 47: THE DISPLAY OF HIS PRESENCE

1. What is the difference between making your goal to win and making your goal to win Christ?
2. Do you expend more energy fighting the enemy or seeking the Lord's presence? Why?
3. What has God done in your life through this study?